D0989388

America Is in Danger

America Is in Danger

GENERAL
CURTIS E. LeMAY

WITH

MAJOR GENERAL
DALE O. SMITH

Funk & Wagnalls
New York

682692

Missouri Western College
ST. JOSEPH, MISSOURI

Second Printing

Copyright © 1968 by GENERAL CURTIS E. LEMAY AND
MAJOR GENERAL DALE O. SMITH

All Rights Reserved.

Library of Congress Catalog Card Number: 68-22203

Published by Funk & Wagnalls, *A Division of*
Reader's Digest Books, Inc.

Printed in the United States of America

Contents

[v]

Introduction

AMERICA IS in danger.

The Soviet Union has been and is now eagerly pressing ahead to acquire a nuclear strategic superiority. Deterrence, *our total defense philosophy*, is not for them. They have already surpassed us in the total megaton yield of warheads. They have already deployed an anti-ballistic missile system and are rapidly improving and expanding it. It is even doubtful that we can now match them in the delivery capability of bombers: we know they lead us in numbers of strategic bombers.

At the same time we have permitted our general war capability to rust. We have scrapped one thousand B-47s without providing replacements. Our B-52s are also on the way out. Our Minuteman force has been reduced to a thousand missiles while our higher yield Titans are phasing out. Our Polaris submarine fleet is static at forty-one vessels. No anti-ballistic missile system has been put into service. We stand nakedly exposed to a first strike. Even our air defense system has been allowed to deteriorate. We have no space weaponry of any sort. Our survival depends almost exclusively on the effectiveness of Minuteman and Polaris. And how effective are they? No one truly knows.

The equivocal manner in which we are waging the war in Southeast Asia is a direct result of the bankrupt nature of our deterrent philosophy. There is reason to believe that we have already lost our strategic military superiority. With such a rent in our nuclear umbrella it would be impossible to exert our real strength in a limited conflict. Our incessant appeals to negotiate are indications of a strategic, if not moral weakness in our cause.

Yes, America is in grave danger. If we have not already lost our military superiority we are well on the way to it.

How has this happened and what can be done about it—that is what this book is about.

Many authors of established reputation and competence in one field make the mistake of asserting equal authority in unrelated areas. In particular, the military profession has been invaded by pundits who set themselves up as popular oracles on military strategy. These "defense intellectuals," go unchallenged simply because the experienced professional active duty officers are officially prohibited from entering into public debate. The end result is that the military is often saddled with unprofessional strategies. Far worse, America stumbles into dangerous military postures.

Let me illustrate this point historically. In 1916 while war in Europe was raging, President Woodrow Wilson banished from Washington a few officers at the Army War College who had the temerity to plan for war. The embryonic planning effort of the professional military to prepare for a war which was then almost inevitable was successfully countered by a host of "defense intellectuals."

A Polish banker, I. S. Block, "proved" statistically in a popular book *The Future of War*, and in numerous speeches, that war was an economic impossibility. His disciples (among whom was David Starr Jordan) were still plugging this doctrine in America in the face of the Battles of the Marne and the Somme.

Just a few months before Sarajevo in 1914 David Starr Jordan, President of Stanford University and a renowned naturalist, said, "It is apparently not possible for another real war among the nations of Europe to take place."

In April, 1917, America was at war. We had neither a respectable military establishment nor a strategy. Our massive military buildup was just getting into full swing when the war ended eighteen months later. The United States provided a relatively small reinforcing army which could not assume independent responsibilities until a year after we declared war. Not one American-designed warplane saw action. Had our allies not held off the enemy while we prepared we would most certainly have been badly mauled.

Before World War II the military professional was again pre-empted by the "defense intellectuals." We had grown a little more sophisticated about planning, however, and had managed to produce the Rainbow series of plans for the *defense* of the Western Hemisphere. The Kellogg-Briand Pact of 1928 had outlawed war in principle. The Washington Disarmament conferences of the 1930s, if not arriving at a treaty had at least condemned "offensive" weapons. Military men were not heard. Billy Mitchell was dead. There was no one who could tell America that wars cannot be won with defensive weapons. And we trained for the next war with wooden guns.

In the Army Air Corps we developed the B-17 Flying Fortress almost clandestinely. Its long range gave it distinctly "offensive" characteristics. Thirteen were ordered in 1937 and with them we worked out the tactics and strategies which carried the war to Germany and Japan less than a decade later.

The capabilities of heavy bombers as war-winning weapons began to be appreciated: in 1938, we intercepted the Italian liner *Rex* 615 miles at sea with three B-17s. Billy Mitchell's prophecies were being realized, but the "defense intellectuals" still controlled national thought. Only the continued clash of arms in Europe, particularly the desperate air Battle of Britain, put the American military professionals back in control of strategic planning. The Secretaries and the President now welcomed the advice of George Marshall, Hap Arnold, Ernie King, and the rest. Under their hands we developed a capable military establishment with winning strategies. But it took two years to get started. Again we were saved by broad oceans and staunch allies.

Today's armchair strategists, glibly writing about military matters to a public avid for military news, can do incalculable harm. "Experts" in a field where they have no experience, they propose strategies based upon hopes and fears rather than upon facts and seasoned judgments.

It never ceases to amaze me that so many intelligent people believe they can become expert in a field where they have had so little training or experience. Like the weather, everyone talks about national defense. But unlike the weather, many of these talkers *do* something about defense.

As Ira Eaker so vividly put it, "I do not object to Walter O'Malley owning the Los Angeles Dodgers but I do not believe he should play first base, although I freely concede his right to do so. I also believe he has been nice to leave the management of his team on the field to an experienced baseball man, Walt Alston.

"Those who see nothing amiss when Massachusetts Institute of Technology and Harvard run a war, would scarcely sanction turning Harvard and M.I.T. over to the first sergeants, the colonels or even the generals. The results would be quite similar."

For myself, I hope to avoid the error of the "defense intellectuals" by steering clear of fields where I have less than a professional understanding. Although I have been intimately associated with matters of foreign, and even domestic, policy while serving in high command positions and on the Joint Chiefs of Staff, I have no illusions that my experience is not primarily military. Good fortune has put me where the military action has been in the past third of a century and I have profited from a great variety of military experience and study.

I must admit that I have a compelling reason for writing this book. It is my deep conviction that we must set straight the many warped and dangerous conceptions of national strategy that are abroad today. If the military professional, once retired, fails to defend his profession against charlatans and dilettantes, I believe he has failed in the final service he should perform for his country.

After a career of seven-day work weeks and flight-bag living, there is a great urge to leave it all to the splendid young men who remain in uniform. But they cannot speak or write what they wish. What they say must understandably be cleared for publication. Therefore it is up to the retired officers to present to the American people the judgments and opinions of the military profession. This I hope to do.

While this study will reflect my personal views, my aim is to present the strategic thinking of the present-day Air Force. There is a recognizable consensus among Air Force officers regarding the art and science of war in the modern world. I hope to record this consensus by analyzing the various strategies which govern our military policy.

Insofar as I am able, I shall avoid the fashionable terminology and euphemisms used by defense intellectuals to describe traditional military events. I shall speak of city or population bombing rather than of "countervalue targeting." The expression "expanding the war" will be used instead of the much overworked term "escalation."

Like the witch doctors, defense intellectuals have created a jargon which tends to becloud understanding. I submit that military strategy and subsequent national defense policies are understandable if clearly presented. Moreover, the average citizen must be familiar with these subjects because, through his franchise, he makes the most fundamental and far-reaching defense decisions.

Gobbledygook has become the union card of defense intellectuals. At a White House meeting with President John F. Kennedy in 1962, I recall being lectured by an articulate defense intellectual who had served briefly in World War II as a bombardier, but whose background was essentially legal and journalistic. For the listening President's benefit he told me how "provocative" Strategic Air Command bombers were, how their "first strike" characteristics were "destabilizing" and liable to result in a "miscalculated" or "spasm" war. He proposed to "burn" these horrible air weapons to achieve one-for-one ratio with Soviet bombers.

After this dramatic and erudite discourse, which left me almost speechless, I began to wonder if my military education had been complete. A lifetime of study and practice of the military art had not prepared me for the pretentious language of the new breed of military philosophers. And *they* were and are the people who have the most influence on our national military policy.

In recent years I have deplored some of the trends which, I believe, threaten American freedom, our Constitutional government, and national survival. Many of these trends are subtle and not always apparent to the layman, even the well-informed layman. To fulfill my proper function as a professional military man I feel obliged to disclose to the American public in this book some of these imperceptible changes and show how they influence the crucial defense issues of today. Then I intend to provide my own analyses as to how these issues should be handled.

I make no claim to objectivity. It is well known that I am partial to air power as a defensive arm of our country. However, I have been and shall continue to be as fair to the other services as my experience will permit. I have a more than average understanding of Army and Navy affairs and a deep respect for the many great leaders in these sister services. I pray that the following pages do them no injustices nor distort their positions.

No one could be more in sympathy than I with strong, positive management techniques. The SAC pioneered concepts of positive control and cost-effectiveness. No course of action was ever selected until every conceivable alternative was thoroughly studied and evaluated. Probable costs were checked against probable benefits. We computerized every activity susceptible to machine analysis long before most businesses or other government agencies adopted these marvelous mechanical aids. Whatever was subject to objective quantification we quantified and fed into our machines. Where the data were *not* subject to quantification we sought out the very best human judgment we could find.

What we did *not* do was to force non-quantifiable data into a quantified mold in order to feed it to the machines. We did not attempt such hocus pocus as to say arbitrarily that leadership is composed of 60 per cent intelligence, 20 per cent health, 10 per cent aggressiveness, etc., and then to assess these "characteristics" in our officers in order to select the best leaders by computers. Yet, today the urge to "quantify" takes on equally ridiculous manifestations.

A strategic weapons system, for example, is a most complicated and complex feature of government. Many material aspects of it can be quantified, such as the range, speed, effects, and logistics of weapons. But when defense intellectuals attempt, in deadpan seriousness, to quantify the effect that X number of casualties will have on the government or the will to resist, they are entering the Land of Oz. Some countries have succumbed, as France did in 1940, with minor casualties. Carthage and Paraguay (in 1870) show that other countries never give up, no matter what the casualties.

Then there is the matter of analyzing our intelligence. Here the judgment factor looms large. How good is our intelligence? How reliable is our collection system? How accurate our analysis? What have we *not* been able to learn? As one Chief of Staff put it, "We never know what we don't know." The enemy attempts to deceive at every turn. We must concede to him the benefit of some success. This is the only prudent, common-sense course.

Such unknowns in the strategic equation are anathema to the quantifier. His computers cannot work unless he introduces data indicating the precise numbers, characteristics, and dispositions of enemy weapons. Everything is covered very nicely until, for example, we discover that intermediate range ballistic missiles are being installed in Cuba!

Suppose that by 1962 we had scrapped our bombers in favor of an all-intercontinental ballistic missile force. We would have had our Atlas, Titan, and Minuteman missiles aimed at targets across the Atlantic only to learn of a new threat just off the Florida coast. With no bombers (and no way at that time to rapidly re-aim our missiles) we would have been at the mercy of the Soviet Union.

I submit that military strategy, like diplomacy or statecraft, is essentially a subjective art. And because it is largely subjective, we must rely for guidance upon those with the most successful experience. Military strategy has no laws or fixed criteria to measure its correctness.

It is characteristic of all professions, and the military is no exception, that professional judgment provides the best measure of success. When a new surgical technique is developed its worth is decided by the medical profession—not by business or the Government. Given certain arbitrary assumptions, any scientist can compute the "best" solution to a particular problem. But who certifies these assumptions? Who decided that a piece of intelligence information is factual or a plant? Who judges that this or that weapon is "destabilizing" or "vulnerable?" Who determines what level of casualties will cause a country to surrender? Unlike experts in other professions, military men are seldom given the last word on certifying strategic assumptions.

No harm is done, of course, until war begins. Then it may be too late to correct our mistakes. It is a strange phenomenon of our land that professional judgment is respected and given corresponding weight in every area of human endeavor but that of the military. Although national defense consumes the lion's share of our taxes and concerns us deeply and personally, we tend to abide by the judgments of those least capable of giving it.

I. Civil Control of the Military

I AM well aware that political considerations can, do, and must transcend military ones when formulating national policy. I have the greatest respect for astute politicians, diplomats, and statesmen. These people seldom overstep their roles and are attentive seekers of bona fide military knowledge and advice. My quarrel is with those who usurp the military professional's position—those who step in front of him and who volunteer and enforce strictly *military* advice and guidance with little knowledge of or experience in such matters. These are the men who have endangered America. Strangely, these individuals are the least apt to give way to political considerations. They usually insist that the military problems of our age—the "proliferation of nuclear weapons," "the arms race," "mistake, miscalculation, or accident" in handling nuclear weapons, or the possibility of nuclear "holocaust"—overshadow all other considerations.

As soon as a man in uniform questions the competence of any civilian to make military judgments, he is charged out of hand with questioning the virtue of civilian control of the military. This is an unfair charge. Such accusations are usually a sly gambit for quieting military opposition to a particular defense philosophy or course of action. The gambit falls upon a fertile field of vague misconceptions of what *kind* and *degree* of civilian control of the military is in the best interests of democratic Constiutional government and national defense.

The bogey of military dictatorship is at the root of the civilian control premise. Yet no country in history has been less susceptible to a military takeover than the United States. Strangely, people fail to appreciate that the principal reason why America has not been threatened by a man on horseback is because the American military profession is itself steeped in the tradition of civil supremacy over the military. Not only is this doctrine fundamental to the American military profession, taught from the beginning of military training and devoutly believed, but the armed forces of the United States have repeatedly fostered and protected this principle.

At times when American military power reigned almost supreme, as during the Revolution, the Civil War, and the two World Wars, the military establishment was only too happy to return control to civil authority. Washington, Grant, Pershing and March, Marshall and Eisenhower, yes, and even MacArthur, were sincere believers in civil control of the military. This did not go as far, particularly in MacArthur's case, as believing that the military man should not speak up on matters which he was particularly qualified by study and experience to discuss. But one must remember that MacArthur scrupulously followed his orders not to bomb beyond the Yalu even at the risk of letting his own army be destroyed.

The President, as Commander-in-Chief, always has the last word and no military man worth his salt would have it any other way.

What frequently beclouds the issue is the haphazard use of the two words "civil" and "civilian." They have been interchanged so often that most people fail to detect the fine semantic distinction between them. Although synonomous, "civil" refers to non-military *government administration*, whereas a "civilian" is a non-military *person*.

No one in uniform ever questions the non-military government administration of the military services. It is clearly set up this way by the Constitution with the President as the Commander-in-Chief. This is the legitimate and traditional civil control of the military.

On the other hand, "civilian control" implies that this non-military governmental control must always be administered by a civilian. Nothing in the Constitution specifies this, and since our first President was also the first soldier of the land, one might question the validity of the idea. The concept can be further questioned when we consider that our first Secretary of War was a general, Henry Knox.

Of course, General Washington pointedly shed his uniform when he became President Washington. All other generals-turned-President have followed suit. This clearly demonstrates that the military firmly believe in *civil* control of the military, that is, control by a legitimately constituted elected government.

It certainly does not mean that military men are beyond the pale and somehow not worthy of civil posts. In fact quite the contrary is true. Our forefathers intended for military men to be active in civil politics. They simply wanted no military government. Nor did they want any President to become too powerful, and for that reason they divided the control of the military between the executive and the legislative branches of government.

They did not feel that because a man wore no uniform he was somehow more trustworthy. This idea is of relatively recent origin. (See *The Eagle's Talons* by Dale O. Smith.) But let us please not call this concept "traditional" or "Constitutional," for it is neither.

The distrust of the man in uniform has led to the recent practice of *civilian command* of the military being justified on the basis of civil control. By civilian command I refer to the detailed direction of military forces by the civilian echelon of the Department of Defense. Traditionally and Constitutionally this has been a *military* responsibility.

Certain laws of recent vintage, however, do distinguish between the civilian and the military. The National Security Act of 1947, for example, clearly specifies that no former regular officer be appointed Secretary of Defense unless he has been inactive for at least ten years. Such a restriction does not apply to the Presidency nor was it applied to the post of Secretary of War. I fail to appreciate how remoteness from military life will enhance a candidate's qualifications for Secretary of Defense, but that is beside the point. Congress no doubt felt that a regular officer too soon out of uniform would somehow threaten democratic government.

This ghost of the man on horseback continues to haunt the halls of Congress and the corridors of the Pentagon. The oversimplified nostrum for protection from this spook is to assume that any civilian supervision of the military is good, while any decisive military action independent of civilian dictation is bad.

The emphasis on *civilian* activity in all areas of military affairs has cut deeply into the traditional roles and responsibilities of the military. The apparent purpose of this, as we have noted, is to avoid military dictatorship. Yet this purpose is as anachronistic as Don Quixote's attacks on windmills. Why, then, does the "civilization" of the military persist? Indeed, it not only persists, but it steadily grows.

At the turn of the century the War Department was filled

with military homesteaders who spent their entire careers in Washington. These officers became superb bureaucrats. Each branch chief of the Army had his own little self-perpetuating sinecure, completely out of touch with field conditions and operating in a sort of detached dream world.

Then came the rude awakening of the Spanish American War. Although not a very big war, it was snarled up beyond belief by the War Department. Without staff coordination, troops went without food, proper clothing, sanitation, and ammunition. When it was over, Elihu Root was appointed to find out what went wrong. It did not take him long to see that the headquarters homesteaders had lost touch with the Army. The remedy was simple. Washington tours of duty were curtailed. A four-year limit was established, then transfer to the field became mandatory. This "Manchu Law" remains in effect today. It was a wise military decision and a sensible solution to a serious organizational problem. Military headquarters in Washington have since been representative of true conditions in the field simply because senior staff officers have recently served there.

However, now we have come full cycle. By civilianizing our military headquarters we have backed into the same condition which Elihu Root found in 1900. Civilians not only are not required to rotate to the field, they have meager, if any, military backgrounds in the first place. Thus they have a built-in detachment from the military establishment. They operate from an unrealistic ivory tower.

There is still another danger in this civilian hierarchy. This new bureaucracy, like any other, develops internal loyalties and group objectives which may sometimes take on more significance than the remoter military needs. Also, its members are a good deal more vulnerable to political pressures than people in uniform. Civil positions frequently have poltical overtones, as do many of the decisions made by the incumbents.

Superficial observers criticize the Chiefs of Staff who may suggest alterations in the budget submitted to Congress by their civilian superiors. Annual military budgets have a direct bearing upon the weapons, military posture, and strategies with which the military Chiefs fulfill their obligations. Not only are the Chiefs responsible to their civilian superiors, but also to Congress and to the American public. The budget is a clear reflection of military judgment, and it is only natural that professional military leaders will have points of difference with their civilian superiors.

It is all very well to say that the judgment of the civilian superiors is arrived at through cost analysis, but cost analysis is not a magic formula available only to those in mufti. It has long been practiced in military staff work under other terms. Differences in judgment arise not because of conflicting methods of analyses, but because different assumptions and postulates are injected into the analyses.

For example, it may be assumed in one instance by the defense intellectuals that manned aircraft will be destroyed on the ground by enemy intercontinental ballistic missiles, whereas military planners might assume a large percentage of the aircraft would become airborne before the nuclear missiles hit. Tracing these assumptions back in the reasoning process, we find that the first group had postulated a tactical surprise and a breakdown in our electronic warning system; the second group had postulated just the opposite. The end result is that the first group considers strategic bombers highly vulnerable and only good if used offensively—thus highly provocative and destabilizing weapons. The military group, on the other hand, concludes that bombers are tried and tested, able to escape an enemy attempt at surprise attack, and a necessary flexible weapon in our arsenal.

We must keep in mind that Congress is charged by the Constitution "to raise and support armies" (and this has been judicially construed to include air forces). Thus Congress has a right and duty to probe into military matters. When called upon by Congress the military Chiefs of Staff are required to answer questions put to them by Congressmen. Codified in 5 United States Constitution 652(d) and 10 United States Constitution 1034, this is the law of the land.

Far from flouting civil control of the military this system of Congressional inquiry represents a fundamental principle of our government—the checks and balances. In this way the Congress and the President share their dual responsibilities for administering the armed forces.

This joint jurisdiction between the Legislative and Executive Branches of the government over the military was established to guard against the possibility of military tyranny and to curb the hands of an overly ambitious President. The specter of Oliver Cromwell controlling Parliament through the army was probably in the minds of our forefathers. Congress was thus given the purse strings by which an army was to be raised and paid. It was also charged with making "rules for the government and regulation of the land and naval forces." Because of this a military leader is often placed in an awkward and ambiguous position. He may receive conflicting instructions from Congress and from his civilian superiors in the Executive Branch. Caught in the middle, the military leader too frequently is accused of disrespect for civilian control when actually he is simply performing his statutory duties which were designed to enhance civil control.

Military dictatorship is a popular topic of discussion today, probably because the military establishment has been kept rather large since 1950. Following V-J Day we thought for a time that we could revert to the token military establishment we had traditionally relied upon in time of peace. But modern technology changed that. The realities of air power and nuclear explosives forced the American people to realize that our only protection was a ready force-in-being. The Korean war illustrated beyond a doubt that there were aggressive forces in the world ready to bury us if they could. Since then we have never relaxed our guard; it is well that we have not. Where would we have been today, for example, if the Cuban missile crisis of 1962 had found us unprepared?

This large peace-time military establishment has allowed many scaremongers to capitalize on the traditional anti-military American attitudes and thus sell books and movies. I deplore this unprincipled literature. It is like yelling fire in a crowded theater. Some of this man-on-horseback talk, I am sure, is encouraged by our enemies to weaken faith in our military leadership and thus to undermine our resolve or capability for self-defense. Some of it, of course, is a perfectly legitimate concern over how a large, perpetual military establishment will change our system of values, society, and government. Dispassionate inquiries of this new phenomenon of American life are healthy; suggestions that military leaders have designs on democratic government are false and harmful.

A hue and cry against imaginary demons in American uniforms can destroy us. One must keep in mind the communist technique of "boring from within." Finding weakness in a system and concentrating attacks on it is good strategy in any conflict.

Having served for over a quarter of a century in some of the highest military positions, I know the suggestion that a military cabal might seize control of the United States is utter nonsense. No American professional man in uniform, steeped in the traditions of Constitutional government, would entertain the thought for a moment. The first institution in our land to extol and foster legitimate civil control under the Constitution is the American military institution.

Freedom of speech and press are the strongest safeguards against dictatorship. History illustrates that the first act of a dictator is to distort and suppress the news. Free speech and press permit the truth to be aired and opposing opinions to be expressed. Dictatorship cannot survive for long when national issues are freely debated in public. Freedom of opinion before a Congressional committee or even within the Executive Branch, is one of the hallmarks of our free society. It would be an unthinking step toward tyranny to prevent military leaders from expressing their honest views before Congress.

II. The Impact of Organization

TO A large extent military national strategy is a product of defense organization. We must therefore examine the organizational birthplace of strategy. It is here that the decisions are made which determine whether we live or die as a nation, and whether we, as individuals, will enjoy an honorable peace or suffer a cruel war. (I will not consider a third alternative—that of surrender—no matter how the pill might be sugarcoated.) These are hard, grim choices which we cannot avoid, and I for one do not believe our present organization for defense is prepared to face them realistically and efficiently.

Our literature is replete with books on management and decision-making. Yet there is little objective, scientific knowledge to aid us with the innumerable and crucial problems of national defense. The best information available comes from successful experience, yet even here we find anomalies and contradictions. Genghis Khan achieved his objectives with a despotic central control, but Hitler failed with an equally tyrannical dictatorship. Athens succumbed to what might be considered an excess of democracy, yet Rome grew to greatness under a similar system of organization.

In the Pentagon today we find champions of the monolithic defense organization who make a case for "unified command" right up to the Secretary of Defense and the President. This philosophy is predominant today. Yet there are others, myself among them (contrary to popular opinion) who believe that greater *de*-centralization of authority would be to our advantage, and who feel that a certain degree of healthy competition and controversy opens up new approaches and novel solutions to defense problems which change continually.

The world is moving too fast today, particularly in technology, for us to be tied to a monolithic organization which stifles all thought outside its own party line of hackneyed solutions. Preconceived solutions to new problems deny us the chance to use the great advances in science and technology. Why go to the moon, for example, if the experience does not somehow add to human security? The discoveries of science and invention are of no real value until they are translated into tools and processes which improve man's life on earth. And one of our first concerns—in fact *the* first concern in the face of danger—is security.

I am not talking solely about gadgets and hardware. I am talking about what people must *do* and how they must operate to be successful in war. The strictly human aspects of techniques, methods, systems, tactics, strategy, doctrine, and policies are even more important than hardware. A superior fighter plane, for example as was the Japanese Zero compared to General Chennault's P-40, came off second best when employed without vision. Similarly, our naval force at Pearl Harbor went down to defeat not because of inferior equipment, but because our defense policies, strategies, doctrines, intelligence, and communications were inadequate to cope with a massive and well-executed surprise attack.

One of the greatest dangers in a military estimate of any situation is to believe, through party-line strategic concepts, that you *know* what the enemy will or will not do. We *knew* that Japan would not attack Pearl Harbor, our best-defended outpost. According to us it would have been sheer suicide for her to attempt it.

Just a few years ago we were victims of the same kind of blindness. We *knew* that the Soviet Union would not put nuclear intermediate range ballistic missiles in Cuba. It was out of character, as defined by us, for the U.S.S.R. to make such a dangerous move. Even after seeing the photographic evidence taken by our reconnaissance planes, our leaders found it difficult to believe, and even more difficult to take the necessary next steps vital to our defense.

How could this have been prevented? By keeping Cuba out of communist hands in the first place. By providing air cover at the Bay of Pigs. By blockading Cuba early in the game—with a tight blockade, not the sham blockade which we attempted later when we might have aggravated the Soviets too much. But these stitch-in-time steps, and others, were never taken. We never believed that the U.S.S.R. might be a real threat in this hemisphere. Now we know, too late.

We must—but do not—have a defense organization which permits controversy, which permits the "unthinkable" condition to be debated freely, which permits the screwball idea to come forth, and which tolerates the maverick officer. The Andrew Jacksons, the Zachary Taylors, the Ulysses S. Grants, the George Deweys, the Alfred Thayer Mahans, the Billy Mitchells, are not nurtured in orthodoxy. They are not products of a party line. And we have not infrequently called on them to save our shirts.

True, we need purposefulness and common direction. We

need objectives and decisions. But this must not rule out innovation, ingenuity, and initiative.

It has long been held axiomatic by most military men that unity of command is fundamental to effective military operations. This axiom has been repeated so often by generations of soldiers that it is rarely questioned. Yet unity of command has not always been marked with military success, nor has divided command always been unsuccessful.

The facts of history and experience reveal that unity of command is a military nostrum which may not automatically cure all organizational ills. As a doctrine and principle of war it must be qualified. Under some circumstances unity of command may hinder effective operations by the denial of initiative and competition. It may also contribute to fixed indoctrination and orthodoxy in outmoded practices and beliefs, thereby leading to defeat. Unity of command may retard the feedback of information which is helpful in correcting erroneous judgments (questioning orders as MacArthur did), and it may encourage rote thinking and behavior which freezes imagination and progress.

Unity of command seems most appropriate in actual warfare of modern times. A commander must be able to apply his forces with the reliability of a well-oiled machine. Commands must be passed unaltered to the last soldier, each carrying out commands explicity if the machine is to operate as planned. As events unfold, the commander must be able to shift and redirect his military machine to take advantage of opportunities as well as to lessen the consequences of failure. Only unity of command permits such rapid and precise re-deployments.

The larger and more cumbersome a military force grows, the more necessity for unity of command. In military circles, therefore, the concept has become a liturgy.

Still and all, it warrants analysis, for even in combat the doctrine may sometimes hinder success. First, plans of any sort are products of prediction and human judgment. Experience shows that prediction is far from precise in any endeavor, least of all in the military field where the enemy works constantly to deceive and hence invalidate predictions.

Second, if information concerning a dangerously changing situation is lacking, a commander may be defeated. At least some slight disunity of command, some authority to initiate or countermand orders, must be granted subordinates if unforeseen hazards are to be avoided or countered. The same argument applies to taking advantage of fleeting opportunities. In war at supersonic speeds, countering action may only be possible at the very instant the opportunity is recognized.

Finally, in point of actual practice, good commanders *do* take liberties with unity of command as the military situation dictates. However, such disturbing deviations tend to be overlooked or rationalized and are seldom discussed. While a subordinate at the siege of Copenhagen, Lord Nelson put his telescope to his blind eye in order not to see the flagship's signal to withdraw. He won the battle and survived the charges of insubordination. The practice of subtle insubordination, less brazenly executed, is not unknown in modern forces, and has led to the common remark, "He should either have been decorated or court martialed."

Unity of command in peacetime presents still other questionable advantages. The military has too often been charged with lagging behind social and technical progress. Could the doctrine of unity of command have something to do with this assumed social and technical lag?

Military objectives in peacetime are not as distinct nor as clearly understood as in time of war. In war, there is the enemy to overcome, battles to win, production to accelerate, supplies to move. Innovation is secondary and seldom even possible because of the press of time. We fight with what we have already developed not only in terms of hardware, but in terms of organization, doctrine, strategy, and tactics.

In peacetime we must advance. We must improve the whole spectrum of military art to bring it abreast with mankind's ever-enlarging field of knowledge. Not only must there be invention and improvement of hardware, but also there must be the doctrine to employ it, the strategy to fit it to national policy and the situation, and the tactics to operate and coordinate it.

Unlike most endeavors, little military progress can be tested empirically short of war itself. Most innovation, then, must rest on *a priori* judgment—from principle to particular. No experienced person is ever fully convinced that these judgments are correct.

Every field of military endeavor requires decisions in time of peace. And when there is no sure way of judging correctness, several judgments or options are better than one. Unity of command tends to decrease the extent of these judgments, although unity of command would, certainly, assure a judgment if one were needed.

Riding, Roman fashion, both the unity-of-command horse and the civilian-control-of-the-military horse, the Pentagon finds itself on a most unstable and confusing platform. These mounts were simply not made to gallop abreast. Until now it has never been conceived that civilians should "command" the military. They are not trained to command military units. They are not subject to the Uniform Code of Military Justice. They are susceptible to political pressures and sometimes lose sight of military objectives, if not of national interests.

Yet there has been a consistent tendency to centralize all power and authority in the hands of the Secretary of Defense, leaving the matter of "command" an empty question of semantics. Not only has this centralization been sanctioned by law, but an extremely ambitious and dynamic Secretary of Defense has been able to wrest every residual shred of authority from his military subordinates, leaving them in the prosaic role of technical advisers. Not infrequently their advice has been overthrown on purely *military* grounds.

Secretary of Defense Robert S. McNamara, for example, all but abolished the Service intelligence functions, and created the Defense Intelligence Agency (DIA), which reported directly to him. Similar "unified" staff agencies have been created in other areas. The Defense Atomic Support Agency, the Defense Supply Agency, and the Defense Communication Agency are vast military bureaucracies which by-pass the Joint Chiefs of Staff and report to the Secretary of Defense.

Nine unified and specified commands, such as the Strategic Air Force, the North American Air Defense Command, the United States Command in Europe, and the Pacific Area Command, report to the Secretary of Defense through the Joint Chiefs of Staff. And let no one be deceived—that office calls the shots.

The office of Defense Research and Engineering was created and given final authority over the Research and Development program and of the development and procurement of weapons. The office of the Assistant Secretary of Defense for International Security Affairs (ISA) runs the military assistance program, and in this capacity has the final word (short of the Secretary of Defense and the President) in calling the shots in Vietnam. This office has become more significant than the Joint Chiefs of Staff National Military Command Center. Here in ISA senior civilians juggle troops and plan air strikes on the basis of their superior "policy" knowledge, and justify this by harking to "civilian control of the military."

I question whether an organization as unwieldy and amateurish as has been created by the Secretary of Defense could ever propagate a successful war. The dismal results in Vietnam attest to this doubt. Never in our history have we suffered such a string of diplomatic, political, and military defeats as we have since 1961. About all that can be said for this leadership is that we have avoided nuclear war. But the avoidance of general war is easy to achieve if we wish to accept graduated surrender in return.

Not all changes introduced by the bourgeoning Office of the Secretary of Defense are undesirable. Many efforts to reduce duplication were overdue, and important monetary savings have been made, although not as many as have been claimed. When one has been able to probe beneath the surface, too often "savings" have been hailed when essential weapons development programs such as the B-70, the Dyna-Soar, and the Skybolt were canceled. To the extent that unity has been sought as a means to avoid rather than solve issues, dollar savings have been gained at the cost of operational flexibility.

Perhaps the outstanding example of the former is in the field of intelligence. Service intelligence estimates have historically varied widely. Contrary to the frequent charge that these differences reflected parochial manipulation, in my experience such variations demonstrate the subjective nature of the judgments involved and the sincere concern of the reporting officers with their areas of interest. Unifying intelligence activities into the DIA may end the annoyance of three separate estimates, but it does not make the new single estimate more reliable than any one of the previous three. On the contrary, our chances of striking an accurate estimate are reduced because the "unified" intelligence is subject to the fashionable bias, and there is no devil's advocate. For example, when Secretary McNamara questioned the estimate of Soviet Army strength the estimate was revised downward. It was well known that he hoped to make a case for the defense of the North Atlantic Treaty Organization with conventional weapons rather than with nuclear weapons. The DIA provided no devil's advocate, no loyal opposition, or jaundiced eye. We have lost the forceful reminder of the uncertainty of intelligence, and run the danger of adopting a "line" without the spur of an alert competitor.

Even if centralization could provide an organization without competing centers of power, its advisability would be questionable. I do not believe a monolithic organization can consistently provide useful answers in a field as subjective as defense policy. Such a goal mistakes the very nature of national security policy. Policy must provide for varying judgments of both ends and means. To the extent that the Department of Defense organization fails to provide for the development, expression, and consideration of opposing views, and for a clear determination between them, policy formulation will suffer and the effectiveness of the Secretary of Defense will diminish.

Many people have a superficial and erroneous view of defense policy development as a problem to which there must be a single, clear, forceful answer. Were this conception accurate, their suggestion of a pyramidal organization topped by an all-powerful decision-maker would be accurate. However, at this level, the "yes, sir; no, sir"; "no excuse, sir" approach to a military problem is inappropriate and can only lead to a continuing cycle of centralization, inadequacy, frustration, and further centralization.

The answer, of course, is to turn defense planning and command back to the professionals in uniform. Perhaps, as in the present Joint Chiefs of Staff, a unanimity can be created and common doctrines arrived at.

Publication of comments and studies by the military profession about professional matters has been generally discouraged and sometimes prohibited by the civilian control element in the Pentagon. This gagging of the military professional has been more prevalent since World War II, for various laws regarding the disclosure of classified information have provided a vehicle for much censorship. What is or is not classified information is often a matter of judgment, and it becomes administratively simple to prohibit publication on the ground that a manuscript contains classified information. Although civilian control over publication serves to discourage professional writing, still more effective is a nineteenth-century attitude in the military itself which says, in effect, that the military should remain apart and separate from the general public and that military writing should be strictly designed for military consumption, as with training manuals or staff studies.

A less biased public view of the military profession could probably be achieved if those who serve in the military as professionals were encouraged to write more about it. As it is, the erroneous folklore of an unreliable military profession continues to be strengthened with biased literature. And until this bias is overcome the national security system cannot attain its optimal effectiveness.

Organizations to unify the three military services have been proposed *ad infinitum.* There is a feeling that if we could only achieve a certain combination of boxes and lines on an organizational chart, the manifold command and coordination problems would be solved. Less thought is given to the organizational changes that cannot be depicted on a chart, such as greater freedom of expression, a common promotion list, interservice transfer, common uniforms, and rotation among services. Might not mixing these systems reveal talents and valuable innovations? Might not informal organizational systems be created which would lead toward more effective interservice unification? Might not such changes be more palatable than the general

staff system which continues to be proposed and which is re-
sisted with such strong prejudice?

Military men who have served with contemporaries in other
services tend to lose some of their own service bias. This is not
absolute, by any means. Even so it is a step in the right direction. When one has good, respected friends in another service,
his esteem for that other service is raised.

Some exchange of officers among the military services is now
undertaken, but the number is so small as to be no more than a
token with minor influence on unification. Service schools provide the best mixing process now practiced, but even here the
effort involves so few people as to hit far short of the mark. It
might be well to increase the interservice exchange program at
all levels as a step toward, if not unification, at least greater
appreciation of the doctrines, tactics, and techniques of other
services.

No one wishes to achieve a case-hardened unified doctrine
that is followed blindly and slavishly by all people in uniform.
Such a one-service outlook would stifle all imagination, ambi-
tion, and progress. Only a few, albeit a powerful few, however,
support the present system with its four largely independent
services, and a remote Department of Defense. Viciously competing over budgets, weapons systems, roles, missions, priori-
ties, properties, and even publicity, the contestants devote only
minimal time to the essential task of national strategy. Few will
gainsay that although competition can be healthy, excesses we
now find in the Pentagon are self-destructive.

The ideal is to strike a balance, but the answer is not to be
found in the civilian Office of the Secretary of Defense (OSD)
no matter how it is organized or how authoritarian it may become. Unification may be achieved at this civilian control level,
but sound military progress and direction will be reduced proportionately. National security already sorely suffers from this

bureaucratic stop-gap solution. Only within the military profession itself can a balanced and productive unification be found.

Every institution, whether it be a government, a military service, a business, or a university has two kinds of organizations. One is written—established by a constitution, charter, laws, regulations, written policies, or something of this kind. This is the conscious organization, the one people believe controls the activity of the institution. The other organization is unwritten, often unvoiced, and sometimes even unrecognized. It might be called the unconscious or hidden organization. It consists of the customs, traditions, habits, value patterns, and standard practices of the institution's members, and it is usually far more significant than the written one. Because it is hidden from view, the unwritten organization is harder to cope with.

To cite an example, nowhere in the Constitution do we find reference to the two-party system which is fundamental, yet unofficial, to our system of government. Nor does the lobbying aspect of the government appear in a formal system, although laws have been passed in a somewhat unsuccessful effort to regulate this traditional and potent practice.

Everyone has experienced informal systems of organization, and almost everyone is well aware of the overriding importance of these informal chains of command which encompass communications, responsibility, and authority. Seldom do the written organizational guides correspond to these informal networks. There are likes and dislikes, animosities and friendships, traditions and habits, varying abilities, talents, and interests, all of which directly affect the organization. No amount of discipline and effort to follow written job descriptions and prescribed channels will eliminate these dominating human factors which establish the hidden organization.

The hidden organization is one of the major influences leading to reorganization of the formal system. When the formal system becomes completely meaningless, there is nothing left to do but change it to conform more closely with the practical hidden system. Reorganizations that fail to consider the hidden organization are generally unsuccessful.

To achieve an organizational evolution, then, it would seem logical to work on the informal level as a first step. If customs and habits can be formed, the formal endorsement will eventually follow. Some major cultural changes have been accomplished in a short period by strong men who have enforced their wishes on a whole people and made them stick. Kemal Ataturk's Westernization of Turkey and his insistence on a new alphabet is an example. But such instances are rare even in history, and certainly not in consonance with the American democratic philosophy. Cultural changes—changes which affect hidden organizations such as those found in the military—are evolutionary in American society, although they do come about to some degree by conscious campaigns of persuasion.

One of the major reasons our system of national defense is in such a deplorable state is that an anti-military bias throughout the land prevents the military from becoming a true American profession. This bias heaps hundreds of amateur administrators on top of the professionals and continually subjects the professionals to barriers to progress in the name of civilian control.

No new National Security Act will end the confusion, proliferation of supervisors, shredded authority, and ceaseless bickering found in the Pentagon until the hidden bias against the military is somehow overcome. This will never happen until the literature on civil-military relations itself becomes unbiased. Unfortunately the dark side of the coin makes better reading because it confirms the suspicious attitude toward the military held by the general population.

It is doubtful that much progress can be expected from any group that is believed to be fundamentally untrustworthy. Checks, limits, supervisions, and investigations of the group will assume overriding importance, so that true progress in the profession will steadily degenerate—and along with it, our national security. Therefore, to foster progress in the military arts we must raise the people's regard for the military profession.

At the very heart of warfare lies doctrine. It represents the central beliefs for waging war in order to achieve victory. Doctrine is of the mind, a network of faith and knowledge reinforced by experience which lays the pattern for the utilization of men, equipment, and tactics. It is the building material for strategy. It is fundamental to sound judgment.

When Peter the Hermit, credited with organizing the First Crusade, made allies of hundreds of strife-ridden European states to march as one against the Infidel, it was one of the most amazing accomplishments of history. However, each state had a different idea about warfare, even though Pope Urban II had clearly established the objective of rescuing the Holy Sepulcher from the Moslems.

Since most of Peter the Hermit's followers were poor and untrained civilians, it is another wonder that they marched as far as Constantinople. Peter's impassioned sermons had gained some capable men-at-arms to the cause who were later able to overcome their doctrinal differences and conquer Jerusalem. But the first two ragged divisions led by Peter himself and Walter the Penniless perished utterly at the hands of the Seljuk Turks. Piles of white bones left on the desert were monuments to the belief that zeal and civilian leadership can prevail in combat against military organization, experience, and common doctrine.

Some typical doctrines are the concept of unity of command which we have examined, as well as the pyramidal organization, the need for decisiveness with caution, gaining surprise through security and audacity, and conserving of resources in order that a maximum effort may be exerted at the time and place of our choosing in order to exploit an enemy weakness and gain a decisive advantage. Such doctrines are not immutable, as we have seen in the case of unity of command. But only professional experience can judge the circumstances under which exceptions and innovations should be made.

We are saddled today with doctrines quite foreign to the doctrines learned through millennia of bitter military experience. Although I will analyze these later in this book, let me mention two such doctrines to show how far from reality we can stray when we become victims of the preachings of modern Peter the Hermits.

We have been pursuing the doctrine of "the pause." This is conceived as a ceasing of hostilities before a military decision has been arrived at, or even before we have achieved a military advantage. The pause is supposed to give the enemy a chance to think it over and ponder the consequences, possibly, of a nuclear attack. Now this pause could work *provided* there was credibility in our implied threat to use nuclear weapons. Without such credibility "the pause" is only an expression of our fundamental irresolution to pursue the conflict to a favorable conclusion.

I am not suggesting that negotiations are inadvisable. On the contrary, no war, even a general war, is terminated without negotiating. But negotiations should be undertaken *without halting the fighting*. We should never allow an enemy to think us irresolute because we are willing to talk. Only when he meets our terms should a ceasefire be ordered.

On his return from Geneva in 1954 Gen. Walter Bedell Smith made a remark after Vietnam had been divided into two states, one communist and one free:

It will be well to remember that diplomacy has rarely been able to gain at the conference table what cannot be gained or held on the battlefield.

There simply is no point in negotiating from weakness, and the strength for negotiating must contain the vital element of credibility.

"The pause" may trap us another way. It may find us with our arms down when the enemy is launching nuclear weapons. It may offer him the slight edge in time and surprise that would mean our national demise.

Another such shortsighted doctrine at work today is that of "graduated and flexible response." This doctrine has a fine-sounding ring to it, but as practiced it is "graduated" but "*in*-flexible." It is graduated in that force is brought to bear against the enemy in increments which never seem quite enough to do the job, and "inflexible" because we fail to apply force at places and times of our choosing where we can profit by our strength and exploit enemy weaknesses. Such a doctrine led to the too-little-too-late Bay of Pigs misadventure. And unhappily we are again pursuing it in Vietnam.

Going back to the Crusades example, we find it interesting to note that the Sixth Crusade achieved its purpose by *not* attacking Jerusalem, the obvious objective. In fact, there was no fighting whatever. Frederick II of Sicily took advantage of the animosity that existed among his rivals, and, reinforced by the credibility of a possible attack on Cairo, he gained possession of the Holy Land for ten years by way of treaty. Forty years of warfare had been unsuccessful in achieving this result. Historians point out that Frederick was more interested in gaining his objective than in punishing the enemy, and for this he was severely disciplined by Pope Gregory IX.

It is possible sometimes to take advantage of enemy weaknesses without fighting, but unfortunately not with the "gradual and flexible response" doctrine we are practicing today.

America can be free for centuries if we adopt sensible military organization and common doctrines for waging war. Of course, the doctrine must be good; dynamically fitted to the environment of its day. But doctrine is the great unseen root of military strength and the basis of any unity. It is not enough to give lip service to unification and set up organizations to achieve it. Unification can never be achieved by superimposing a bureaucratic structure. It will only be realized when military doctrine has more commonality among and within all of the armed services.

III. The Strategic Situation

ANY ASSESSMENT of strategy begins with the time-honored military "estimate of the situation." This rests upon the logical premise that we can hardly chart a course for future navigation until we know where we have been and where we are today. An estimate of any situation is fraught with many "unknowns," and the assumptions we make about these "unknowns" are the cause of such a wide divergence among strategists and strategies.

As an experienced professional I distinguish hard facts from "unknowns" and "assumptions." I am also prepared to be proved wrong by history and therefore demand flexibility and options in any military policy. The defense intellectuals, however, believing they can quantify assumptions and theories, thereby transforming "unknowns" into hard facts. They need no flexibility or extra options. They are so sure of themselves that they refuse to hedge their bets even when the stakes are national survival.

Let me cite an example which has given me real concern in recent years. One of the cogent reasons given by scientific analysts for the lessening need for manned strategic bombers was that the Soviet Surface to Air (SAM) anti-aircraft missiles would shoot down too many of the relatively slow-flying bombers. There was little doubt that a SAM missile had shot down Francis Gary Powers' U-2 over Russia, and another U-2 in 1962 over Cuba. From these two specifics, together with some inconclusive intelligence (much drawn from Soviet boasts and film clips of SAM's blasting I-28 jet bomber target drones), and analogies drawn from the performance of our own Nike and Hawk anti-aircraft weapons, a conclusion was reached which appeared to doom the high-flying strategic bomber.

Although the evidence and the preponderance of figures seemed to be against me, I persisted in believing that the analysis was far from conclusive and that the manned strategic bomber could still be used without suffering prohibitive losses from the Soviet SAMs. History, and the judgment of hundreds of capable and level-headed bomber and ex-bomber commanders, were on my side. Such practical evidence was cavalierly tossed aside by the decision-makers, however, and to this day—long past the eleventh hour—no replacement has been planned for the aging B-52s save the jury-rigged fighter bomber, the FB-111.

The verdict on this debate has now been made with the air attacks against SAM-defended North Vietnam. The box score at the end of 1967 revealed the relative weakness of SAM defenses against determined, skillful, and well-equipped air invaders. Only about 2.5 per cent of the SAMs launched against penetrating aircraft have hit home. And our airmen continue to widen their edge with improved evasive action, better radar countermeasures, and more effective methods of attack.

Well, what does this mean? It means that one of the telling arguments for the elimination of manned bombers has proved just as false as the argument that Columbus would sail off the edge of a flat world. It means that the decisions—vital decisions to our national survival—concerning the need for replacement of strategic bombers, were made with the wrong kind of evidence and later proved false. It means that the computers, and those who believed so implicitly in this method of analysis were dead wrong, because wrong data were fed into the machines. It means that common human judgment based on practical experience was right.

One might surmise that, in the face of this new evidence, our leaders would re-think their earlier decisions about the survivability of bombers. But there is little indication that this is being done. They are still studying the problem. Will we still be studying when a nuclear ultimatum is hurled at us?

Thus an "estimate of the situation" can upset a whole line of strategic thinking. We must, in analyzing the situation of "today," keep an open mind, give full weight to history, to successful experience, and to sober, unquantified human judgment. We must be prepared to hedge our bets so that we will not be caught as we now are—*without the weapons necessary to preserve our independence.*

How did this happen?

American military doctrine preaches that because motives are obscure, we should only report enemy *capabilities* in estimating the situation. Indeed, capabilities are far more tangible and understandable than motives. And the doctrine obviates much speculation which at the tactical level might be somewhat naïve. But when wrestling with strategy at the national level we must fully consider enemy intentions insofar as we can assess them.

The "boilerplate" for an estimate of the situation first calls for an analysis of friendly forces. Let us briefly examine the evolution of our air doctrine and our roles and missions in order to peg the position of our thinking today.

From August 1, 1909, when the War Department acquired

its first airplane from the Wright brothers, until the present day when the Advanced Manned Strategic Airplane (AMSA) is still under debate, the roles and missions of military aviation have been fraught with heated controversy. The airplane was first assigned to the Signal Corps, that branch of service charged with scouting and reconnaissance. The airplane, like the balloon, was ideally suited for this mission. Controversy soon materialized, however, when visionaries began to see other roles and missions for the airplane, such as direct combat functions.

Air combat broke out in World War I. First came air-to-air engagements to deter the scouting role undertaken by both sides. Then came the bombing role against troops and behind-the-lines targets which demonstrated limited success but much promise. Next came the escort role to support the bombers. Even the concept of airlift and vertical envelopment was planned, but the Armistice came before they were tried. Thus all the roles of air power were revealed in a limited sense in World War I, although there was most certainly no consensus as to their effectiveness.

In the Meuse-Argonne between September 12 and 16, 1918, air power was used for the first time as a massed striking force. Prior to this, engagements were usually between individual aircraft. Gen. Billy Mitchell planned this revolutionary attack in which over fifteen hundred combat aircraft from all allied countries took part. Targets were attacked ahead of the ground forces in relays of five hundred planes. This was the first attempt to apply the theory of "isolation of the battlefield." The success of this air offensive went largely unnoticed—only those who flew really had the opportunity to see the results of air operations.

"The manner in which war is waged varies from age to age and with the advent of new weapons," wrote Field Marshal Montgomery. And the airplane created a revolution in warfare.

The British were the first to experience it. In 1916 British air-craft attacked targets in the Saar basin of Germany, but poor results caused Sir Douglas Haig, commander of all British troops, to dissuade the imaginative airmen from straying from the direct support of the surface forces. The concept of the independent air role, however, was born, never to be subdued for long. Although the German zeppelin raids on London did little military damage, the terror they brought to the city was a foreboding of things to come. More than any other event, these attacks led to the creation of the Air Ministry by the end of 1917, and to a British Independent Air Force in June, 1918.

Those in the United States who envisioned air combat roles as potential rivals to land and sea power pursued a relentless campaign to gain more recognition for military aviation. But not until 1920 was the Air Service created as a combatant branch of the Army.

Reaction had set in rapidly in America following World War I. Even the ex-Chief of Air Service, American Expeditionary Forces, Gen. Mason M. Patrick, reported in 1921 that the war "clearly demonstrated" that observation for surface forces was "the most important and far-reaching mission of aviation in war." General Pershing's final report suggested little promise for aviation. Thus the conceptual struggle between the airmen and the traditionalists entered the Billy Mitchell era, enlivening the press during the years between the wars.

Billy Mitchell claimed that air power was the first line of defense for the United States. This was heresy to the Navy who religiously guarded sea power as the first line of defense. It led to the famous tests off the Virginia Capes in 1921 when the captured German battleship *Ostfriesland* together with a number of other vessels were sent to the bottom by aerial bombs. Still little change was made in the roles and missions of air power. Aviation remained tied to surface forces, principally as an auxiliary, with observation its major role. Strangely, it was not the success of military tests or the oratory of prophets, or impassioned writings which gave American aviation its long-delayed boost into the twentieth century. It was the shock and tragedy of the air mail fiasco of 1934.

President Franklin D. Roosevelt, annoyed over negotiating subsidy rates, cancelled all civilian air mail contracts in 1934 and ordered the Air Corps to fly the mail. The antiquated and poorly instrumented military aircraft were not up to the task. Repeated crashes caused a national scandal, awakening the public to the poor condition into which military aviation had been allowed to sink. The subsequent "Baker Board" led to the purchase of modern military aircraft and the creation of the General Headquarters Air Force, the first significant step toward an independent United States Air Force. Even so, the Baker Board, except for the one dissent of Jimmy Doolittle, reported "independent air missions have little effect upon the issue of battle and none upon the outcome of war."

With these developments the theoretical roles and missions began to take on substance. A four-engine bomber, the B-17, was built, and by 1938 we had intercepted the Italian liner *Rex* 615 miles at sea. The forces of reaction immediately restricted land-based air power to no more than 100 miles from the shoreline, but the realities of long-range flying were so apparent that the independent military role of aviation was never again seriously threatened.

With the German march into Poland on September 1, 1939, exponents of air power were vindicated. Germany employed her *Luftwaffe* as a semi-independent military force, first, knocking out opposing air power and, second, bombing objectives ahead of and in support of the advancing ground forces. Poland was subdued in less than ninety days. At this period dive bombing with the JU-87 (Stuka) was a kind of extended artillery. This *blitzkrieg* pattern was repeated against Denmark, Norway, the Netherlands, Belgium, and France with overwhelming success. Nazi "Operation Sea Lion," the invasion of Britain, would no doubt have been equally successful had not the independent Royal Air Force successfully opposed the *Luftwaffe* in the great Battle of Britain. Not only were German invasion fleets badly damaged by RAF Bomber Command but RAF Fighter Command took such a toll of the invading Nazi air forces that Hitler postponed "Sea Lion" indefinitely.

The concept of bombing the enemy's industrial establishment, even its cities, had been debated in the United States Army Air Corps since the translation of Giulio Douhet's *Air Warfare* by the Air Corps Tactical School in 1933. The concept was gaining more adherents in Britain under the aegis of Air Chief Marshal Sir Hugh Trenchard, who, with Douhet and Mitchell, was one of the triumvirate of early air-power theorists.

The moral compuction against city bombing began to lose force after the German bombing of Coventry. Retaliation and re-retaliation led to all-out "strategic" air warfare by Allied air forces against enemy homefronts. The ultimate expression of this "strategic" war was found in the fire-bombings of Hamburg and Tokyo, and in the atom bombing of Hiroshima and Nagasaki.

Strategic bombing was phenomenally successful as a war-winning tactic, but the break with tradition in which war had been waged primarily against combatants, and the moral revulsion caused by the indiscriminate killing in city bombings, caused much controversy following the war over the advisability of continuing the strategic bombing role. Realism prevailed, however, and the "strategic" role of the Air Force was written into the statutory roles and missions in the National Security Act of 1947.

Other roles and missions of air power took on importance during World War II. The question of air power's superiority over surface fleets was decided once and for all at the Battle of Midway (1942), which was fought entirely by air actions. The fact that most damage was caused by carrier aircraft was incidental to the fact that battleships were no longer able to cope with bombers.

Tactical air power in support of ground operations became co-equal in importance to the ground operations themselves. Air power provided vehicles for vertical envelopment tactics: paratroops, gliders, and air supply. As air power continued in its vital reconnaissance role, aerial photography became the primary source of intelligence. Meteorology was advanced by air observations. And air power provided a massive line of communication circling the globe and hauling vast quantities of supplies and numbers of troops.

The first role of military aviation was always anti-air. Once air superiority had been achieved, the many other missions of air power could be exploited. When D-Day arrived for the invasion of Normandy, everyone asked "Where is the *Luftwaffe?*" It had been largely destroyed in the air and on the ground by superior Allied air power.

At the end of World War II the United States was the sole possessor of the atom bomb and had fielded the greatest military force ever seen. Yet within eighteen months, under the pressures of an internationally immature public and an optimistically innocent conception of world politics, this mighty military force was dissipated. United States security then rested solely upon its nuclear monopoly, its reputation, and the exhaustion of its only potential enemy.

The National Security Act of 1947 established the Air Force

as a co-equal arm of the service to the Army and Navy. No longer was air power an auxiliary to surface arms. But this legislation did not clarify the Air Force mission. It soon became apparent that the passage of the National Security Act had not settled the matter of roles and missions assignments among the services. Secretary of Defense James Forrestal met with the Joint Chiefs of Staff at Key West on March 11–14, 1948, and achieved an agreement of sorts. Although the Air Force was given the primary strategic warfare responsibility by statute, the Navy was permitted to develop weapons which would have a strategic capability, such as long-range carrier attack planes. At a later meeting that year in Newport, an effort was made to resolve the obvious anomalies created at Key West, but with no more success. However, it was generally understood that only the Air Force would build and operate long-range land-based bombers. The Navy was permitted to develop every other kind of military aviation.

Responsibility for strategic warfare again became an issue in 1949 with the debate over the proposed super-carrier, the *United States*. The value of the B-36 strategic bomber was questioned in the "Revolt of the Admirals." But both the large strategic bomber and the super-carrier prevailed. At this point, and in consequence of the bitter debates, the House Committee of the Armed Services complained: "The basic reason for this continuing disagreement is a genuine inability of these services to agree fundamentally and professionally on the art of war."

When the Korean war broke out in 1950 the Far Eastern Air Force had little tactical aviation to support the ground forces. Moreover, the co-equal doctrine, coordinated targeting, forward controllers, and close cooperation techniques at all echelons of command—doctrines which had been developed and successfully employed in World War II—had been largely forgotten. The inadequate air support of the early fighting caused the Army to seek to control and operate its own supporting aviation. Marine units were so organized, with the division commanders commanding integrally assigned Marine Air Wings.

Air Force doctrine held that if air power were fractionated to commanders with limited objectives, air power's ability to concentrate and strike rapidly with great force and in line with broader strategic objectives would be put in jeopardy. When the Army also attempted to gain control of battlefield air transportation, the same "rapid concentration" and "full utilization" arguments were used by the Air Force to retain its control.

As tactical air power grew during the Korean war, and as old tactics and techniques were relearned, the Army's disputes grew less demanding. Yet, from a conceptual standpoint, the argument remains unresolved today: Should the Army or the Air Force control tactical aviation?

Roles and missions again took the spotlight when ballistic missiles were developed in the mid-1950s. The Air Force maintained that any missile with a range extending far beyond the battlefield was a strategic missile. In 1956 the Secretary of Defense ordered the Army to limit its ballistic missiles to a three hundred-mile range. All intercontinental ballistic missiles and intermediate range ballistic missiles became Air Force weapons.

Intensification of the Cold War came when the Soviet Union demonstrated a nuclear capability in 1949, exploded a thermonuclear bomb in 1953, and demonstrated a modern long-range air force. An obvious ICBM capability appeared after Sputnik's flight in 1957. Concern was then raised over the possibility of nuclear war breaking out by accident under some high state of tension and alert. A search was made for what was believed to be a less provocative strategic weapon system, which the Navy was soon to demonstrate in the solid-fueled Polaris.

The question of seaborne missiles then arose. The nuclear-tipped Polaris submarine-launched missile with an initial range of nearly a thousand miles was definitely "strategic." I recommended that this strategic weapon be incorporated into the Strategic Air Command, but service tradition prevailed. At least a common targeting authority was established under SAC, however.

The development of air refueling and lightweight megaton bombs permitted not only Naval aircraft but Air Force tactical fighters to reach and bomb strategic targets. This new technical fact has continued to becloud the roles and missions issues to some extent, although the fierce jurisdictional struggles of the past have abated. The Air Force has become resigned to sharing a portion of its strategic warfare mission with the Navy.

The future will probably see a struggle for jurisdiction over space roles and missions. The Air Force was first authorized to conduct manned space experiments on August 25, 1965. On that day the President announced his approval to proceed with the Manned Orbiting Laboratory (MOL). However, the nonmilitary National Aeronautics and Space Agency (NASA) created in 1958 has been undertaking manned space experiments since 1961. The major roles and missions conflict now seems to be between NASA and the USAF rather than between the Air Force and its sister military services.

Secretary of the Air Force Dr. Harold Brown has listed a number of roles and missions for the Air Force in space. They include navigation, meteorology, communication, anti-satellite, and early warning missions. Air Force leaders have suggested other roles such as anti-missile, or even offensive roles, which are politically unacceptable in the present environment.

We recently secured the Kremlin's agreement to a treaty barring the orbiting of weapons of mass destruction from outer space. This did not deter the Soviet from building the Scrag missile and advertising it as an orbital weapon of very high yield. In order to preserve the détente we have not challenged this near violation of the treaty. We have no evidence that the U.S.S.R. has ever put a loaded Scrag into orbit, although we have tracked many similar Soviet space vehicles and wonder. We have no way of telling for sure.

I believe that we not only have a legitimate mission to build a space craft which could intercept and inspect suspicious satellites, we have a clear and pressing *responsibility* to do so in the interests of national defense. I believe also that we should develop the capability for an orbital weapon as the Soviets have.

Disputes between Air Force, Army, and Navy have been heard in relation to the Vietnam operations, but these are more involved with command relationships and strategies than with service roles and missions.

During the postwar years important reorganization of United States forces has been carried out including the establishment of the SAC, and the introduction of the B-36 bomber. However, little else was done before Korea to prepare militarily for the growing Soviet threat. We were told by the best economists of the land that our national budget could stand no more for defense, that a higher proportion would threaten the overall economy.

It was not until the Korean war that the United States became alarmed enough to rearm. Almost immediately the defense budget was tripled and an effort was begun to modernize our force. The economy prospered.

When SAC was formed shortly after the war, the equipment centered around the wartime B-29 heavy bomber, and later, the modified B-29 which we called the B-50. SAC later got the huge eight-engine B-36 which had been laid down during the war. As the crisis in Europe developed, however, the six-jet B-47 medium bomber began to come into the inventory. We eventually developed an air refueling technique with the B-47 which gave it world-wide range, but in the beginning it was necessary to have overseas bases in order to reach the possible targets in Russia.

Some observers charged that our overseas bases were provocative and caused the Soviets to begin an arms race with us. A cursory glance at history will suffice, however, to show that the Soviets began pressing for a long-range nuclear capability even before the war was over. They commandeered at least two of our B-29s which had made forced landings in Siberia. The early Soviet TU-4 was almost a duplicate of our B-29. But soon the Soviets were able to build creditable heavy bombers of their own. Also, when they learned about the Manhattan Project they managed to get in on the ground floor with the help of such spies as Dr. Klaus Fuchs, Alan Nunn May, Julius and Ethel Rosenberg, and others. After the war when we generously offered to share the nuclear secret with them through the Baruch Plan, they refused. From the beginning the Soviets were determined to match and surpass us in strategic nuclear capabilities. There can be little question that they are still at it, racing at top speed.

After the Korean War began, our military budget permitted the production of the eight-jet B-52 heavy bombers which became the backbone of SAC. Soon the propeller-driven bombers were dropped from the inventory and SAC became an all-jet nuclear bomber force capable of world-wide attacks. It was a most formidable force and, we believed, able to deter any major Soviet aggression.

Along with the sharpening of our SAC weapon went the development of a comprehensive air defense. This was accomplished during the same post-Korea period when we built an elaborate network of radar and control stations to warn of enemy air penetrations and to direct our fighters to intercept.

Thule Air Base was built in northern Greenland, and the Distant Early Warning (DEW) Line was constructed on a crash basis across the top of the world. Jet fighters improved with the North American F-86D, and later the supersonic F-102, F-104, F-106, and F-4. Command integration with the Royal Canadian Air Force was achieved through the North American Air Defense Command (NORAD). Countless practice contests were conducted between SAC and NORAD to sharpen both our offensive and defensive swords. The skill and coordination of these great air forces achieved a peak of near perfection. Not only did we feel secure at home from aerial attack, but we were convinced that we could destroy the entire military capacity of the Soviet Union without losing a man to their defenses.

But then the Soviets outflanked our vast air defense system with thermonuclear ballistic missiles. We had no defense for these weapons. *We still do not.*

Let us now take a quick look at the historical situation inside Soviet Russia. Since the Berlin Blockade of 1949 we have been forced to regard the U.S.S.R. as our likely enemy. After our marriage of convenience with the U.S.S.R. during World War II, we almost talked ourselves into being friendly, but grew suspicious when she tried to capture Iran by failing to withdraw her troops following the war. We turned away when she remained entrenched in the defeated eastern European countries. By not reacting to this, we thought the Soviets might feel more secure. With "friendly" neighbors, the Russians would perhaps be less bellicose. But we grew alarmed about her imperialistic intentions when she attempted to incorporate Greece and Turkey in 1947 through subversion. Thanks to the resistance we exercised with the Truman Doctrine this probe was checked and Greece and Turkey remained this side of the Iron Curtain.

Although the North Atlantic Treaty Organization did not exist in 1948, the "hot wind of the East" threw the Western nations into each other's arms. At that time I was in charge of the United States Air Forces in Europe. The cooperation I received in setting up the airlift, in building supply depots, and in establishing lines of communications, airfields, and navigational aids was truly magnificent. Weisbaden, my headquarters in Germany, was just two and one-half hours from the Soviet border. The chances of Soviet invasion seemed high. Czechoslovakia had fallen to communism earlier in the year and western countries were threatened by subversive elements. My principal airfields in Germany were ahead of our troops. It was vital that I have airfields in France and Belgium upon which to fall back. Although the laws of France and Belgium denied America the right to base troops on their soil, these laws were conveniently overlooked. To guard against fifth column propaganda and subversion we had our military trains take wildly circuitous routes to confuse the local communists and enemy agents. It worked.

Such subterfuges, however, were not enough. We needed a true alliance. I made such a recommendation to Gen. Lucius Clay in Germany and on my return to the United States, to the Secretary of War, Robert A. Lovett. Both took up the issue on the political level.

When Soviet troops closed our legal access to Berlin in 1948 we were very close to war. The Berlin Blockade was just one of a series of Soviet probes against us since the end of World War II. They have been repeatedly testing our strength and our resolve. When we demonstrate weakness, they move in. When we stand up to them, they withdraw, as they did after about a year of the Berlin Blockade.

The fall of China to communism came the next year. We had been so preoccupied with the Berlin Blockade as to almost overlook this cataclysmic event in the Orient. Our eyes, however, were opened still wider to the truly imperialistic nature of the Kremlin.

Soviet aggression flamed into proxy war in 1950 when she induced the North Koreans and later the Chinese to attack southward across the 38th Parallel. This was the line between Soviet and United States forces in Korea which had been established by mutual agreement during our "strange alliance" with the Kremlin. Thanks to President Truman's magnificent stubbornness, when the communists attacked across the 38th Parallel we accepted the challenge and rushed armed assistance to our South Korean allies. A seesaw war in which our military hands were severely tied by political direction found us accepting a *status quo ante* in 1953. An armed truce is still in effect today, with no clear resolution in sight. We keep two divisions in Korea and supply a huge South Korean army. It is a stalemate.

The Korean war demonstrated for the first time in history how fear of the nuclear bomb dominated our policy and restrained us from winning a war we were entirely able to win. It was an encouragement, on balance, to the Sino-Soviets.

When Stalin died in 1953, we had hopes that Soviet policy would soften. However, the ruthless suppression of popular revolts in Hungary and East Germany a few years later revealed that the new rulers had no intention of pursuing policies of peace. Although Chairman Khrushchev was a smiling and somewhat popular leader I could see little change in his international policies from those of Stalin. It was he who planted IRBMs in Cuba which led to the nuclear confrontation of 1962. Nor have I witnessed any true détente since the Brezhnev-Kosygin team took over from Khrushchev in 1964. I fear that the so-called détente is the wildest kind of wishful thinking.

In the early 1950s we had established the greatest peacetime alliance of nations in history—NATO. This, combined with the billions our Marshall Plan had pumped into its economy, caused Western Europe to prosper and refurbish its defenses. The Soviets were checked in Western Europe and their subversive influences all but destroyed.

We again attempted this successful pattern with the Southeast Asia Treaty Organization (SEATO), the Organization of American States (OAS), and many bilateral agreements throughout the world. These alliances, however, never achieved the sense of urgency, the drive and unity of purpose, that NATO did.

Again and again we hoped for a softening of U.S.S.R. policy only to be disappointed. In the early 1950s we learned through intelligence of the massive Soviet effort to outflank us by building great ICBMs tipped with megaton explosives. This threw official circles into somewhat of a panic. There was much talk in the press about a "missile gap" and *it was no hoax.* Had not the Air Force undertaken all-out measures to close the gap by creating our own ICBM force in record time, we would have been subject to the clearest kind of nuclear blackmail. Just how far the "backward" Soviets had got in this forced march to missile supremacy was illustrated by the orbiting of Sputnik in 1957. Since that time we have successfully developed Atlas, Titan, and Minuteman ICBMs. The *military* missile gap has now been closed (although there are now some frightening unknowns which I shall discuss in later chapters). The space-exploration gap, a by-product of the missile gap, persists today.

In the late 1950s a movement was growing which was to have a profound effect upon our strategic posture. For want of a better term, I shall call it the arms control movement. The underlying philosophy of this arms control movement was that, since the Soviets were now armed with multi-megaton ICBMs which we could not stop, any nuclear war would bring down a rain of destruction upon us which would be unbearable and unacceptable. Therefore, general nuclear warfare was out of the question and nuclear weaponry would be used for deterrence, period, but never in anger.

Once these basic premises are accepted, almost anyone will agree that warfare must remain at the non-nuclear level if waged at all, and that this can only be achieved through some sort of international agreement, formal or implied.

It has often been said that the present military situation is a "balance" or a "standoff." This is illusory. The fact that wars do not occur or that one country does not dominate another is not necessarily a direct consequence of a military balance or imbalance. Many non-military factors may be more responsible for the condition of "peace." Political issues, domestic as well as international, usually have more to do with hostility than do the existence or absence of weapons or armed forces. Nor does it necessarily follow that a military superiority leads to conquest. As we have seen, after World War II the United States had a nuclear monopoly, yet the Soviet Union felt secure enough to provoke us with such international banditry as the conquest of China and the Berlin Blockade.

Because the United States no longer enjoys a nuclear monopoly it is fashionable to say that a *mutual* deterrence exists which provides a sort of international stability. This hardly makes sense when recent history has shown that America, even with a distinct superiority, does not need to be deterred from waging war. On the other hand, decreasing American superiority can create a precarious military imbalance with less possibility for Soviet deterrence.

In their massive efforts to excel in the nuclear arms field, the Soviets have achieved some frightening "firsts." In 1961 they detonated the first sixty-megaton nuclear explosion (capable of being boosted to a hundred megatons) at Novaya Zemlya in the Soviet Arctic. A massive series of nuclear tests followed on the heels of a deceitful surprise abrogation of the three-year test ban moratorium. This massive nuclear capability combined with the Soviet work-horse military missile boosters which have enough power to project 26,500 pounds into orbit, leads one to believe that Soviet ICBMs are tremendously more destructive than ours. In fact all reputable estimates give them ten times the yield of our Minuteman. We believe we have a *numerical* superiority of intercontinental missiles (we can never be sure), and that our superior bomber fleet combined with our Polaris submarine fleet, will compensate for the higher warhead yield of Soviet missiles. But here again we are indulging in wishful thinking. I used to believe we had an edge on experience, too, and I am sure that we still do with respect to air operations. But the Soviets have demonstrated such remarkable skill in operating their space vehicles that it would be foolhardy indeed to grant ourselves an edge in skill at this new art of missilry.

As our once great bomber fleet continues to waste away, with no adequate replacements in sight, our general war edge (if it truly exists at all) is narrowed still more. Although our Minuteman and Polaris missiles continue to improve in reliability, accuracy, and numbers of warheads, these incremental advances could not compete with a massive Soviet ICBM capability which might, in effect, bury our missiles in their holes.

Ever since World War II the Soviet Union has maintained a much larger army than the United States. The Red Army is particularly strong in armor. Her large tactical air force is well-equipped and trained to support her army. The much smaller NATO conventional forces could probably do no more than hold temporarily against a full-scale Soviet attack in Europe. However, the Soviet leaders are aware of the firm United States commitment to Western Europe and are unlikely to risk a general nuclear war by attacking NATO.

In other geographical areas the Soviet advantage in conventional forces is reduced by inadequate transportation facilities. Our superior airlift and advantages in naval power enhance Western capabilities to fight limited wars, particularly outside NATO, but the expanding Soviet merchant fleet is reducing even this American advantage.

Wars of "national liberation" are openly supported by Kremlin policy. These have broken out into small limited wars in places such as Vietnam, Laos, Malay, and the Congo. The increased commitments in South Vietnam by both sides have created a war situation equalling the Korean war in scope. Here neither the Soviets nor the Communist Chinese are directly involved, yet their resources permit the North Vietnamese and the dissident Viet Cong to carry on the fight. We find ourselves heavily involved while the communists harass us with a relatively small commitment.

In the field of insurgency the Soviet Communists have a still important advantage which is the product of several factors:

1. It is often easier to destroy than to build; to capitalize upon existing hardship and dissatisfaction than to build a consensus of hope, trust, and cooperation.

2. In many areas political leaders are inexperienced, and restricted by an imagined fear of colonialism. They are without the support of a unifying nationalism or a vigorous middle-class, and are unable to rely upon a tradition of governmental responsibility or a well-trained corps of civil servants.

3. The dogmatism and discipline of the communist mythology and its promise of rapid material advance appeal to the understandable impatience of poor nations. Its authoritarian approach is more understandable than the highly sophisticated doctrines of a free economy and self-government.

4. The conspiratorial nature of the communist movement provides a ready framework and cast of mind for clandestine operations.

5. The communist acceptance of ends justifying means raises no problems of conscience at even the most deceptive, immoral, or cruel methods.

6. By its very nature guerrilla warfare places the defender of the *status quo* on the tactical defensive, which in turn requires a much larger effort by the government in power than by the insurgents. Nevertheless, in the last few years we and our allies have gained valuable experience in counterinsurgence. More effective doctrine, new training, better equipment, and preventive programs promise to decrease the communist advantages.

In spite of the magnificent Soviet recovery since World War II, the Soviet Gross National Product (GNP) remains at approximately 40 per cent of ours, and whereas the last few years have seen a spurt in our own economy, the U.S.S.R.'s growth rate has tended to lag. It is true that Soviet leaders get more international and military mileage from a given size GNP by drastically restricting home consumption and holding down the production of civilian commodities. Soviet economic aid sometimes appears to be more carefully directed for its propaganda advantage, but this same technique means that their economy is less resilient and flexible in responding to an emergency. The U.S.S.R. has much less slack than we—slack which can be converted to military purposes if the need arises.

Since we revealed to the world on television our photographic reconnaissance techniques over Cuba in 1962, the Soviets have been careful to camouflage their ICBM construction. I question seriously whether our intelligence is as good as we think it is today. We know that they are working at top speed to develop an ICBM defensive capability and what we see in the May Day and Revolution Day parades shows no slackening of their ICBM developments.

In his military Posture Statement submitted to Congress on February 1, 1968, Secretary of Defense McNamara reported that the Soviet ICBM force had grown from 340 to 720 "launches" in the past year. Considering that Russian missiles pack ten times the warhead yield of our own Minuteman missiles, the Soviet Union has clearly surpassed the United States in the ICBM field. Another missile gap confronts us.

I am not at all happy with our present military posture and as current policies are being translated into weapons and forces, I grow less so. There are some very disquieting unknowns. Moreover, our position relative to the U.S.S.R. has been in decline since 1960 and continues to decline. On top of this there are some strategic "fashions" at large which I feel are soft-headed and which, whatever our strength, can lead us to a shocking defeat, either militarily or politically.

It is the habit of military men to be pessimistic, to suspect trickery from the enemy and blindness at home. I hope my estimate is on the dark side. Yet I keep reminding myself that the reason military men are pessimistic is that they have so often been defeated by trickery or blindness.

IV. Deterrence

IN RECENT years the "spectrum of conflict" and "escalation" have become hackneyed concepts which refer to the presumed continuum of gradually intensifying conflict from peaceful competition at the lower end of the spectrum to nuclear holocaust at the upper end. Herman Kahn has dramatized this with a series of escalating scenarios in his book *Thinking about the Unthinkable,* and so many other authors have discussed the concept that escalation is assumed to lead inevitably to the nuclear holocaust.

The implication is that since there is a spectrum of conflict, there is a spectrum of particular strategies to match. I shall attempt to describe and evaluate various strategies of the day in the context of general, limited, and counterinsurgency war. In subsequent chapters I shall go into more detail of alternative strategies, the military postures required to pursue them, and the related environmental and political situations.

There are various aproaches for analyzing general war strategy, and one of the problems with the current strategic debate in the United States is that there is frequently neither

[49]

broad agreement on terms of reference nor a clear picture of the strategic objectives of the various protagonists. However, the various proposed general war strategies seem to fall into two groups: 1, those with the sole objective of deterring such a war, and 2, those with the dual objectives of deterrence and capability to fight a general nuclear war if deterrence fails. These differing objectives give rise to varying recommendations regarding the size and composition of the strategic force, including its targeting doctrine.

Those who believe that general nuclear war would mean the end of civilization as we know it, perhaps of man himself, usually assert that this awesome result is universally obvious. Consequently, they maintain that a relatively small strategic nuclear delivery capability is sufficient to assure the stability of deterrence. If the enemy is so foolish as not to understand this basic nuclear "fact" and wishes to waste his national resources on unusable nuclear weapons, let him. There is no need for us to follow this erroneous route. A few thermonuclear weapons on our side should be able to deter him, they say. Such deterrers are willing to accept parity or even inferiority in numbers, technical sophistication, or damage-inflicting capability. It is difficult to categorize this group because it includes subgroups of its own. The two more commonly accepted divisions are "minimum deterrers" and "finite deterrers."

Minimum deterrence is the most extreme expression of this view. Its adherents hold that very few weapons indeed are necessary to insure deterrence. Typically this view pays little or no regard to complexities of the military environment, such as aborts of delivery systems, human errors, and active and passive defenses. They talk with pseudo-authority about our "overkill" capability. In fact, this group is marked by a shocking naïveté combined with a burning missionary zeal. No single estimate of the number of weapons required is accepted by all minimum deterrers, but fifty thermonuclear missiles is a fairly typical "ball park" figure.

Finite deterrence is a somewhat more sophisticated version of minimum deterrence. Its proponents are knowledgeable enough to appreciate the need for a larger nuclear force. An enemy first strike, friendly aborts, misses, and active and passive defenses are admitted to make necessary a larger initial force even to inflict the damage level deemed necessary by the minimum deterrer. Moreover, the finite deterrer usually foresees the need for a higher level of destruction to make deterrence stable; that is, a deterrence not easily overcome by some enemy breakthrough or surprise. Thus his number of weapons increases again.

Advocates of finite deterrence do not agree on the number of weapons required, but their estimates tend to fall within a range of 500 to 1000. One thousand is a round figure which has been used frequently in studies by the United States Arms Control and Disarmament Agency. It is interesting to note, too, that our Minuteman force has been leveled off at a thousand weapons by the Office of the Secretary of Defense in spite of recommendations of the Air Force for a much larger force. Finite deterrers agree that enemy choices affect the size of our force, but a growing Soviet intercontinental ballistic missile force has not caused us to enlarge our own.

Minimum and finite deterrence concepts are frequently related to the concept of parity. This doctrine is the strongest one abroad today both inside and outside of official circles. It is believed by this school of thought that a mutual nuclear deterrence or standoff is feasible, if each side had roughly the same number of nuclear weapons. Once parity is achieved and a stable mutual nuclear deterrence realized, both sides can gradually reduce the number of weapons by agreement to create a minimum, finite deterrence. Then, if it could be fully realized that nuclear weapons would never be used at all, both sides would eliminate their nuclear weapons altogether and the nuclear genie would be bottled for good.

Although the strategy of parity is the most dominant concept of its sort at large today in America, most military men scoff at it. With few exceptions, however, the so-called "defense intellectuals" of the Kennedy-Johnson Administration advocate parity as an ultimate goal, although not many admit it publicly. I would place most of the civilian decision-makers in this category.

What upsets the parity notion is the proliferation of nuclear powers. Obviously, parity can only be practiced in a bi-polar nuclear world. Thus, this problem of nuclear weapon proliferation has assumed an overwhelming importance in our foreign policy. The proliferation issue has even taken precedence over the perpetuation of the North Atlantic Treaty Organization. Our refusal to assist our ally France in the development of her nuclear *force de frappe* unquestionably led to her alienation and *de facto* withdrawal from NATO.

The minimum, finite, and parity deterrers all regard deterrence as a relatively stable condition. Others, notably military men, think that deterrence is only possible in an atmosphere of strategic superiority. Anything less than superiority destabilizes the political climate and threatens deterrence, they claim. And, significantly, superiority advocates assert that a failure of deterrence need not be fatal under conditions of nuclear weapon preponderance. Therefore these strategists hold that deterrence can be strengthened by always maintaining superior strategic forces and that provisions can and should be made to fight and survive a general nuclear war. They tend to regard security as one of the primary national objectives. Consequently, if necessary for superiority, they would devote a larger proportion of our gross national product to defense. Mixed strategic forces of missiles and bombers, active and passive defenses, secure command and control systems, and much better intelligence systems are advocated by those who espouse strategic superiority. Emphasis on research and development, tactical innovations, space applications, and the development of nuclear science and techniques are all germane to the objective of military superiority.

Hardened and hidden weapon systems such as Minuteman and Polaris are considered stabilizing by most defense intellectuals. The same people believe that bombers, anti-ballistic missile weapons, and civil defense are destabilizing. The word stabilizing refers to a political stability or détente brought about because the employed nuclear weapons would, in their lights, not be threatening in nature. Arguments for "first" and "second" strike weapons are involved in this controversy.

The categorization of nuclear delivery vehicles into "first" and "second" strike weapons provides the bedrock for premises upon which rests an elaborate edifice of logic concerning our military posture, not to mention our foreign policy under the Johnson Administration. How sensible is this categorization of weapons? Cannot any weapon be triggered first as well as second depending upon the will (or reaction) of the intelligence behind the trigger?

The assumptions behind the first-second strike dichotomy have been given in these oversimplified terms: a Polaris missile is a second strike weapon because, hidden beneath the waves, it is not in the push-button category where the decision to fire it must be taken the moment we believe aggressive enemy action has been observed. Such arguments go on to rationalize that a button for launching Strategic Air Command bombers might be pushed by accident or by misreading the radar screen and mistaking geese for missiles. With Polaris the President would have time to recheck.

In other words, a second strike missile is conceived of as one which can survive a first strike by the enemy and then retaliate after a deliberate decision has been made. This is a fundamental assumption. Is it valid?

In theory a second strike weapon is not a weapon which can easily be destroyed by surprise attack. It is not a weapon which must be fired in haste because an attack might prevent its being used at all. Therefore, a country would not be forced by the physical vulnerability of its weapons to use them first. Thus a second strike weapon is assumed to be non-provocative of war and stabilizing.

Not only do Polaris submarines fit this second strike category, but so do missiles like Minuteman, which, because they are "hardened" beneath tons of earth, concrete and steel, have a high degree of invulnerability. But aircraft are not usually placed in this category. Aircraft, because of being berthed in "soft" airfields, are believed to be highly vulnerable to surprise attack.

The little understood tactics of air and strip alert tend to make aircraft considerably less vulnerable than they might otherwise be. It is conceived by the Air Force that should an enemy surprise attack occur, those aircraft in the air would escape damage. Those aircraft on alert, moreover, would take to the air before enemy warheads could detonate near the airfields, provided adequate warning time were given—something on the order of fifteen minutes. Warning, of course, would come from long-range radar. The Ballistic Missile Early Warning System (BMEWS) in Alaska, Greenland, and England provides at least fifteen minutes of warning time against an attack by enemy missiles. Over-the-horizon radar now under development will provide more warning time.

A nuclear delivery system utilizing aircraft is admittedly more subject to human fallibility than a system involving missiles. Bomber force survival rests upon the quick and positive reaction of the many elements of the system, from BMEWS warning to combat crews. If one link in the chain is broken, such as a communications breakdown somewhere between the BMEWS radar and the North American Air Defense Command headquarters at Colorado Springs, there is a chance that many of our bombers could be caught dead on the ground by a volley of enemy ballistic missiles.

However, this possibility is no worse than the unknowns of what an attack would do to our hardened missile sites. Blast, electromagnetic flux, and a host of other effects from very high yield thermonuclear warheads—the kind many Soviet missiles are equipped with—have never been tested against our operational missile complexes.

Many alternative systems of control and communications at the missile sites, together with constant drill, tend to reduce the human element of possible error to a minimum. But we are up against a stone wall in our efforts to determine the vulnerability of our hardened missiles to nuclear blast. The atmospheric test ban prohibits the tests which would give us this knowledge.

Although a decision to launch nuclear armed bombers must be made in seconds, it is erroneously believed by many that such a decision is tantamount to ordering a nuclear strike. It is not. Launching of bombers is primarily a defensive measure to prevent them from being destroyed on the ground and there is no more likelihood of their being used offensively than before launch. Only a positive coded order from the President could ever cause them to fly beyond friendly territory. It is from such a mélange of legitimate reasons and vague misconceptions as these that bombers are considered "soft" and "provocative."

Too many people with too little knowledge have been feeding such unrealistic pap to an unquestioning American public. The consequences are catastrophic. Today our strategic bombers are going to the trash pile with age and we have no follow-on models.

Obviously, the survival equation can become imbalanced if erroneous assumptions are introduced. Are there other questionable assumptions? Second strike reasoning implicitly assumes that the hard or hidden missiles would be deliberately held back until the enemy first-strike warheads had actually exploded in America. Moreover, the enemy is assumed to accept our defense intellectuals' logic. Is this really the way we—or our enemies—would wage a nuclear war?

There would certainly be some strategic warning: the kind of warning we had before Pearl Harbor, for example. Whether this warning would be accurately analyzed, which we failed to do before December, 1941, is really not a serious concern in the missile age. Before the Pearl Harbor attack we knew that relations with Japan were strained to the brink of war and that the Japanese fleet was at sea. We assumed that the Japanese were planning to pursue further conquests in Southeast Asia rather than strike us at Pearl Harbor. Our alert status in Hawaii, therefore, was a guard against sabotage. Today, no such error would be possible. Whatever the strategic warning, we would alert our Air Defense, Strategic Air Command and Fleet Ballistic Missile Force. They would all be prepared to launch our nuclear delivery vehicles at a moment's notice. Even if strategic warning pointed to a Soviet attack in Europe or Asia, American strategic forces and warning systems would be placed on a high state of alert. No distinction would be made between bombers or missiles at this stage of tension. The military lexicon does not use the first-second strike categorization.

Let us assume that during this state of emergency, a flock of geese crossed through a radar beam, as certain laymen have concerned themselves about. And let us assume further that the geese cause a blip in a radar scope at a Distant Early Warning (DEW) Line Station. What would happen then?

To begin with, flocks of geese not infrequently appear on radar scopes and they are about as easily identified by radar as they are by the naked eye. They do not fly quite as fast as jets, or as high. Nor do they make as big blips. It would be a neat trick for bombers to fly so that their radar return resembled geese, but so far this has not been accomplished nor does it seem a worthwhile deception in view of ballistic missile characteristics. Certainly no one could make missiles behave like geese.

When BMEWS was being tested in 1961 prior to becoming operational, it picked up some unidentified blips which were later identified as moon reflections. Wild stories are still being written of how close we came then to triggering off World War III. In fact, there was never the slightest danger of such a horrible accident, though one must admit it does make an excellent piece of fiction. If only the consequences of such fiction were not so frightfully influential on our national policy!

A commander is always concerned about the readiness of his forces. He conducts exercises and dry runs repeatedly in order to peak up his training, coordination, and communications. These exercises, however, fall short of the real thing and hence there is an element of doubt as to just how good his elaborate military machine actually is. One of the best exercises is a surprise alert. Any object passing through a radar fence will provide an ideal excuse to test the warning system, even after the object has been identified as a friendly transport or even a flock of geese. For this reason, SAC might order its bombers into the air. But no one in authority is deceived that anything but an exercise is taking place. And the possibility of our launching an accidental attack under these circumstances is pure nonsense.

So the assumption that bombers are in the "push-button"

category because of the possibility of ambiguous warning bears no relation to reality. If enemy bombers penetrate our warning system, *we will know it*, and we shall *not* be fooled by geese or friendly aircraft.

On the other hand, what about our Polaris fleet hidden somewhere in the North Atlantic? How will it get commands to commence firing? Presumably this information will be sent by code from the President's command post, for only orders from the President can authorize an expenditure of nuclear weapons.

He would be giving orders to the Polaris submarines based upon precisely the same information that might cause him to give orders to SAC bombers and ICBMs. If this major decision is ever made there seems to be no logic in his ordering bombers or ICBMs to strike first while withholding Polaris launchings unless he chose to hold back a reserve. He can delay the decision in both instances without seriously risking either strike force. In such an eventuality, there would be little reason to launch one kind of weapon and withhold another for the sake of security. What then is the difference between first and second strike weapons?

If one were in the President's position, would one give orders for bombers to attack and at the same time hold back "second strike" Polaris and Minuteman missiles until the enemy weapons had actually struck? Or would one attempt to blunt the enemy attack and destroy as many enemy weapons on the ground as possible? In this scenario, we presume that there are no antiballistic missiles to blunt the enemy attack. Granted, the President could not eliminate the enemy attack altogether nor protect all of the American population. But, as some strategists have calculated, he might save as many as fifty million lives by rapid retaliation with all available weapons.

This is sometimes referred to disparagingly as a "spasm" response. But one must keep in mind that if the die is cast and many nuclear weapons have unquestionably been launched against America, this would be no time for restraint.

The United States has no preventive war or first strike policy. Unquestionably United States policy is purely defensive and strategic nuclear weapons are designed for second strike "assured destruction," as Secretary of Defense McNamara has said. Nevertheless, if nuclear war becomes a fact we must take every measure to prevail, whatever the inevitable cost. As a secondary objective, Mr. McNamara has specified that we must "limit damage to our population."

So we must presume in this first scenario that the President will launch an all-out counterattack as soon as he is certain that the enemy has launched an attack against us. And it does not seem reasonable to suppose that he will wait until Washington, D. C., has been eliminated, if he has that option.

Let us suppose next that the President were either a casualty himself or that he deliberately held back the Polaris missiles and ICBMs until the first wave of enemy missiles had struck. Friendly bombers would have long been airborne and safe from destruction. They would be flying toward their positive control points without danger of an inadvertent or accidental attack. But a number of our ICBMs would certainly have been rendered non-operational by the enemy attack. How many? We cannot say, because there is no knowing the actual reliability, accuracy, warhead capability, tactics, and many other variables of the enemy force. And as I have noted, we have little empirical evidence of the vulnerability of our ICBMs under attack conditions. Regardless of the brainpower expended on such problems, the answers are never more than educated guesses based upon arrays of other educated guesses. Only warfare itself provides the kind of evidence upon which we could place full confidence. So we must assume that the withholding of our ICBMs for a second strike would degrade their effectiveness to some indeterminate degree.

Would our Polaris weapons be similarly endangered? From all indications these hidden missiles would be almost completely invulnerable. But is this assumption valid? Some of the greatest countries of history have succumbed by relying on "invulnerable" defenses, the last one being France with its Maginot Line. The experts who predicted this invulnerability were cruelly surprised when the enemy made certain breakthroughs, technical or tactical, and kept them a secret. It is therefore a military axiom not to put too much faith in the "invulnerability" of any weapon system or fortification because we never can be absolutely sure of our calculations. As Adm. Arleigh N. Burke said (and he was one of the architects of the Polaris system when Chief of Naval Operations), "The Polaris is a near perfect weapon but it is not enough."

We learned much about hunting submarines from the air during World War II and acquired some useful knowledge of their habits and vulnerabilities. Large modern nuclear-powered submarines (now called ships, not boats) which stay submerged for weeks and cruise at high speeds are a quantum improvement over the World War II boats. Nevertheless, they are still similar to their predecessors.

For example, they still make noise when cruising. Nuclear engines can hardly be quieter than battery power and a noiseless propeller may never be invented. So their noise can be tracked with some degree of success by sonobuoys or other listening devices.

Also, these submarines are big pieces of metal, and magnetic detection equipment has had some success in the past. A technical breakthrough in this area might be disastrous to the presumed invulnerability of Polaris.

In addition, submarines still present a reflecting surface for high frequency "sonar" sound emitted by a hunter.

Finally, they cannot stay submerged forever, and it is no secret that some American ships are berthed at Holy Loch, Scotland. Considerable publicity has been given to the numbers of Polaris submarines we have built (forty-one) and to the numbers we keep on station (fourteen).

With this information, it would not require much imagination for enemy strategists to work out a plan: develop hunter-killer submarines or surface vessels faster than our Polaris submarines, lie doggy outside of Holy Loch and tail United States vessels when they come out. Keep this up until the technique has become well perfected and the submarines are unsuspecting. Have a tail on all submarines on station and, at a predetermined H-hour, let them have it with nuclear-tipped homing torpedoes.

This same H-hour, of course, would trigger the Soviet ICBMs and bombers. In this way there would be no second strike at all from our Polaris submarines. And, since Polaris submarines do not likely send many radio messages for fear of revealing their location, the President would probably never be sure that his second strike Polaris force had been lost until he ordered the delayed retaliatory "second strike" launch. Then nothing would happen.

The outcome of the war would depend on the effectiveness of our crippled ICBMs and our undamaged but too small force of airborne bombers—*we would probably lose.*

Now it is only logical to assume that a surprise attack would not be launched until the enemy perfected a Polaris-destroying technique together with an effective anti-ballistic missile system (ABM). And if we provide the enemy with the invitation by relying almost exclusively on Polaris and Minuteman missiles as a psychological deterrent it would be a safe prediction that enemy energy and ingenuity would be bent in this direction. There would be no relatively invulnerable airborne bombers to contend with. No mobile intermediate range ballistic missiles exist in Europe. No ABMs in America or Europe would blunt the attack. A depleted continental air defense system would even permit enemy bombers to penetrate our skies. Only Polaris and Minuteman would stand in their way, and these only for a reduced second strike.

Suppose the retaliatory residue of Minuteman still would be more than the enemy wished to endure. Without launching an attack, might not the enemy reveal the technological breakthrough which would nullify Polaris and then make us squirm? Knowing that we could no longer rely on Polaris, could we then prevent the enemy from salting Cuba with IRBMs to cancel any residual numerical advantage we might have in the Minuteman category? Would not our diplomacy be drastically revised if we knew we were second best? This would not be defeat by combat, but defeat with a whimper.

Now let us examine another hypothetical situation whereby the United States would deploy defensive systems to include continental ABMs of the Nike-X or Sentinel variety as well as a beefed-up air defense system with improved manned interceptors (IMIs). Backing up this formidable defense would be new advanced manned strategic aircraft (AMSAs) as replacements for B-52s. These forces would supplement but not replace hardened Minuteman and Titan ICBMs together with Poseidon-armed nuclear submarines. This is a weapons mix which I recommend.

At the outset, this military posture would provide the President with a maximum flexibility and the greatest possible number of strategic options. Should deterrence fail, at least some final protection would be available with ABMs and a modern air defense. This might save as many as eighty million lives (by official estimate) on a Soviet first strike. This also assumes an ABM defense that the Soviets have not learned to penetrate. Quick and early retaliation to blunt the remaining Soviet ICBMs (since it is known that many Soviet sites have a reload capability) is part of this equation.

Simultaneously, United States advanced anti-submarine warfare forces (ASW) would attack every Soviet submarine which had been held under surveillance. This would blunt the formidable Soviet sea-launched nuclear missile capability.

A war fought from such a base of nuclear superiority, maximum options, a traditional balance of friendly offensive and defensive forces, and with quick-strike retaliation would leave the United States sorely wounded, but viable and victorious.

More important, such a posture would suggest the capability of a first strike—of initiating nuclear war. Such a suggestion is absolutely necessary if the United States is to prevail in the diplomatic world. Many Americans shudder at the idea of our initiating a nuclear war, but they forget that it was precisely this suggestion—backed by known superiority—that gave President Kennedy the winning hand in the Cuban missile crisis.

Deterrence cannot be achieved with a second-strike facade. Conceding the enemy the first blow simply invites him to find a way to smother our retaliation. Strategy on our side then becomes stagnated, case-hardened, and ritualistic.

Deterrence cannot be assured in a no-win vacuum. It must rest not upon the ability to withstand a first strike and retaliate effectively, but on the ability to launch a first strike and win if necessary. This requires a comprehensive defensive system including an effective ABM, not a "thin" token force as now planned by the Johnson Administration.

Defense is never provocative. A porcupine invites no attack. It signals the desire to stay at peace. It is the essence of deterrence. When we use the word provocative we tend to project our own thinking into what is presumed to be Russian thought. It might be more accurate to see what the Soviets themselves say about an ABM disposition.

A most articulate Soviet commentator on nuclear strategy, Maj. Gen. Nikolai Talenski, argued for the ABM in the Soviet magazine *International Affairs* in these terms:

> Only the side which intends to use its means of attack for aggressive purposes can wish to slow down the creation and improvement of anti-missile defense systems. For the peace-loving states, anti-missile systems are really a means of building up their security.

He went on to say:

> The creation of an effective anti-missile missile system enables the state to make its defenses dependent chiefly on its own capabilities, not only on mutual deterrence, that is, on the good will of the other side.

I find this logic hard to refute.

To return to the concept of first and second strike weapons, the idea has been considerably oversimplified. If the President decides to use his nuclear weapons, certainly bombers or missiles or both will be fired on a decision based upon identical information of enemy action. One or another *kind* of weapon will not be safer to use, or less free of accident. Launch information will never include a flock of geese crossing the DEW line, but there is, of course, always a remote chance of a *political* misinterpretation of the opponents' motives. Kaiser Wilhelm was not convinced in 1914 that Czar Alexander's mobilization was purely defensive. (Some historians are not sure of this today.) So the Kaiser struck first by ordering the execution of the Schlieffen plan. It is conceivable that the world situation today could present a parallel political decision. It is doubtful if the *kind* of weapons would affect such a decision.

More likely national intentions as demonstrated by high-level statements and political actions would pull the trigger. And if and when that day comes we had better have the *kind* of weapons we can win with.

It is well to observe that the first-second strike notion is not reasoned on a "war" situation but on a "deterrent" situation. The major premise is that nuclear war would be so horrible that it must never happen at all. Therefore weapon systems must be developed which are purely for retaliation and even incapable of rapid launch simply because this must never happen. In other words, weapons must never be *used* at all, yet they must provide the leverage to deter the enemy from striking us.

There is something missing in this logic. First of all, it is entirely defensive; and a wholly defensive military policy could lead to some embarrassing political complications. How could we have defended Europe from communism, maintained the freedom of Berlin, or insisted on the removal of IRBMs from Cuba if our nuclear forces had been solely capable of second strike? How can we ever be sure that our deterrent has not been overcome by a Soviet Union technological breakthrough?

This kind of reasoning presupposes a static situation which will permit our "invulnerable" forces to remain so indefinitely. The dynamism of modern technology is one fact to which we cannot shut our eyes. There can be no static or "stable" military forces in a world of rapidly expanding technology.

However, the second strike philosophy dominates our national strategy. It affects our military and foreign policy decisions. It paints a beguiling picture of a stable world with reduced tensions and sober negotiations freed from the fear of nuclear war. But the second strike philosophy is invalid. It rests upon a series of naïve and dangerous assumptions that a defensive-offensive nuclear posture can always be given a capability of "assured destruction," that our intelligence is infallible, that the Soviet Union is striving for peace rather than conquest, and that the Soviet ABM development is no better than ours.

Generally speaking, those who stress the horror of nuclear war, and foresee a resultant stable deterrence, oppose any move toward reducing that horror. This is, they insist, not because they are sadists but because they do not wish to see deterrence weakened. Consequently, minimum, finite deterrers and believers in parity favor city targets, that is, urban and industrial centers. They feel strategic nuclear weapons should be targeted against those things the enemy would hate most to lose: lives, cities, and industries. They maintain that any state will be deterred by the assured destruction of something like a quarter of its population and industry. (The Office of the Secretary of Defense seems to revise this figure downward from one year to the next.) Since they believe any general nuclear war would be disastrous, they have no interest in providing the means by which one could be fought.

The other major targeting option is counterforce. This, as I have noted, is the targeting of enemy missile sites, airfields, and other military works. Advocates of strategic superiority believe deterrence is somewhat tenuous and that we therefore may actually have to fight a general nuclear war. We can do so and survive, I believe, if proper preparations are made. Within the field of counterforce there are at least three discernible positions:

1. "Pure" counterforce implies the destruction of all enemy strategic forces regardless of the collateral damage to industry or population caused by attacking co-located targets. In other words, if an enemy airfield is located in a city, we would destroy it regardless of what incidental damage might be done to to the city. The rationale for this choice is that enemy nuclear

forces pose such a threat to the United States that we cannot afford to be humanitarian by foregoing attacks on military targets just because they are situated close to population centers. As our intelligence improves and our weapons become more accurate, another argument will become common: that higher accuracy and lower explosive yields will permit destruction of co-located targets without major damage to adjacent cities. In other words, it will be more possible to sharpshoot without hitting bystanders.

2. Counterforce-plus-avoidance follows a somewhat different scale of values. This is an attempt to signal the enemy that we have no wish to harm his population, in hopes that he will avoid such targets in our country. Here, although the destruction of the enemy's nuclear forces remains primary, it is tempered by indicating to him as clearly as possible that we do not intend to attack his cities. Proponents of this strategy suggest that this might be done in several ways: by not attacking a co-located target at all, by accepting a lower probability of destruction and attacking with fewer or smaller weapons, or by placing the aiming point of the weapons on the side of the target away from the population complex. At best it would be hard to signal the enemy this limitation in our strategy. It might be misconstrued as weakness or an inability to hit the obvious targets. The choice of means for signaling would depend upon the relative importance of the military target, the assumed value of the associated city, the technical characteristics of our weapons, and the degree of choice of weapons available to us. In all this the major reason for avoiding enemy cities would be to encourage a reciprocal policy. I see little chance of this "avoidance" strategy ever working.

3. Counter-force-plus-bonus is the opposite idea of counter-force-plus-avoidance, in that population destruction incidental to counterforce attacks would be considered desirable for intra-

war deterrence of retaliation. It is felt by some that this approach would also provide the best pre-war deterrent posture because of the associated danger to cities. Of course, since such a concept might not be appreciated until after the shooting started, it loses its attractiveness as a deterrent strategy. Some strategists feel that the shock reaction to such a targeting philosophy would lead to quick enemy surrender. I doubt this because of the consequent unlikeliness of being able to communicate with a mangled country. Arms controllers look upon this approach as pure holocaust which would lead to blows and counterblows until both sides were utterly destroyed.

I personally do not subscribe to the counterforce-plus-bonus targeting scheme because I believe it would waste warheads which should *all* be directed at the enemy capacity to harm us. However, I do not see the ultimate horror predicted by arms controllers. One or both sides would stop before we have an Armageddon.

I submit that strategic nuclear warfare should be fought on the basis of "pure" counterforce. This strategy promises the most for victory with a viable post-war world. There will be enough unfortunate misses in this strategy to provide intra-war deterrence and thus end the conflict quickly. Communications, too, should be adequate to accept a surrender.

For a nation to adopt a policy without suitable alternative should that policy fail would be the height of folly. Yet this is exactly what the minimum, finite, and parity variants of "stable" deterrence in the present Administration would have the United States do. None of these strategies offers any means for coping with the possibility of general nuclear war. In fact, in their singleminded emphasis upon deterrence they arrive at a strategic posture (with a relatively few high yield weapons targeted against cities) which increases the frightfulness of a nuclear war. Moreover, by so increasing the destructiveness and carnage of a nuclear war, these strategists paradoxically undercut the credibility that our nuclear deterrent would ever be used at all. Thus the threshold of provocation at which an enemy would be willing to challenge us is lowered. For this reason the total amount of conflict, particularly in the form of limited and guerrilla wars, tends to rise.

Anyone who seeks an absolute end to the possibility of war might as well resign from the human race. Pacifists with their perennial utopian quests can harm the human race as much as conquerors. Most will agree that Chamberlain's appeasement (and ingenuous encouragement) of Hitler, for example, regardless of how well meant, was a major contribution to the origins of World War II.

It is reasonable, however, to expect that mankind can govern its affairs in such a way as to limit the possibility of war, or even its violence. To this end, much brainpower has been expended by intellectuals, with a great burst of activity in the last two decades. No doubt the awesome power of nuclear weapons coupled with the fear of an unfriendly and powerful rival nation has caused this accelerated search for more international stability. The findings, nonetheless, have been disheartening.

Generally speaking, two schools of conflicting thought have tackled this great problem. One, the traditional one, and the one upon which our national policy has rested since the Korean war up until recently is that of *military superiority*. Through our military superiority, goes the argument, the rival will be deterred from attacking. This has worked.

The other concept is new to modern military thought and has been arrived at through pure intellectual speculation. It is born of the despair of achieving a true military superiority. If, the intellectuals ask, the United States wins a war but loses a large proportion of its population, has it really won at all? Answering this in the negative, they then take a leaf from the book of ancient wars when stability was sought through the exchange of hostages. By making hostages out of millions of people in each country, they reason, stability will be assured.

In other words, if each country has intercontinental nuclear weapons aimed at the other's cities, and neither can stop the other's missiles from falling, each country's cities are hostage to the other. The result of this mutual threat of the most frightening kind is believed to provide a mutual or stable deterrent to war.

The hostage system is useful but not infallible. When Rome demanded the sons of the aristocrats of Carthage as assurance that Carthage would not again disturb the peace of the Mediterranean, Carthage sent them. But this was not enough for Rome. She built a great navy, invaded, and defeated Carthage at Zama.

Today's stable deterrent hostage principle conceives of so many hardened or hidden offensive weapons on both sides that a surprise attack would not prevent a devastating counterattack aimed at the other's unprotected cities. Conversely, it is argued, soft or unhardened and well-targeted offensive weapons such as bomber airfields are only good for a first strike and thus cause instability by threatening or inviting a surprise attack. Refining this further, as we have noted, this school argues that our national strategy should point toward a finite agreed number of hardened or hidden offensive weapons on both sides. The final step in the reasoning is that defensive measures taken against these offensive weapons, such as the use of ABMs or even passive civil defense, should also be equated, or, better, mutually eliminated so that neither side would gain a strategic advantage from a strong defense.

Correlative to this concept is that of conventional "limited" war. It is conceded by the "stable deterrent" school that international conflict may lead to certain ancillary wars, but with the "stable deterrent" each side would be constrained from employing nuclear weapons of any sort. Using nuclear arms, goes the thesis, would probably lead to an "escalation" resulting eventually in unleashing the mutual intercontinental thermonuclear holocaust.

Here is a basic inconsistency. If the "stable deterrent" were truly effective, the use of nuclear weapons in limited wars would not cause the mutually destructive exchange to be triggered on the rival cities. In other words, if the argument that the deterrence produced by hostage cities holds true, it should hold true whether or not nuclear weapons are used tactically against purely military targets.

Should the postulated limited war be a central one, that is, a war between the two principal antagonists, goes the argument, each side would voluntarily limit itself to conventional weapons rather than risk the mutual nuclear exchange. Thus, war would be fought something along the lines of World War II.

There can be no doubt that the believed strength of an enemy's defenses and his counterattack capability have always been a deterrent to war. Whenever an enemy is thought to have superior power, the deterrence is comparably stronger. However, one must always realize that in war, or in the contemplation of war, there is usually a wide disparity between what is so and what is believed to be so. This fact tends to weaken the "stable deterrent" argument.

It is doubtful that any political or military analyst could ever find an equality of power between two countries. The elements of national power are infinite, varying from the confidence and resolve of one individual to the emotional heat revealed in a legislative body which has been provoked by an international incident, or from the aim of one rifleman to the speed of an ICBM, or from the patriotism of a school teacher to the callous opportunism of a racketeer. National power cannot possibly be measured by counting ICBMs. The sources of national power are dynamic, ever-changing and inconceivably complicated in comparison with a near-equal rival nation. National power, too, is directly affected by political or foreign policies. If the U.S.S.R., for example, were as unaggressive as Switzerland, the world power structure would be considerably altered. Hence it is extremely difficult, if not impossible, to equate the power of two nations regardless of how armaments are measured, balanced, and manipulated, simply because armaments alone provide only a fraction of the total power of any state.

Stable deterrent philosophers argue that today there is a novel function of intercontinental nuclear warfare which makes it possible to achieve an equatable destructive capacity. There seems to be no reason why the same logic would fail to apply in a world without nuclear weapons. Two opposing land powers of an earlier century, each with a comparable military force, could conceivably fight until every city was destroyed and every human being on either side was killed. This has never happened in history, however, because no matter how equally matched, no state has had the kind of collective resolve that would permit continued fighting to the point of suicide. One or the other belligerent party has always given up long before reaching the point of mutual annihilation.

Is there any reason to believe that states will behave differently under nuclear attack? After one or two massive exchanges of destructive power, it would seem very likely that one or both of the contestants would abandon the fight. The side most likely to continue would be that side which *believes* it is ahead and *believes* it could survive. As always, the first side to lose hope of winning would capitulate.

Those of the stable deterrent school will argue that even one or two nuclear attacks in force would cause so many millions of casualties that the contemplation of any such exchanges whatsoever is out of the question. Most military attention has been paid to offensive means of warfare. Each side contemplates the destruction of enemy weapons on the ground; and, at the very least, the spill-over of these attacks is bound to obliterate many cities and fill the air with lethal fallout. Today it is argued, neither side has adequate defenses against such attacks.

Thus, if the present stand-off situation prevails, goes the argument, limiting the "stable deterrent" seems to be a way to stop the arms race and possibly turn back the clock so that both sides will prefer to fight with conventional weapons. The fallacy in this lies in the fact that the dynamism of power is bound to oscillate, and one side or the other will probably develop the means for blunting attacks to the degree that they might be endured and countered. Even now, means are available to provide rather effective defenses, but public understanding is apparently insufficient to cause the necessary steps to be taken. Rather than take reasonable measures for defense, more confidence seems to be placed in the stable deterrent philosophy and related palliatives.

Nor will the argument hold up that parity with a large number of nuclear weapons on each side presents a stable situation. Arms controllers assert that an increase of a few more, or a technological improvement, will not change the balance of power significantly. Students of military history point out that a minor military advantage such as an inconspicuous improvement in ICBM accuracy can cause a major difference in the fortunes of war. More important, a *believed* advantage or disadvantage, such as the effectiveness of an ABM system, can spell the vital difference between defeat and victory—even though the beliefs may have no relation to the facts. Often this advantage cannot be measured or predicted in advance of the actual conflict. A typical example is seen in the German advance in 1940 across Belgium and Northern France. The German Army overcame "impregnable" fortification (The Maginot Line) with fewer troops and less armor than the Allies had. What was the elusive quality that accounted for its overwhelming victory? This and similar historical riddles might be pondered by the advocates of "stable deterrence."

Consider for a moment the advantage the Soviets would have with an effective ABM system and shelter program. They could launch an all-out surprise attack against us without too much fear of our inevitable retaliatory strike. If we were not equally prepared in ABM defense, the Soviets would have achieved a rather stable deterrent *in their favor*. The same would work in reverse if we first achieved effective defensive systems, active and passive, which could assure the safety of most of our population.

Gen. Austin W. Betts, the Army's Chief of Research and Development and its leading authority on missile defense, dismisses the possibility that the ABM might upset deterrence. "Buying seat belts doesn't mean that you intend to smash into the car of someone you don't like," he said.

There are other basic weaknesses in this stable deterrent hypothesis. It conceives of a rather static political world, which does not exist today. One cannot contemplate balancing anything unless the materials in the scales achieve some sort of unchanging character. In world power-politics, this is patently impossible. In terms of technology it is equally farfetched. One cannot predict what the changes and technical breakthroughs might be, but one *can* predict with certainly that any agreement on balanced numbers or kinds of nuclear weapons would be out of date before the agreements were fulfilled.

Since the end of World War II, there have been at least three complete changes of strategic weapon systems. From B-29s and B-36s to B-47s and B-52s to the B-52s and ICBMs. Since scientific and technical progress seem to advance at an ever-increasing geometric rate, some weapon systems actually become obsolescent before reaching operational status.

Stable deterrent writers have an answer to this one, too! "Limit and inspect research and development!" This measure would seem even harder to achieve. It is like telling men to stop thinking, to stop inventing. Who can tell what kinds of research for peaceful purposes might have world-shaking military application? The discovery of fissionable uranium was not in connection with any military research program; nor was the invention of the airplane or the rocket—or the railroad, telegraph, telephone, automobile, or radio.

One can say with some confidence that regardless of arms control agreements, men will continue to think, to experiment, and to invent. The knowledge of the world cannot be destroyed, and it will always provide springboards for the acquisition of more and more knowledge.

Possibly the designers of the stable deterrent hypothesis have been influenced by the traditional British principle of "balance of power." One must look at this principle carefully to realize that the British were never quite content with a true balance of power, even had that been possible. What they sought were combinations of alliances which tipped the balance pretty obviously in their favor. In the nineteenth century, when this principle flourished, Great Britain maintained a fleet able to outgun any combination of fleets which might have been allied against her. This was hardly a balance. It was only when the balance became real, when the German High Seas Fleet approached parity, and when the Triple Alliance and the Triple Entente began to balance land power, that a most *un*stable situation occurred. The balance was so unstable that Germany felt her only chance for survival lay in superior tactics—i.e., to mobilize rapidly and attack, as she did in 1914.

True international stability will probably not be realized

today until one side or the other achieves a clearly recognizable advantage. This does not mean, necessarily, that the stronger will inevitably devour the weaker. The weaker may yet have power enough to punish the stronger aggressor, even though the underdog is eventually defeated. This fact, together with world opinion and economic motives, has protected the independence of many weak states throughout history. One wonders whether the philosophy of international communism will permit this for long, particularly if the alliance of free states becomes irresolute and ineffective.

To assume a stable situation when, in the words of ex-President Eisenhower, "two atomic colossi confront each other across a trembling world," is to oversimplify and misread history and political science. A mechanical balance of any significance in the social environment is not possible. The physical science model is inappropriate.

Consider, for example, the effort to equate two individuals in a contest as closely controlled, regulated, and inspected as a prize fight. Could one say that because the two rivals weigh the same they are equally matched? Could a "stable deterrent" exist on this basis? Unmeasurable factors such as courage, speed, stamina, reaction time, motivation, muscular coordination, experience, coaching and so on, would more than likely establish the winner. War, like physical conflict between two individuals, is an art. There are so many factors which determine success, and so many situations which react with the innumerable human factors, that the combinations are infinite. One thing is certain: that side which plays the game most skillfully, provided it has resources comparable to those of its opponent, wins the war.

In an interview, Dr. Edward Teller, the "father of the H-bomb," made this remark about parity:

. . . Have you thought seriously of having parity with a bear? He has two arms and you have two arms. That seems to be parity, and you might feel absolutely safe. Except that perhaps the arms of the bear may be a little stronger, and somehow bears keep their secrets better. The Russians, on top of that, are better able to evaluate whether parity is really proper in their sense of coexistence. Their idea of parity may be a little different from our idea of parity.

States, like people, can become so provoked as to lose all consideration of the consequences of their acts. An enraged country may go to war against impossible odds, with no logical chance of victory. This is another example of weakness in the concept of deterrence—the possibility of the *illogical* reaction. Thus did Paraguay fight against an overwhelming alliance of Brazil, Argentina, and Uruguay in 1864. So did little Serbia stand up to the great Austria-Hungarian Empire in 1914. And thus did England and France declare war on Germany in 1939 when they felt themselves to be grossly inferior.

Almost any country can be pushed too far, as was Hungary in 1956. It then feels compelled to fight regardless of the consequences. Patrick Henry's remark ". . . give me liberty or give me death" is not an isolated human decision.

Probably no military force, regardless of how superior it may be, could ever assure an absolute deterrent. People have been known to fight against whatever odds if sufficiently provoked. As our frontiersmen used to say, "the only good Indian is a dead Indian." They meant that no matter how outnumbered or outgunned, the Indian might still fight.

The only reliable deterrent to war is that achieved by the skillful manipulation of the many elements of national power, of which the military is only one. Foreign policy, rather than naked military power, is the key to peace.

Certainly if military superiority cannot provide an absolute deterrent, neither can nuclear parity. And when war has been started, nuclear parity will result in no more than mutual slaughter of populations with little chance of either side exploiting an advantage. On the other hand, military superiority will at least assure that we continue to dominate the enemy, dictate terms, and establish our pattern of government in the postwar world. In other words, the "stable deterrent" policy does not permit a war to be won once the deterrent fails, yet millions are killed. In a war fought under a military superiority policy, we could expect far fewer casualties since there would be no deliberate destruction of the civil population, and the political outcome should be in favor of the stronger.

Military superiority presupposes that our forces are able to defeat enemy forces under whatever circumstances hostilities may dictate, across the whole spectrum of conflict. One must realize that our armed forces are not entities in themselves in a political vacuum. They are tools of our political leadership and may be employed in any manner this leadership directs: offensively as in the Mexican War, or defensively as at Pearl Harbor; in declared war as in 1918, or in undeclared war as in 1950; in counterinsurgency as in the early days of Vietnam or in limited war as against Spain (we did not invade); or even in ways and places inconceivable at the present time. Certainly, any adjustment of our forces must be done in consonance with an adjusted foreign policy and revised political commitments. Military forces cannot be considered out of this context.

Does this then throw out any hope for arms control or disarmament? Not by any means. There have been many periods in our history when we have disarmed unilaterally, not the least of which was as recent as 1946 when the military budget fell to less than $11 billion. At this time we were laboring under the mistaken impression that we had nothing to fear from our former ally, the Soviet Union.

Since arms control and disarmament are inextricably related to foreign policy, it is safe to assume that when the political frictions of the world subside, reductions in arms will follow. But let us not put the cart before the horse.

No military or political measures can assure an absolute deterrent to war. Deterrence of war rests on as complicated a human decision as the causes of war itself, and is far more susceptible to political acumen. Deterrence is a product of what is *believed* about enemy and friendly forces, of national aspirations, and of the emotional heat of provocation. It is a state of mind, a matter of intentions. Attempting to equate forces, nuclear or otherwise, will if anything destabilize international relationships.

Combined with able diplomacy, military superiority has had real success in promoting peace, particularly when that superiority rests in the hands of an intrinsically peaceful country. With an umbrella of nuclear superiority capable of fighting and winning a general war, we can employ an infinite number of lesser strategic options along the spectrum of conflict. But now we are losing our military superiority. It is high time that we devote our utmost energy toward regaining it as quickly as possible.

V. Our General War Strategy

THE TERM general war usually refers to wars of the magnitude of World Wars I and II. Very little restraint was exercised and the issues involved amounted to stark national survival. Such a conflict is normally between major powers whose total resources are employed. General war might be placed at the highest end of the war spectrum, although one must make the distinction that "general" does not necessarily mean unlimited war. There still are some restraints, and it does not follow that a general war would involve unlimited and unrestrained nuclear bombing of cities and populations.

It should be recognized, however, that the restraints imposed in general war are usually predicated upon military necessity rather than upon humanitarian motives. Of course this point can be contested for there are always political interests at work even in general war. Some historians contend that poison gas was not used in World War II because it was considered immoral. Others assert that gas was not used because it offered little military advantage for either side. Certainly flame throwers, fire bombs, and napalm were used without compunction.

One would be hard pressed not to call this thermal warfare, chemical warfare.

In a war for survival governments seem able to rationalize the morality of violent acts. In World War II there was little objection to city bombing. The tragedy of many friendly combat casualties also has a tendency to lessen the concern shown for the enemy. Military leaders, who in the past have been given wide discretion on this score, for the most part exercised their power sparingly on the basis of military necessity as opposed to malice or revenge.

Some restraints are traditionally exercised in general wars of the modern age. Prisoners are not executed except in rare instances. Usually prisoners are given adequate care under the rules of the Geneva Convention. Chiefs of state and senior officials are not usually targets. General war could, of course, reach unlimited proportions should either of the combatants become desperate enough to feel that all-out violence might provide an outside chance of, if not victory, at least a stronger negotiating position in a stalemate. The Viet Cong practice this.

It is often predicted that a future general war would involve the exchange of strategic nuclear weapons. But general wars are most likely to occur as an outgrowth of lesser conflicts or as a result of a series of emotional provocations. It does not necessarily follow that general war will start with an all-out strategic nuclear exchange. It is more conceivable to me that only one or two multimegaton weapons would be exchanged in the first stages of such a war. I say this not from military considerations but from what I have learned in dealing with political leaders who make such decisions. I frankly think that it would be a rare President or an unusual Kremlin leader who would risk everything in a strategic war by launching most of his deployed thermonuclear weapons. A far more likely course, it would seem to me, would be for him to launch one or two nuclear missiles to see what the consequences might be, both in terms of enemy response, domestic opinion, and the reactions of friendly and enemy allies.

However, a general war started hesitantly and equivocally by either combatant would put the initiator in a very dangerous position. The almost certain retaliation might be all-out, and the hesitant initiator would, of course, have gained the onus of having started the nuclear war in the first place. If the time should ever come to initiate a general nuclear war I believe it should certainly be started with enough power to win that war in the shortest possible time. Unfortunately, few political leaders think in this vein.

In my opinion, a general nuclear war will grow through a series of *political* miscalculations and accidents rather than through any deliberate attack by either side. Let me stress the point that I said *political* accidents, not military accidents. The dominant school of thought believes that control of nuclear weapons must be denied military leaders because a commander might exceed his authority and independently start a nuclear war. Military-instigated war has never occurred or even been contemplated in America; and I am hard pressed to think of an instance when it has happened elsewhere unless the military leader was acting within his authority as concurrent chief-of-state. Military leaders are not prone to start wars. Politicians are.

The conflict growing out of Sarajevo was a political decision. So was the attack on Poland in 1939 and the subsequent British declaration of war. The beginnings of World War I might readily be considered a series of political accidents. And Hitler anticipated that his Polish adventure would remain limited.

When I led the Strategic Air Command I operated on the premise that we should have some warning of enemy preparations to attack us. Toward this end we spent a great deal of our energies learning what the opposition was doing day to day. Believing I could foresee an attack, I was prepared to beat him to the draw and attack all of his bomber and missile bases. In accordance with the Joint Chiefs of Staff my purpose was to destroy his war-making capability, particularly in the strategic nuclear area. Of course, I had no authority to order such attacks. All I could do was have the capability and hope that the orders would be given if necessary.

This was the counterforce strategy which we examined briefly in Chapter IV. Our weapons were not directed against cities and people but against enemy military forces, particularly against those forces which could do us the most harm. Some key war-making industries, like nuclear plants, were included. This strategy, I felt, was most sensible because it would limit enemy casualties and leave his civilian society relatively unharmed so that we would not have to rehabilitate him following the war. The strategy of counterforce was basically defensive.

There was a catch to it. To get most of the enemy forces on the ground we would have to attack first. This would be an offensive-defensive kind of strategy. Of course, we would never make such an attack unless we were sure the enemy was preparing to attack us. A strategy which rested on our initiating a war ran against the American philosophy. Thus the strategy of pre-emptive counterforce gained a bad name and has been discarded by the civilian strategists in the Office of the Secretary of Defense.

Even so, the possibility of pre-emption still seems to be in our strategic deck of cards. Gen. Earle G. Wheeler, Chairman of the JCS, suggested this in testimony on March 6, 1967, before a committee of Congress. He said one Soviet aim is "to reduce U. S. confidence in our ability to penetrate Soviet defenses, thereby reducing the possibility that the United States would undertake a pre-emptive first strike against the Soviet Union even under extreme provocation." Of course, the second strike philosophy in OSD is rapidly undermining any residual pre-emptive posture we might have.

One school of thought declares that a pre-emptive or counterforce strategy would be extremely provocative. To exercise it we would have to sit on alert with a great number of bombers and missiles prepared to attack on a moment's notice. The decision would be based largely on intelligence information. Since this intelligence might be misconstrued it has been assumed by many that a war might be started by *us* through erroneous information or misinterpretation of the evidence. Thus was developed the second strike concept, which I have discussed in Chapter IV. The second strike idea, as we have seen, is that our forces would never attack until the United States had first been attacked by enemy nuclear weapons. Should deterrence fail, this strategy means the almost certain nuclear devastation of the United States.

It was conceived by the second strikers that if our SAC forces were sitting on the *qui vive* ready to attack on the basis of intelligence, then the Soviet forces would be doing the same thing. This would lead to a most unstable world situation, which might, it was thought, stimulate uncontrollable tensions and the outbreak of nuclear war. War itself might be brought on purely by the provocation of the particular military dispositions.

It is interesting to note that this never did happen when I maintained precisely those dispositions. Nuclear war never occurred as long as we were actually sitting on the alert with a counterforce posture. One might think that this was because the Soviet Union did not have a comparable SAC force. Nevertheless the Soviets did have one of considerable power, and they still never seemed particularly provoked by our counter-force strategy. The fear of provocation was, to my mind, mostly a straw man.

Another reason for the pre-emptive counterforce strategy which I proposed was the fact that we had not then perfected a completely tight air defense system nor any ballistic missile defense system at all. Therefore, our only defense in case of a general war in which some high yield weapons might fall on us was to destroy those weapons before they had an oppor-tunity to be launched. Once we had adopted a second strike posture, however, with much of the philosophy that goes with it, it became highly likely that American cities would be struck by the enemy nuclear weapons in case of a general war.

The second strike proponents argued that a general war must *never* occur under *any* circumstances. So our posture today is designed to be non-provocative and to deter rather than to win. There *is* a difference, as we have seen. Pure deterrence is a highly esoteric way of regarding our national defense, but it is nonetheless the fundamental rationale behind our strategy today.

In January, 1967, Secretary of Defense Robert S. McNamara provided a Joint Session of the Senate Armed Services Com-mittee and the Senate Subcommittee on Department of Defense Appropriations with a dissertation that has come to be known as his 1967 Posture Statement. The published version of this testimony ran to 209 mimeographed pages and contained both frank and frightening enlightenment on the United States mili-tary posture, present and future.

I am perpetually amazed at the placidity of the American public—not to mention Congress itself—in the face of the stark meaning of what Mr. McNamara has laid down as the basic United States military policy. Perhaps it is because Mr. McNa-mara, or at least his speech writers, made the policy statements sound like clear arguments for strategic superiority when the facts he presented pointed directly to the second strike parity concept.

It also amazes me how, when so many words were cascaded in his frequent testimony and press releases, Mr. McNamara managed to omit some of the most significant details. For example, when he accounted the precise number of people who would be killed in case of nuclear war under various conditions, he seldom revealed the assumptions upon which these assessments are based. As a simple illustration, what are the targets in these hypothetical exchanges of United States and Soviet intercontinental nuclear missiles? Are we or they aiming at weapons sites? Or are cities the targets? The selection of one or the other assumption (among many others equally sensitive) could cause radical differences in the millions of casualties which he so confidently predicted.

One of Mr. McNamara's most flagrant bits of deception and one which he managed to get away with repeatedly almost without challenge is the manner in which he stated the United States superiority in strategic weapons. His definition of strategic weapons was adjusted to reveal a United States superiority in numbers which, in fact, was not so at all.

For example, he lumped all of our submarine-launched Polaris weapons in with the numbers of our Minuteman and Titan ICBMs and then compared the aggregate with the number of Soviet ICBMs plus a small number (130) of Soviet submarine-launched ballistic missiles. However, he did not use the same ground rules in counting Soviet ICBMs as he did when counting American missiles. He did not count *all* Soviet sea-launched high yield nuclear missiles, because they are short-range and therefore not in his strategic category.

One should then ask: "What is the range of the Russian submarines and destroyers that carry these short-range nuclear missiles? Can they not easily strike our coastal cities with their short-range cruise-type nuclear missiles? Is not the capability of a weapon to destroy New York or Washington sufficient cause for classifying it as strategic?"

Our Polaris missiles *must* be long range because we cannot get very near Soviet territory with our submarines. But in peacetime we cannot stop Russian submarines and surface vessels from cruising up and down our coastlines at will. Not to consider *all* Soviet sea-launched high-yield nuclear missiles in the strategic classification, including those carried on destroyers, is pure sophistry. This, according to public information, would add something like 350 nuclear missiles to the Russian total.

A footnote in the Posture Statement readily admits to additional, but unspecified, Soviet submarine-launched cruise missiles but writes them off stating that their "primary targets are naval and merchant vessels." If the open sources of intelligence are anywhere near correct, that these weapons mount a half-megaton warhead or better, then they could and probably would be employed strategically as necessary. The fact that a weapon system may be specified as an anti-naval design does not preclude its use against cities as well.

Another feature of Mr. McNamara's numbers game with Congress and the American public is to overlook the size of ICBM warheads. Again I refer to unclassified sources when I say that warheads of Russian ICBMs may be as much as ten times as powerful as our Minuteman warheads. So it may be entirely erroneous to presume that we are militarily superior with 934 ICBMs versus the Soviet 340.* If Russian warheads are truly ten times as powerful as ours, a better comparison would be a United States to Soviet Union ratio, in terms of explosive power, of 934 for the United States to 3400 for the Soviet Union. The picture begins to look considerably less rosy than

* As noted in the 1967 Posture Statement.

the one the former Secretary of Defense would have us see. And this is not all.

On February 1, 1968, Mr. McNamara submitted his last Posture Statement to Congress; it revealed the chilling news that the Soviet Union has *doubled* its ICBM force in the past year. The Soviet "hardened and dispersed" ICBM force, McNamara said, *has grown from 340 to 720* launchers between October 1, 1966, and October 1, 1967. This compares with a U.S. growth of 934 to 1054 Minuteman and Titan ICBMs. This new ratio indicates that the U.S. has roughly 1,540 megatons on its ICBM warheads as opposed to 7,200 Soviet megatons. The ICBM firepower advantage of the U.S.S.R. over the U.S. last year was about 3 to 1. This year it is 5 to 1.

Yet Mr. McNamara with his accustomary statistical legerdemain still expresses the conviction that the United States holds an edge. His aim "to halt the momentum of the arms race" has certainly succeeded *on our side*. But since the Soviet Union has doubled its ICBM force *in one year*, it appears that Soviet arms production is accelerating at a frantic pace.

It is clear that the Soviet Union is now bending every effort to gain a massive strategic superiority—and our own defense policies have assisted them.

As few as seventeen large-yield Soviet ICBMs could severely damage the seventeen densely populated urban complexes in the United States that contain over one-third of our population. The Soviets have forty ICBMs for each United States urban complex. The United States, on the other hand, to cover some 175 dispersed Soviet cities, would need 7000 missiles to provide the same ratio of forty per target. Yet we plan to have only 1054 missiles from now on. This is just one reason why it is delusory and oversimplified to compare number of ICBMs. Geography and demography between the United States and the Soviet Union are unequal. But still that is not all.

When the United States had a fleet of over a thousand B-47 medium bombers, these were classified as strategic weapons, for, indeed, intercontinental nuclear bombing was their mission. The Russians had and still do have similar medium bombers, the Badger TU-16, which is being replaced with the supersonic Binder TU-22. But we have scrapped all of our B-47s, over a thousand of them. When the Air Force planned its phase-out of aging B-47s it also planned replacement with advanced versions. OSD approved the scrapping of the B-47s, but never the replacements.

Close to a thousand Soviet Badgers, however, are still operational, some with the Soviet navy. Yet Mr. McNamara does not classify these old but still formidable weapons as strategic. The inconsistency of this reasoning seems to escape most analysts.

In comparing "U. S. vs. Soviet Intercontinental Strategic Nuclear Forces," Mr. McNamara lists 680 intercontinental bombers for the United States versus 155 comparable bombers for the Soviet Union. A footnote states, "In addition to the intercontinental bombers shown in the table, the Soviets possess medium bombers capable of striking Eurasian targets." This is true as far as it goes, but because it was not admitted that these Badgers could strike American targets, using air-to-air refueling, of which they are capable, I can only conclude that there was a deliberate intention to delude the reader.

The general nuclear war problem was also discussed by Mr. McNamara in his 1967 Posture Statement. General nuclear war forces, he maintained, should have two basic capabilities:

1. To deter deliberate nuclear attack upon the United States and its allies by maintaining, continuously, a highly reliable ability to inflict an unacceptable degree of damage upon any single aggressor, or combination of aggressors, at any time during the course of a strategic nuclear exchange, even after absorbing a surprise first strike.

2. In the event such a war nevertheless occurred, to limit damage to our population and industrial capacity.

The first capability is called by the confident-sounding phrase, "assured destruction," and the second capability, "damage limitation." These phrases, "assured destruction" and "damage limitation," are used liberally in the discussion of the current national strategy of the United States. It is well that we understand precisely what they mean.

As the first capability implies, "assured destruction" is assumed to be that capability which will permit us to destroy the Soviet Union as a viable nation regardless of what the Soviet Union may do to us in a first strike. The strategy of assured destruction is an effort to provide both deterrence and some control over the proliferation of armaments. Since the outcome would be unacceptable to the attacker he would be deterred from any reasonable deliberate attack.

The word "assured" is perhaps somewhat inaccurate. If the chips were down, there would be nothing assured about our capability. Of course, our objective is to be assured, but aspirations and certainty that the capability exists are not the same.

We could never be certain of overcoming our enemy unless confident of an overwhelming superiority through precise and highly reliable intelligence information. It is the very nature of the latter condition to be fraught with doubt. I question whether either of these conditions prevails today. Therefore, our first capability is a long way from being assured even though Mr. McNamara uses this comforting term.

"Damage limitation" simply means the defensive consequences of our general war strategy. Our capability in this defensive area is *very* limited. We have, as you must know, absolutely *no* defense against thermonuclear ballistic missiles. The planned "thin" anti-ballistic missile system is years from fruition and even then will not protect us against a Soviet attack. We do have a limited capability for defending ourselves against enemy bombers, but this is gradually being reduced through the current policies of the Administration.

The McNamara Posture Statement notes that the first capability, or our offensive capability of "assured destruction," will contribute to our defensive capability. This is so, of course, provided that we strike enemy bomber and missile bases soon enough to catch their delivery vehicles on the ground. Under the second strike philosophy which we now subscribe to, our capability to stop enemy offensive forces is almost academic. What good would it do to destroy a launching site when the missiles had already been sent against us? The same holds true for airfields.

The Posture Statement notes that "deterrence of a deliberate Soviet (or Red Chinese) nuclear attack upon the United States or its allies is the overriding objective of our strategic forces. . . ." By starting with this fundamental premise, the offensive capability, or "assured destruction," is conceived to be a first priority with respect to the commitment of our resources, regardless of cost.

Before the advent of nuclear weapons our national objectives were reversed. It was usually the policy of the United States first to defend itself and second to achieve some sort of offensive capability. As protection against nuclear weapons became less and less feasible, the concept of deterrence became more accepted as a kind of defense in itself. Certainly if you hold a big enough stick it would seem reasonable to presume that the enemy would not attack. This of course is a pretty good rule of thumb, and has been throughout the history of conflict, but it is *not* something which we can always consider an absolute assured defense. Mankind and even nations have the habit of acting irrationally at times. Even when they act rationally we might not understand their motives because we cannot know all the factors that go into the making of their own decisions. Therefore *deterrence*, although essential, should be considered with some reservations. Deterrence, of and by itself, is not a policy on which we can place sole reliance for national survival.

We must assume if we are to truly defend our country, that there is always a possibility of deterrence failing and that in such an event we should still have the capacity to protect our people. In other words, because the big stick might not always scare off an attack, we should equip ourselves with a shield as well.

We have *no* shield today. If deterrence fails, we are dead.

It is implicit in the philosophy which guides the Johnson Administration that no matter *what* we do, if deterrence fails, all is lost. The doctrine will not admit that we *can* protect ourselves. Therefore there need be no defensive forces whatever. This is fundamentally a handwringing attitude of despair.

In March, 1966, Secretary McNamara testified that the following considerations were guiding United States programs:

Against the forces we expect the Soviets to have during the next decade, it will be virtually impossible for us to be able to ensure anything approaching complete protection for our population, no matter how large the general nuclear war forces we were to provide, including even the hypothetical possibility of striking first . . . the Soviets have the technical and economic capability to prevent us from achieving a posture which could keep our fatalities below some tens of millions; they can increase their first strike capabilities at an extra cost to them substantially less than the extra cost to us of any additional Damage Limiting measures we might take.

From this policy of hopelessness there seems to be no reason to try to protect ourselves. In fact, it would be a waste of national resources. We might just as well disarm to a minimum deterrent.

With this premise of despair, Mr. McNamara also made a seemingly logical case that should we develop strategic anti-missile forces it would give us such an advantage that the Soviets would, in turn, develop improved ICBMs to penetrate our anti-missile system. This he believed would spark a new arms race and accelerate the cost of weapons development on both sides of the Iron Curtain to prohibitive levels. In the long run, he asserted, we would end up where we were before we built a defensive ABM system. Each side would soon be able to penetrate the other's defensive systems with improved ballistic missiles.

This sort of reasoning rests upon so many imponderables as to be entirely specious. In the first place, *all* new military technological developments are eventually counterable, yet they can provide a significant advantage to that side which gets them first. To assume that the enemy would concurrently achieve penetration aids, for example, to circumvent our ABM system at the same time we were bringing such a system into effect, is crediting them with superhuman qualities—unless we gave them our plans in advance. True, they may achieve some penetration capability, but if our ABM system is built with this in mind, the chances are, if we move first and fast and keep on improving it, we would gain a significant superiority for some time to come.

In other words, military technological advances are more likely to be sequential, rather than concurrent. For every new offensive weapon or tactic, a defensive counter follows: the machine gun by the tank, the tank by the bazooka, the battleship by the bomber. For every defensive measure, a superior offensive measure eventually materializes. Armor-piercing shells have penetrated the thick armor of the battleship, chaff and low-level tactics have confused radar, deep-diving submarines have confused sonar.

After a new weapon or tactic is developed there is normally

a lag before a counter to this system is likewise developed. In the interim the new weapon system has significant advantages. It might even protect a country from annihilation or be responsible for winning a war.

Once the counter to a new weapon system has been invented and put into use, then, of course, the cycle repeats itself. And new offensive or defensive systems must be developed.

You may call this an arms race, but it is the same kind of an arms race mankind has been running since the dawn of time. Certainly in this age when weapons hold such terrific powers of destruction, it is not the time to suggest that we no longer need to seek protection, pure physical protection, from these very overpowering lethal weapons. Quite the opposite should be our aim.

Nor can I subscribe to the proposition as the Johnson Administration does that an arms race is to our economic disadvantage. Although I shall examine this matter in some detail later, I must note here that I sincerely believe any arms race with the Soviet Union would act to our benefit. I believe that we can out-invent, out-research, out-develop, out-engineer and out-produce the U.S.S.R. in any area from sling shots to space weapons, and in so doing become more and more prosperous while the Soviets become progressively poorer. This is the faith I have in the free enterprise economy over the rigidly planned and programmed socialistic system of our rivals.

Perhaps President Johnson's policies with respect to defensive weapons systems can best be revealed by examining the history of the development of our embryonic ABM capability. Although both the United States Army and Air Force began studies for missile defense as early as 1955, the OSD did not authorize the Nike Zeus program before 1957. Preliminary tests on Kwajalein Island of the Army's Nike Zeus system against Atlas ICBMs launched from the mainland proved successful in 1962.

OSD, however, noted then that Nike Zeus could not discriminate between warheads and decoys where interception took place above the atmosphere, from 50 to 150 miles out. The decoys, of course, in the form of balloons which might be ejected from a missile when in space, would travel right along with the warhead and it would be impossible to determine which one of the blips on the radar screen was the true warhead. There was no evidence that the Soviets had developed ICBMs which could throw out decoys, but it was conceived by our scientists that the state of the art would make this a possible ploy. Thus, on the basis of this presumed future capability of the Soviet Union to develop decoys for their ICBMs which might confuse our Nike Zeus radars, the Nike Zeus was not put into production.

The policy against ABMs has been defended by OSD cost-effectiveness studies. Cost effectiveness rests upon an implicit assumption that we can predict the future effectiveness of a military weapon system, but we have most assuredly learned from a great deal of military experience that any new weapon takes months or even years of use by tactical field units before it is shaken down and becomes truly effective. A weapon, in truth, is a useless machine until it marries with the troops in the field. They must test it again and again under combat conditions. There were hundreds of modifications to the B-52 which came about through knowledge gained of this great airplane while it was flown under simulated conditions of air warfare. I know of no successful complicated weapon system that has not undergone this same process of adaption to practical use through trial and error in the field.

The philosophy of cost effectiveness, however, conceives that we can, through deliberate cerebration, determine just how effective a weapon system is going to be before it is developed. Now certainly we can and must make the best estimates possible, but we should not place implicit reliance in any system of prediction—and that is what cost-effectiveness analyses actually are.

Moreover, we should always hedge our bets. Cost effectiveness does not do this, for such a system of analysis is designed to select the *one* "best" weapon in terms of both usefulness and cost. If the selected weapon fails, there is nothing to fall back on as a second choice. And since it takes five to ten years lead time to develop a complicated weapon, we are in deep trouble if the weapon proves to be a lemon.

What I am saying is this: perhaps we should have deployed our Nike Zeus even though it did have some predictable limitations in not being able to discriminate between actual warheads and decoys. I must admit that at the time I did not think it was ready and recommended only an increase in research and development. But by deploying Nike Zeus, by putting it in the hands of troops and exercising it against actual re-entry vehicles again and again, we would have learned a great deal about the system which no amount of technological study and development could ever teach us.

In 1963 the Army designed the Nike X system. This was to include the Nike Zeus and another missile, the Sprint, which would fire rapidly and intercept at close range (twenty-eight to thirty miles) those incoming warheads missed by Zeus. The Army very cleverly brought in this Sprint development to take care of the decoy problem which OSD had conjured up. It was conceived that on re-entry the lighter decoys would fall behind or burn up in the atmosphere. A new multifunction array radar (MAR) system would be able to discriminate and handle many targets simultaneously.

This Nike X system worked remarkably well in those tests

that could be run without actually exploding nuclear warheads in the atmosphere. Nevertheless Nike X was not put into production, although about $250 million each year for ten years had been invested in the development, or roughly $2.5 billion.

An advanced version of the Zeus, now called Spartan, with a 400-mile range is now under development. This, combined with Sprint, will constitute the Sentinel "thin" system which was approved for deployment in 1967. This "thin" system is an ineffective stop-gap measure apparently approved more for political purposes than for sound defense.

It is quite interesting how this game of one-upmanship has been played between the Army and the OSD. First, the OSD claimed that Nike Zeus could not discriminate between a true penetrating warhead and a balloon decoy. So the Army solved this problem with the Sprint. The Sprint would fire after the warheads and decoys had penetrated the atmosphere. In the atmosphere the decoys would fall behind and radar would then discriminate which blips represented the true warheads. Once this technological development was presented, OSD had a new reservation: Since the Sprint would explode a great number of defensive nuclear warheads over our heads it would be necessary to have fallout shelters for all cities being defended. It was maintained by OSD strategists that unless we had an elaborate fallout shelter program to protect citizens from the radioactive debris caused by dozens or hundreds of defensive missiles going off over our cities that there was no sense in having an ABM system at all. This objection proved erroneous when Norris E. Bradbury, director of the Los Alamos Scientific Laboratory, said, "the anti-ballistic missile does not involve the question of too greatly contaminating the atmosphere." When this became well known, OSD changed its tune again: Perhaps the enemy would aim his missiles upwind of the cities but out of range of the Nike X. Then, with dirty surface bursts, fallout would engulf the cities and kill the people.

So the need for fallout shelters became the next straw man erected by OSD to delay the ABM deployment again. It was evident that the shelter program had become an unpopular political issue and thus was a splendid ally for those desiring to kill the ABM.

Mr. McNamara lumped most of these arguments in his testimony before the subcommittee of the Committee on Appropriations before the House of Representatives in 1966:

> I would strongly recommend against deployment of Nike X because Nike X itself can be completely negated by an attack outside of the effective zones of that defense system. Such an attack would be successful if we did not have a widespread shelter system because the detonation of the warheads outside of the effective range of Nike X would allow fallout to be distributed across the country by the prevailing west to east winds. Even if we were to have a national fallout shelter program at a cost of something on the order of $2.5 billion, I would still be inclined to recommend against Nike X unless at the same time the Congress are willing to take the other action necessary to provide a balanced defense. It would be necessary, I think, to strengthen our bomber defenses and to provide certain other defenses as well. Were the Congress willing to take all of these actions I would still recommend against the defense system, including Nike X, at this time because as I say I believe the Soviets would with relative ease and at low cost to themselves offset our defenses by strengthening their own strategic offensive forces.

By 1967 the fallout shelter problem was largely solved. Testimony of Secretary of the Army Stanley R. Resor on February 21, 1966, set minds at rest on this score and deprived Mr. McNamara of an earlier caveat. Shelter for 141 million people had been identified and by 1970 adequate protection would be available for virtually the entire population of the country.

With the fallout shelter argument invalid, Mr. McNamara moved confidently to his current position that the Soviets are capable of building adequate penetration aids into their warheads which would circumvent any defensive missile system we might devise. He also made the point that the Soviet penetration aids would be considerably cheaper to manufacture than our ABM system. This raises the arms race issue by implying that we might lose the race through useless spending.

The chairman of the JCS in 1966, Gen. Earle Wheeler, United States Army, testified in favor of the deployment of a Nike X system at the same hearings where Mr. McNamara testified against it. General Wheeler said, "I must say that the Joint Chiefs agree and have agreed for some time that it would be desirable from the viewpoint of our over-all strategic posture to have an anti-ballistic missile system."

He went on to say that an effective fallout shelter program would save the lives of possibly 20 per cent of the population of the country. "Nike X," he said, "is the next most promising savior of American lives. Depending upon the type of attack made by the Soviet Union, that is, their targeting philosophy and so on, the actual number of lives saved could be determined." General Wheeler agreed that the Soviets might well undertake programs to circumvent an ABM system, but he thought that if this started an arms race that the United States could better afford the cost than the Soviet Union could. He noted that the Soviets had already embarked upon a tremendous expenditure for military and space equipment. The Chairman told the subcommittee on March 6, 1967, that the Joint Chiefs had voted unanimously for deployment two years before and that they were still of that mind. He said further that Mr. McNamara was increasing the risk of accidental nuclear war by his refusal to order immediate deployment of an ABM system. In speaking for the JCS General Wheeler said,

We believe that the Soviet offensive and defensive buildup does increase the risk of nuclear war. Deterrence is a combination of forces in being, and state of mind. Should the Soviets come to believe that their ballistic-missile defense coupled with a nuclear attack on the United States, would limit damage to the Soviet Union to a level acceptable to them, whatever that level is, our forces would no longer deter. The first principle of our security policy would be gone.

I should say here that, while I certainly agree—and so do the Joint Chiefs—that the basis of deterrence is the ability to destroy an attacker as a viable nation, as a part of this, there is also the ability of the nation to survive as a nation—in other words, the converse of the first point.

Secondly, lack of a deployed U. S. ABM increases the possibility of a nuclear war by accident and by nth country triggering.

Thirdly, failure to deploy a U. S. ABM creates a strategic imbalance both within our forces and between the United States and the Soviet forces. It could lead to Soviet and allied belief that we are interested only in the offensive, that is, a first strike, or that our technology is deficient, or that we will not pay to maintain strategic superiority.

We also believe that damage to the United States from a nuclear strike can be reduced by an ABM system in a meaningful way.

Now, of course, nobody can say at what point of nuclear destruction a nation is no longer a viable society. We do know, or at least we have estimates, that the Soviets lost something like twenty-five million people in World War II. These losses are not exactly comparable, of course, to what would happen in a nuclear war, because they lost twenty-five million people perhaps over a period of some four to five years.

We are talking here of the loss of twenty-five or more million people in a matter of hours, and the psychological shock and other effects would be considerably different. Nevertheless, one nation will probably survive best in a nuclear exchange. The thirty, forty, or fifty million American lives that could be saved by Nike X, therefore, are meaningful, we believe, in every sense of the word. Accordingly, the recommendation of the Joint Chiefs that we now initiate deployment of Nike X is based fundamentally on the requirement to maintain the total strategic nuclear capability or balance clearly in favor of the United States.

With the burdensome expense of the war in Vietnam which has cost us almost $2 billion a month, the cost of the Nike X system becomes a political stumbling block. Mr. McNamara lumped every conceivable expense into a proposed ABM program in order, it would seem, to make the cost appear prohibitively high. In 1966 he talked of a $2.5 million shelter program with another $2.5 million spent by private parties. He then added $6.5 billion for an air defense airplane, the F-12 program, and another $2 or $3 billion for a surface-to-air missile defense program against penetrating aircraft. After thus adding every imaginable ancillary expense, the Secretary estimated the cost of an ABM system would run between $30 and $50 billion. Splitting the difference, the figure of $40 billion was bandied about in 1966 and the public became understandably concerned over such an astronomical expense.

However, OSD failed to emphasize that the inflated $40 billion figure would have been spread over a ten year period at roughly $4 billion per year. This does not seem so expensive when measured against a Vietnam expense of about $25 billion in 1966 alone. And the war in Vietnam will not save a single American city.

More recent and realistic estimates made of the United States ABM system run between $20 billion and $40 billion for an "extensive" system which might protect fifty cities. A less extensive system was also talked about which would cost up to $20 billion. This economy size ABM would be designed primarily to protect our offensive missile silos, and would incidentally protect twenty-five nearby cities. This has sometimes been referred to as "Posture A" and would consist of about a thousand Spartans and a hundred Sprints. I prefer this latter version because with its deployment we could repeatedly test its effectiveness and prove it out with the usual changes and retrofits. Then if we chose to we would expand it with more assurance of success.

Always ready with a new objection, Mr. McNamara maintained it would be political mayhem in this country to try to select the twenty-five or fifty cities for ABM protection. I have more faith in the wisdom and common sense of the American people. No one is being politically injured by our having no protection at all today. I wish someone were!

As a stop-gap, the Secretary of Defense proposed a third and still thinner deployment, the Sentinel, costing possibly $4 billion and designed to protect us only from Chinese ICBMs. This to my mind is simply another tactic for sabotaging a useful United States ABM system and will hardly cause any Soviet reaction.

As long as the Johnson Administration is permitted to dream up superhuman capabilities of the Soviet Union for countering an ABM system, we will, I fear, never field an effective one. And we shall remain nakedly exposed to a murderous attack.

The point to be considered is that the President, as well as the people of the United States, are banking on Mr. McNamara's judgment alone against the unanimous judgment of the JCS and the Chairman. All of these uniformed leaders have favored an effective anti-ballistic missile system after the Nike X had been demonstrated.

I can hear some of my contemporaries saying now, "But you, Curt, were not enthusiastic about an ABM," and in one respect they are right. In the early days of Nike Zeus development I was skeptical of its ultimate value. First, it looked too difficult and expensive a technological problem to solve. I was for putting more of our wealth and energies into perfecting our offensive weapons—bombers and missiles. At the time this simply appeared to be more cost effective. But the Army proved me wrong and I am glad they did. They made the Zeus work and they even developed what seems to be an effective Sprint to fill in the Zeus gaps.

I shall not go so far as to say that I became enthusiastic about the resultant Nike X system even then, but my resistance was weakening. A second reservation I held then and still hold to some extent is involved with a principle of defensive strategy. I believed that we should develop an "area" rather than a "point" defense.

It has long been Air Force strategy that the enemy intruder must be detected, intercepted, and destroyed as far from his target as possible. A deployment of this sort permits repeated efforts to knock out the intruder if you miss him the first time. It gives the defender a cushion of time to perform his interception and inhibits surprise.

Such defense in depth requires widespread installations and long-range intercepters. It is expensive. It is much cheaper to guard specific installations or cities with a "point" defense, but it is not as sure. Point defense is a last minute proposition giving the defender no second chance in case of failure.

Nike Zeus was a point defense system, and I tried to get approval from OSD for the Air Force to work on an area defense. There are many ways this might be done. At one time we studied the problem of placing defensive missiles in orbit. These then, when triggered, would home on the hot boost phase of Soviet ICBMs and theoretically destroy them before they cleared their own country. This same idea was examined by substituting aircraft for space vehicles, the idea being to fire homing anti-missile missiles from aircraft cruising near or over enemy territory. The scheme promised to provide a true area defense against enemy missiles and I still believe we should develop this feasible capability.

There were two major reasons why the area defense against ICBMs failed to get off the ground. First was the United States policy not to place "weapons of mass destruction" in orbit. At the instigation of the United States, a United Nations General Assembly resolution against orbiting nuclear weapons was passed in 1963. In 1967 a treaty was consummated between the United States and the Soviet Union with similar terms. This gained unanimous approval from the Senate. Our space policy shuts off any ICBM defense in space. When the treaty was debated in the Senate no one seemed to recognize this handicap to our defensive posture.

The second reason why the space-based ABM idea cooled off was because of our second strike policy. How, for example, could we discriminate between peaceful launch and a belligerent launch? Under the second strike reasoning we simply would have to wait until the enemy warhead was unmistakably on a course bound for our cities or weapon sites. Thus a point defense guarding these specific targets would be adequate.

All of this presupposes that the enemy will launch everything at once. I cannot accept this, and still believe we could catch many of his missiles on the boost phase of their launch should we have to opt unequivocally for nuclear war.

If the space-based ABM is ruled out for political reasons, there is no reason why we cannot develop an air-to-surface missile for our Advanced Manned Strategic Aircraft (AMSA) which would home on enemy ICBMs either before or after launch. The Air Force is developing such a weapon in the AGM-69A short-range attack missile (SRAM), but it is contingent upon the FB-111 carrier, the AMSA, and other questionable factors.

As we study this ABM business the solution does not look so formidable. When warheads plunge down through the atmosphere they are highly vulnerable. A near miss with an ABM is as good as a direct hit. We do not have to "hit a bullet with a bullet" as detractors have said. The incoming warhead can be put out of commission in a number of ways:

1. by nuclear blast and shock,
2. from cooking it in the heat of the ABM explosion,
3. by disturbing its electronic circuitry and guidance,
4. by damaging its heat shield and thus causing it to burn up on re-entry, or
5. by forming a nuclear screen of radiation particles such as X-rays, which would render it useless.

The President has vainly sought an agreement with the Soviet Union that neither side will build an ABM system. Bi-lateral talks never developed but we have provided the Soviets with a splendid opportunity for delaying our ABM deployment while they busily perfect theirs.

The argument made repeatedly by Mr. McNamara with the Olympian authority of his high place and the vast public information machinery of OSD to push out The Word, was this:

The Soviet Union would be forced to react to U. S. ABM deployment by increasing its offensive nuclear force with the result that, first, the risk of a Soviet nuclear attack on the United States would not be further decreased, and second, the damage to the United States from a nuclear attack in the event deterrence failed, would not be reduced in any meaningful sense.

General Wheeler has noted that Mr. McNamara's judgment assumes the Soviet reaction to Nike X deployment will be "equal, opposite, feasible, and possible," and that the JCS does not think this would happen. I certainly endorse this view. Also, the Soviets would pay dearly to counter our ABM.

In one way of thinking, an ABM system on our side would reduce the Soviet weight of attack. A study headed by Gen. Austin W. Betts, Chief of Army R & D, in which many scien-

tists participated, concluded that the most likely Soviet response
to the ABM—and the most "cost effective"—would be, not to
build more missiles, but to make greater use of penetration
aids in missile warheads; this would require a reduction in their
total megatonnage. Certainly this would be a move in the right
direction.

On November 10, 1966, Mr. McNamara publicly admitted
that Russia had begun to employ an ABM system around Moscow and Leningrad. Unclassified sources had been reporting
this for years. The Galosh ABM was displayed in a Moscow
parade in November, 1964. The Griffon ABM was unveiled
even earlier, in 1963. Some reporters claim the Soviets have an
extensive area ABM defense in operation, the Tallinn. Mr. Mc-
Namara insists this is an air defense system, although why the
Soviets should spend so much on air defense when our bomber
force is shrinking escapes me. The JCS share my view on this,
according to General Wheeler. The Soviets know very well
that our offensive forces are increasingly dependent on missiles
rather than strategic bombers.

If the former Secretary and the President are wrong in their
independent judgment, we might have to absorb a nuclear
attack from the Soviet Union without a defense. This would
mean the death of a large portion of the American populace
and certainly the end of America as we know it. I am sure
conditions would not be appropriate then to condemn Mr. Mc-
Namara and Mr. Johnson for their error in judgment. What
good would it do anyway? Should we not, today, for Heaven's
sake, hedge their presumed infallible foresight? Better yet,
should we not seek more sensible leadership?

The arms controllers have been battling against the deployment of an ABM system for ten years. They consider it "provocative" and inducive to another arms race. The fallacy of this
reasoning was best pointed out by Soviet Premier Aleksei
Kosygin during his visit to London early in 1967:

What would you say is more of a step toward tension in the military field, an offensive weapon or a defensive weapon?

And his answer to his own question:

The system that warns of an attack is not a factor in the arms race. On the contrary, it is a factor that reduces the possibility of the destruction of people.

It embarrasses me that this expression of common sense must come from a Soviet leader. Why do some of our political leaders not see the obvious?

The "assured destruction" concept provided arms controllers with the rationale to halt the so-called arms race. The United States proposed at Geneva to freeze the production of nuclear delivery vehicles and convert nuclear material in existing warheads to peaceful purposes. In November, 1965, a committee headed by Jerome B. Wiesner, former White House scientific advisor, and Roswell Gilpatric, former deputy to Mr. McNamara, recommended to the President that the United States do this. Specifically the committee proposed an uninspected moratorium on ABMs and a freeze followed by a one-third reduction of strategic delivery vehicles. Inspection was proposed to be "unilateral," that is, by intelligence methods only. Reasoning behind this was that "assured destruction" was so little affected by Russian force levels that we could take greater risk with arms control. Since "damage limitation" (counterforce) weapons could not do their job in any event, it was not vital whether the Soviets adhered to force reduction or not.

Not long before this Mr. Gilpatric had provided us with the new model defense posture in an article he wrote for *Foreign Affairs:* With an "assured destruction" capability on each side, all manned bombers would be retired. Air defense interception would be phased out and there would be no ABM employment. It is pretty obvious that the United States strategic posture has been moving steadily in this direction under the firm hands of Gilpatric's former chiefs, Robert McNamara and Lyndon B. Johnson.

It is also obvious that the second proposition of Mr. McNamara's strategy, that of "damage limitation," is an empty statement, for without an ABM system, and under a second strike philosophy, whatever damage limitation might occur would be extremely fortuitous and unplanned. We have neither an active defense nor a strategy of counterforce. What we have, we think, is a threat to strike back with enough punishment to deter a first strike against us. We have no intention of protecting ourselves from this first strike. This is Mr. McNamara's first proposition, or "assured destruction." There is nothing at all to the second proposition of "damage limitation." Our posture today assures "damage maximization."

How "assured" is Mr. McNamara's "assured destruction" even today? If it were truly assured *and the Soviets believed it so,* we could bank on a world free from nuclear attack. But we must make a shaky assumption here. We must assume that we can forever cause our enemies to hold us in awe. From the standpoint of history, we know this to be impossible. Why, then, should we rest our very national survival on what we believe to be enemy intentions?

It has long been axiomatic in the military profession to base our plans and conjectures on enemy capabilities rather than enemy intentions. Capabilities can, with good intelligence, be measured rather accurately. The number of ICBMs, their characteristics, the numbers and capabilities of tanks, the deployment of divisions, location and numbers of airfields, and so on are capabilities—hard, tangible, and factual things.

Intentions, on the other hand, are volatile and sway with a changeable political climate. Intentions can be reversed overnight, as they were in Blair House Conference in 1950, or the

German-Soviet non-aggression pact of 1939. We are always being surprised by intentions. No one, no matter how highly placed or how learned, can always predict intentions in advance, not even our own.

Any outside observer would have thought in August, 1941, that the United States had no intentions whatsoever of getting involved in the European war. It was just a few months before Pearl Harbor and the vote in the House of Representatives to extend the military draft for just eighteen months was 203 to 202. Those in opposition wanted to shrink the size of the standing army. There could have been no better notice to our future enemies that we had no intention of fighting any war.

In 1950 just prior to the Korean war, Congress made a substantial cut in the military budget. It seemed unlikely that we would react as we did to the invasion of South Vietnam. Intentions, even our own, are hard to predict.

And the strategy of deterrence rests to a large extent on enemy intentions not to attack us.

Deterrence also rests on our capability to absorb a first strike and to retaliate with devastating force. How assured can we be of this capability? Let us first see if we truly can absorb an enemy nuclear attack and be able to strike back.

What effect will a ten-megaton Soviet warhead have when it explodes over a Minuteman complex? We have made countless studies of this with paper and pencil, computers, and underground nuclear tests. Components of our silo complex and missiles have been tested repeatedly and continue to undergo careful examination. Nevertheless, this kind of testing and forecasting is highly theoretical. Let me illustrate this.

One would think that with the advanced state of nuclear physics we could predict the explosive yield of nuclear bombs with some accuracy, and usually we do. But we have had, in our nuclear testing, some eye-opening surprises when the predicted yield of the exploded device varied significantly from the yield actually measured.

Now predicting the yield of a nuclear bomb in a scientifically controlled test is a relatively easy task compared to predicting the security of a hardened missile site against a multimegaton nuclear blast, or compared to predicting the reliability and accuracy of the Minuteman missile itself after such a shakeup. So, until we actually test a silo complex under a high yield nuclear blast, we shall never know how effective our "assured destruction" retaliation actually is. Until then we are making some pretty big guesses. This is a frightening unknown, and Mr. McNamara's bombastic confidence in our retaliatory capability does not quiet my fears one bit.

There are other unknowns in this "assured destruction" equation. We know that our ICBMs will fly the course and we know that they are amazingly accurate. But we have never launched one in full wartime configuration with a nuclear warhead and then exploded it. The chances are high that it would work as predicted, but I have often been disappointed by the optimistic assurances of weapons designers. I want to see it work as it was intended to work. Not just once but several times. Particularly I want to see it work if I am to rest the life of my country on it.

And there are still other doubts about this "assured destruction." Will our warheads penetrate the Soviet ABM system? This we can never know. We can never be absolutely sure of our intelligence. We can never know the extent of Soviet ABM technology. What breakthroughs have they made? They are not likely to tell us. No matter how many penetration aids we build into our warheads (and we do not have many right now) —aids of shielding against radiation, heat, and blast; aids of decoys like balloons or chaff; multiple warheads to deceive enemy radars, and aids to cause chinking courses to get off the predictable ballistic curve—no matter what we build into our missiles it may not be just the right kind of defense against the enemy ABM system. And, also, because of the nuclear test ban, we never will be able to conduct very accurate tests of our new penetration aids, let alone guess at what kind of tricks the Soviets have up their sleeves to stop our missiles.

Therefore, considering the unknowns of the security of our missile bases, the unknowns of our missile reliability and the unknowns of the enemy ABM system, "assured destruction" sounds like a hollow boast—or a dangerous delusion.

What is the answer? What can we do?

We can first hedge our bets with other kinds of weapons systems—the bomber system, for example, which is now termed, euphemistically, the Advanced Manned Strategic Aircraft (AMSA).

(This tortured terminology was no doubt dreamed up to avoid the word "bomber," since recent literature has associated bombing with all the evils of war. Yet when our B-17 and B-24 bombers of the Eighth Air Force were taking heavy losses in World War II, these bombers were regarded with some respect and their crews were heroes.)

Secretary of the Air Force Harold Brown has aptly said that "military doctrine must be alive and responsive to shifts in national policy—whatever the individual frustration which may be caused by shifts in the prominence of particular types of weapons and military units." The inference here is that some people like myself want bombers for nostalgic purposes. I have never had any love for bombers and would be the first to scrap them when they can no longer do a good strategic job. But not before, as some people would have us do.

The Secretary revealed some doctrinal ambivalence in the same *Air Force* magazine article, however, by doubting whether the technical knowledge gained in the XB-70 supersonic bomber program was worth the price of a billion and a half dollars spent on it. The XB-70 would have been a valuable offensive weapon system hedging our bets on the ICBM system and immeasurably strengthening our deterrence. The waste came in canceling the program before its major purpose was realized. Cancellation also deprived the United States of a flexible weapon system which would have been responsive, in Mr. Brown's words, "to shifts in national policy."

In fairness to Mr. Brown, I must say that he has come out in favor of a mixed force of bombers and missiles. However, we are already too late to save ourselves from a very dangerously weak general war posture in the 1970s. A policy to be worthwhile must be carried out and Mr. Brown has always counseled delays in building new bombers.

The second measure we can take is to test our weapon systems thoroughly under simulated wartime conditions. This means we should avoid treaties like the atmospheric nuclear test ban which denies us the right to determine the effectiveness of our weapons. I admit that the Soviet Union is similarly handicapped, but I am convinced that Soviet tests with very high yield weapons and simulated ABM situations just before they agreed to the ban gave them answers in this area which we do not have. In other words, I think that they know more about the ultimate effectiveness of our weapons than we do ourselves. Perhaps, for political reasons, we shall now have to live with the limited test ban treaty, but let us not box ourselves in further by subscribing to an underground test ban, or some similar nonsense like an uninspected freeze in production of offensive and defensive strategic nuclear weapons which we have already proposed to the Soviets. If we have not yet learned of the U.S.S.R. proclivity for breaking treaties when it suits her convenience, then maybe we deserve to be cruelly surprised as we were in 1961 with her breaking of the nuclear test ban and in 1962 with the Cuban missile crisis.

The third answer to this dilemma is to continue striving for better weapon systems. There must be no relaxing in research and development. There should be no thought of a "technological plateau" which could become a self-fulfilling prophesy, and no freezing of our offensive and defensive systems into stylized patterns as we have done with our "assured destruction" posture. We must move forward constantly.

We must RACE!

International life, as always, is a choice between the quick and the dead. And we need a whole new team of competitors. We need some *winners*.

As we have seen, actually we do not have a general war fighting strategy. We have a general war *deterrent* strategy. Should deterrence fail I think we would be hard pressed to fight a general war simply because we have not permitted ourselves to admit frankly the possibility of such a violent conflict. As Secretary Brown said in his posture and budget statement before the Joint Session of the Senate Armed Services Committee and the Senate Subcommitee on Defense Appropriations on February 2, 1967, "The failure of deterrence—whether due to an enemy's miscalculations or irrational acts—would be catastrophic." Hence not much attention is paid to this possibility beyond the one retaliatory strike of strategic offensive forces.

Mr. Brown suggests that our strategic offensive forces might be aimed at similar enemy forces "which had not yet been launched against us," but this seems to present little hope of damage limitations for us when the likelihood seems high of the enemy having already launched most all of his strategic offensive weapons at us. One must constantly keep in mind that our policy is actually based upon the *second* strike. Retaliation only.

A general war strategy should, of course, be predicated on multiple options and a flexible use of our strategic forces. This is so simply because we have never yet exactly foretold how a general war would start, how it would be fought, or what constraints would be placed on its propagation. There are no recent scientific advances known to me which have sharpened our powers of prescience, and I have every reason to believe that the next general war, if it is ever fought, will follow no preferred patterns. This is one of the reasons why I want a mixed force of both missiles and bombers.

OSD does not agree on the need for AMSA. OSD believes we can do as well as need be with our obsolete B-52s plus 210 FB-111s added to the force in the early 1970s.

The FB-111 is a bomber version of the General Dynamics variable wing F-111 fighter, formerly called the TFX. This airplane will provide us with an inferior stop-gap weapon system but it will be better than nothing. The F-111 has had painful growing pains, and at best the bomber version will have a range too short and a payload too light to perform a complicated deep penetration of enemy country with much chance of returning.

Secretary Brown has conceded that the Soviets would have a capability in the mid-1970s to deploy a long-range interceptor comparable to our F-12, and to field an airborne warning and control system as well as an advanced surface-to-air missile. Against this formidable air defense system an AMSA will certainly be a necessity. Yet the Secretary notes that we cannot know for sure if the U.S.S.R. will truly achieve this sophisticated air defense system. By voicing this doubt the Secretary tacitly accepts the repeated delays and incessant studies of the AMSA that Mr. McNamara insisted upon.

The "cost effectiveness" argument for military development and procurement rests upon a thorough analysis of the military requirement and the concept of operation. This is termed "concept formulation" and by its very nature the reasoning process must presuppose a certain national policy and military strategy. Yet national policy changes by the month, while military strategy is a function of rapidly developing technology. For these reasons, the military man rests a good deal of his judgment on principles of war and personal experience. Thus he is in a far better position to adjust his strategy and weapons to fulfill the dictates of a changing national policy. For example, the use of B-52s to bomb Viet Cong jungle headquarters with conventional bombs could never have been justified on a cost effectiveness basis, yet these big eight-engine bombers are performing a necessary tactical function under existing national policy.

Getting back to general war strategy, then, just what should our strategy be? I submit that we must first calmly accept the possibility of the failure of deterrence—of the necessity of fighting a general war. I do not subscribe to the second strike strategy, but let us accept it for the moment. When deterrence fails, the enemy will strike us. What then?

Immediately we assume that the enemy will hit us with almost his total strategic offensive force. Actually, we must grant him the option of hitting us with all or any part of this force in a variety of ways. If he has developed an effective missile and air defense system, he may not feel the need of hitting us with a full-blown attack. Do we then launch a full-scale second strike?

Here again we should grant *ourselves* the option of retaliating with one or all of our strategic nuclear weapons. But we cannot afford to now. We can afford but *one* option if we have no defensive ABM system. Without a defensive system we must try to knock out his *entire* remaining offensive force (assuming that he has hit us with only a portion of it). We must strike back with everything we have.

We may be hit by one or two nuclear missiles as a Soviet warning measure or threat. But because we cannot defend ourselves from a devastating attack, we are compelled to strike back with all-out force in order to blunt his remaining offensive force. Our present posture locks us into this unlimited nuclear war response. Our military posture, rather than our national policy then, would have dictated our strategy.

Let us examine some of the factors which might influence the President's judgment under the above conditions. First, the Soviets would have to have high confidence in their defensive ABM system. If we felt, however, that we had developed a relatively effective ABM system and the necessary penetration aids to circumvent the Soviet defenses, the President might demonstrate this by lobbing one or two weapons at Russia. If they actually penetrated this might limit the exchange at that very point with a standoff. The general war might then be waged in a strictly tactical sense—as an intercontinental "limited" nuclear war.

But if our missiles failed to penetrate, and if we had no similar ABM defense, quick surrender would be our only salvation.

A limited response to a limited attack would be feasible only if we had ourselves deployed a relatively effective ABM defense system. Without such a system, our only material defense would be to destroy all Russian missiles and bombers on their bases. To do this our force would have to be much larger than it now is. This would be the "counterforce" posture which I have long advocated and which OSD threw out for the deterrent second strike force of "assured destruction."

By having a retaliatory force too small to destroy all of the enemy offensive strategic weapons, we really do not have a logical counterattack to his limited first strike. We could destroy his cities, but what good would that do? He would undoubtedly come back at us with everything he had left. And with no ABM, doomsday would be upon us.

Any way we analyze it, it would be to our advantage both to have an ABM system and a counterforce offensive strategic weapon system. We have neither today.

Let us look at it one more way. Let us assume that the

U.S.S.R. throws everything at us in a surprise first strike, something Rear Adm. Chester Ward and Phyllis Schlafly suggest in their book *Strike From Space*. How do we respond then? Assuming we have something left to respond with, as Mr. McNamara does, would we strike back at his cities? This would certainly bring on a final blow from the enemy. He would hit what was left of us with reloaded nuclear missiles and bombers launched from sites we had not touched. This strategy, it seems to me, is a purposeless mad-dog kind of exchange with built-in defeat for the United States. Yet this is the strategy of the second strike "assured destruction" which we now follow.

A general war could also start in Europe where the last two have started. Maybe the United States would be slow to join the issue in spite of NATO commitments. Maybe when we did join we would wish to confine the conflict as it was in the last two experiences to Europe. What good would our "second strike" strategy then do us?

These are simply a few ways in which a general war might be fought. There are hundreds of others, and our strategy should be designed to meet every imaginable contingency.

Only that country which plans to strike first in a deliberately planned aggressive war, as Germany did in 1914, can rest its general war posture on a single strategy. In America, our general war strategy should be designed to prevail and defeat the enemy under a variety of circumstances, and not to rule out a first strike. We should recognize that the onset of general war may blur any distinction between first and second strike. In any event, the enemy must appreciate that we have a first strike capability. The Berlin crisis of 1961 and the Cuban missile crisis of 1962 should leave no one with the feeling that the United States is not fully capable, psychologically and politically, at least, of striking first. But the current attrition of our strategic force is denying us this option. Molding a strategic force (as we now are) which limits first strike capabilities prevents us from being able to employ many valuable options in pursuit of national policy.

To provide us with the multi-option general war capability which I advocate, we must:

1. Develop a nuclear missile counterforce superiority in all categories (land, sea, and air launched) not only in terms of numbers and accuracy, but also in terms of warhead yield and ABM penetration capability.

2. Develop and employ an AMSA force.

3. Deploy an effective ABM system.

4. Modernize our air defense system.

5. Maintain an effective shelter program.

6. Continue to seek new strategic options, both offensive and defensive, through research and development, tactical innovation, military study and test. This includes space defense, which I shall discuss in another chapter.

General war in its various terrible guises is a distinct possibility. Military men and OSD policy-makers alike charged with defending our country should be prepared not only to deter this war but to protect the American people and to win the war if necessary. For deterrence is best achieved through a real and convincing ability to win, not just to punish.

As Deputy Secretary of Defense Paul Nitze said as long ago as 1960, the second strike retaliatory capability "provides us with no rational military strategy if deterrence fails. . . . If deterrence fails the only reaction open to us is retaliation in support of a purpose that no longer exists—the purpose of deterring the enemy from taking the action he has already taken."

I, for one, prefer a rational strategy which will permit us to win and protect ourselves. This is the essence of national defense. Anything less is idiotic.

VI. Limited War

LIMITED WAR is somewhere down the scale on the spectrum of conflict from general war. The Korean war definitely falls in that category, and most people feel the Vietnam war also fits the definition even though it began as a counterinsurgency conflict. I propose to take some poetic license here, however, and talk about the Vietnam war in a following chapter under counterinsurgency. I see no reason to become a victim of hardening of the categories. Also, the present conflict in Southeast Asia warrants a chapter by itself.

It might be well to voice a caution here of becoming overly concerned with various artificially contrived categories of war and their definitions. I have cut the spectrum of conflict into three segments only for the convenience of analysis. The defense intellectuals might not agree with this for they consider "limited war" as something rather unique to history. There is nothing sacrosanct in my divisions of warfare, however. War may well take on characteristics which appear in no definitions. Looking at history, it would be hard to categorize the American Revolution. For the Colonies it was general war, I suppose, even if as a nation we did fight it half-heartedly. But for England it was somewhere between counterinsurgency and limited war. The Mexican War was defiinitely limited for the United States, but general for the Mexicans, who lost their capital city and their vast northern provinces which are now our southwest states. Because our definitions depend on where one stands in the war, to be consistent we shall regard all wars from our own position.

The term "limited war" came into vogue in 1961 when our decision-makers began to feel that any nuclear detonation in anger would set off an all-out city-destroying nuclear exchange. This notion was closely related to the escalation concept that war, unless carefully controlled at a sub-nuclear level, would soon climb to the imagined nuclear holocaust. One can see this philosophy at work today in the stagnant propagation of the war in Vietnam.

Limited war, then, is essentially a war fought with non-nuclear explosives. The Air Force has argued the case that a limited war could be fought with small tactical nuclear weapons used against purely military targets. I am sure that such a war *could* be fought under certain ideal conditions. But I feel quite certain that our present civilian decision-makers will never *permit* such a limited nuclear war to be fought. When things get so bad that these decision-makers are ready to order nuclear war you can rest assured that we shall have our backs to the wall and be in a hot general war situation with no holds barred.

Exponents of the limited war doctrine advocate national defense postures geared to non-nuclear limited war because, they point out, such wars will occur more frequently than general wars. There can be no question of this. History has shown quite clearly that most armed clashes between nations are caused by conflicting objectives somewhat less important than national survival. The point is not often made, however, that we can afford to lose a *limited* war simply because our objectives are less than survival. On the other hand, we can never afford to lose a *general* war where we at least feel that defeat would be worse than death, or comparable to it.

Because of this I have always maintained that our military establishment should first be constructed to fight and win a major war. If we have any military resources left over after this, then we can safely procure weapons especially suited to fight limited wars.

There is truly little difference between many general and limited war weapons, such as defensive fighters and missiles, for example. But some uniquely general war weapons such as B-52s are so costly that we might not wish to commit them into dangerous limited war combat. Certainly it would be out of the question to waste an intercontinental ballistic missile with a non-nuclear tip. Bombers can still be used to carry chemical bombs, however, where their probability of loss is not great. The point is that we need to hold back these expensive weapons in reserve as insurance against general war.

Where we find most of the limited versus general war differences is in Army and Naval surface forces. (I make the distinction here between Naval surface and Naval sub-surface forces, since surface forces, including aircraft carriers, have been relieved by the Office of the Secretary of Defence of the strategic warfare mission.) Submarines, however, with Polaris missiles and nuclear attack submarines designed to hunt out similar offensive strategic vessels are definitely in the general war category.

Some people have suggested that the Army promoted the limited war doctrine, and this might be well documented by the military literature of the 1950s. In that decade it appeared that the Air Force had dominance in the nuclear area, and defense budgets tipped in the direction of air power. Thus, to retain its position, Army leaders, joining with the arms controllers to develop a philosophy of non-nuclear or limited warfare, took this segment of the warfare spectrum as their own exclusive domain. The Air Force, absorbed in the nuclear segment, allowed itself to be cast in a supporting role to the Army's limited war responsibility. This has been vividly evident in Vietnam. There was not even an air deputy to Gen. William C. Westmoreland in South Vietnam until 1967. And the commander of our "fire department" limited war force, STRIKE Command, is an Army general. Thus the doctrine of "cooperation" between co-equal air and ground forces under a unified command which was so jealously guarded by the Army Air Forces during World War II (and which proved eminently successful, I might add) has given way to the Air Force's subordinate "support" role to the Army. This was about where we came in before World War II.

Army ground forces are heavily committed in the kind of limited war we are now fighting and in the type of combat we contemplate for the future. We now have eighteen Army divisions as opposed to fifteen in 1960. The Kennedy and Johnson Administrations have often complimented themselves on this shift of emphasis to limited war forces, and since the extra divisions came in handy (without calling up reserves) for the Vietnam war, the policy seems vindicated.

I would have had no quarrel with building up our infantry muscle had it not been associated with a reduction of our general war posture. To my mind we were (and are still) gambling dangerously with our national survival in order to win limited wars which, even if lost, would not directly threaten the existence of our country. At worst, defeat in a limited war creates, not an immediate danger but a long-term threat to our national existence, which would give us time to fall back and regroup.

I think the Army simply climbed on the band wagon. I believe that the current limited war concept resulted from strategic planners and policy-makers seeking to resolve international conflict without employing nuclear weapons. Our limited war policy is still theoretical. We have not fought one against a nuclear power. In our recent limited wars we have unilaterally avoided the use of nuclear weapons. One reason for this is our decision-makers' belief that a nuclear explosion would cause escalation of political problems, solidifying loose enemy alliances against us and alienating our friends. They seldom contemplate that the opposite effect is considerably more likely. Against a winner, enemy alliances break up. Friends grow more ardent as victory approaches. Another reason, I think, is an effort to set a good example—to sweep the hated nuclear weapon under the carpet in the hope that opposing nuclear powers will do the same. The effectiveness of example has never proved very successful in history.

I feel that the limited war concept which has dominated our national strategy and patterned our military posture is false and unrealistic. It rests fundamentally on fear rather than on cool, logical analysis. Let us hope that we do not become so enamored with this non-nuclear chimera as to be surprised by the Soviets, who have a disturbing tendency to call a spade a spade, no matter how black the mud it shovels.

Much against the wishes of American policy-makers, the North Atlantic Treaty Organization continues to postulate a war in Europe as probably taking the form of a limited *nuclear* war. By "limited" they conceive of nuclear weapons being employed against strictly military objectives, rather than against strategic objectives in the form of industries, transportation, utilities, and possibly cities themselves. This is sometimes referred to as "tactical" nuclear employment.

It might be possible for a nuclear war to be fought in this

limited manner but the chances are against it. Even in World War II, and to some extent in World War I, strategic targets (industrial and transportation) came under heavy attack. Would there be any more chance of creating city sanctuaries in World War III simply because each side now has a bigger stick?

If the nuclear bombing were confined to Europe, I believe the United States would be compelled to take a very limited part in the war. Should we become deeply involved I cannot imagine how the United States and the Soviet Union could avoid hurling nuclear thunderbolts at each other.

Another school which has gained considerable prominence believes that a non-nuclear war on the order of World War II might be fought in Europe. Turning back the clock to 1945 would be a neat trick considering that the European countries themselves would be fighting a *general* war and that they have never been known to use many restraints once they locked horns. Also, since at least three European countries have nuclear arsenals, I doubt if they would keep them locked up for long.

Associated with the limited war concept is the "flexible response" strategy. (Sometimes this is called "graduated response," which is a more descriptive term.) Flexible response was pushed into prominence by civilian strategists of the Kennedy-Johnson Administration, since it appeared to offer an alternative to nuclear conflict. The speechwriters in the Presidential campaign of 1960 made a big issue over the then current policy of "massive retaliation," suggesting that this policy of President Eisenhower's was an inevitable and quick nuclear response to any aggression. The policy never was intended to mean this, but campaign oratory and literature managed to make people think so.

In 1954 when we stationed large numbers of American soldiers on European soil, we and our Atlantic Alliance partners still felt that the Soviet ground capability was greatly superior to ours. A deterrent with tactical nuclear weapons against invading forces from the East was believed to be a necessary precaution. NATO never has matched the ground strength of the Warsaw Pact countries and in every NATO review a positive tactical nuclear response to a strong Soviet attack has remained Western policy.

President Kennedy complained of not having enough military options. This European strategy seemed to him to present nuclear war or surrender. In actuality, it was still well within the capability of the Supreme Allied Commander, Europe (SACEUR) to respond with non-nuclear force to a less than massive invasion. SACEUR could have, for example, used nonnuclear power in opening the route to Berlin in 1949. But with inferior ground forces SACEUR might have been defeated in doing so.

My feelings, however, were that if NATO had maintained a decisive non-nuclear air superiority we could have isolated the battlefield and pounded enemy ground forces into submission against any kind of a limited probe. We would not have needed superior strength on the ground. We did not have numerical superiority in Normandy in 1944. Our domination of the air gave us victory against the superior numbers of a well-drilled and well-equipped German army.

It has always puzzled me why we have never adopted an air strategy for Europe. A dominant air superiority could provide the West with the only sensible and feasible non-nuclear strategy.

Misreading the "massive retaliation" policy which President Kennedy inherited became deeprooted. The policy, in the public mind, meant instant and unlimited nuclear warfare as a response to any minor enemy probe. When the doctrine was voiced by Secretary of State John Foster Dulles before the Council on Foreign Relations on January 12, 1954, he spoke of "local defenses" and pointed out that they "will always be important." "But," he went on, "there is no local defense which alone will contain the mighty land power of the communist world. Local defenses must be reinforced by the future deterrent of massive retaliatory power." This made sound military sense and is as valid today as it was in 1954—or 1944—or 1934. No mention was made of nuclear power, but Dulles' opponents began putting words in his mouth as soon as the speech reached the press. Nuclear power might have been implied by his remark that we cannot let the aggressor "prescribe battle conditions" that give him the advantage. If the enemy is "glutted with manpower," said Secretary Dulles, "he might be tempted to attack in confidence that resistance would be confined to manpower. He might be tempted to attack in places where his superiority was decisive."

History has proved Secretary Dulles dead right. The aggressor *has* attacked where he had a superiority, as in Vietnam. But unfortunately we did not "respond vigorously at places and with means of [our] own choosing." We confronted him directly on his own terms. But this is a discussion for a later chapter.

Just after President Kennedy took office, Khrushchev again tightened the thumb screws on Berlin. The thought of nuclear war over Berlin was abhorrent to the President, and he cast about for suitable alternatives. He called up the reserves to give us more ground manpower. No logical plan was advanced as to just how this reserve manpower was to be used, but at least the President's decisive action signalled his determination not to pull out of Berlin. The crisis subsided.

It might be noted that this ground power option was available to President Kennedy as a legacy from the previous Administration which had espoused "massive retaliation."

However, defense intellectuals wanted something besides options. In truth, they wanted *no nuclear* option. They wanted to bottle the nuclear genie altogether and *never* fight a nuclear war under any circumstances. They thought this objective could be achieved unilaterally because the Soviet Union would eventually come to see that this non-nuclear war stance was in its own best interests as well. Consequently these defense intellectuals ever have since been twisting and turning in their efforts to denuclearize NATO and to adopt non-nuclear strategies. The campaign goes on today and is making some headway although it appears that NATO will have ceased to exist by the time its strategy becomes wholly non-nuclear. I might add that when this day comes there will be little need for NATO in any event because it will not be able to defend itself.

When NATO defense officials met at Brussels in May, 1967, Mr. McNamara got them to embrace the doctrine of "flexible response." This culminated a six-year campaign by our Secretary of Defense. I venture to say that many of his NATO opposite numbers agreed to this strategy with tongues in cheek knowing full well they were not prepared to take on the Warsaw Pact in a land war. However, the apparent political détente has made them brave, and an unrealistic strategy to please their rich and powerful ally was a reasonable calculated risk.

Of course, "flexible response" does not call for the all non-nuclear war that the defense intellectuals aspire to. But it does call for an *initial* non-nuclear response. This would provide time, so the reasoning goes, for a "pause" to enable both sides to think over the consequences of nuclear exchanges and to permit negotiations.

The "pause" idea is one of the most idiotic to come out of the Pentagon third floor. If the Soviet Union plans for war in Europe you can rest assured it will move with lightning dispatch. The talkative Chairman Khrushchev made no bones about such a war being nuclear from the outset. In an interview in 1964 he said, ". . . the losing side will always use nuclear weapons." With this in mind the aggressor would have to start with them. You can also be assured that negotiations would have *already* failed, otherwise there would be no war! Why then would a "pause" bring new negotiations?

This "pause" concept is about as nonsensical as the thought that ceasing to bomb North Vietnam will bring Ho Chi Minh to the conference table. Any fighter could tell these dreamers in the Office of the Secretary of Defense that negotiations occur when pressure is *applied*, not when it slacks off. A man does not yell "Uncle" when you let go of his arm.

Early NATO military planners believed that only nuclear weapons would halt an advance of Soviet land armies. We therefore deployed all kinds of battlefield nuclear arms with their delivery vehicles, taking meticulous care that the warheads remained in the hands of United States personnel. This definitely put us in the driver's seat with regard to the decision—on our side of the Iron Curtain at least—for nuclear war. Combined with our agitation for "flexible response" and a "pause" I can readily understand how our European allies felt. What if we reneged? What if we decided that defeat in Europe would be better than a nuclear war which would lead to worldwide holocaust? By holding back our nuclear weapons, of course, our civilian population, an ocean away, would be relatively safe as they were in the past two World Wars—but not our European allies. And they might have no wish to suffer a cruel defeat gracefully in order to save mankind from a nuclear storm.

Therefore France decided to build her own nuclear force. We took every peaceful measure to prevent France from doing so, but only succeeded in alienating her as an ally and as a member of NATO. Now the German Federal Republic is having similar second thoughts and with our planned troop withdrawals from NATO you can rest assured that Bonn will re-evaluate her position.

The British with their own nuclear weapons have been frightening themselves, as have we, with the thought that some day they might have to use them. There has seemed to be no defense à la the Battle of Britain that could protect the tight little island from a devastating nuclear attack.

Of course Britain could retaliate with their nuclear V-bombers consisting of about 150 Vulcans, Victors, and Valiants. This might prove a minor deterrent to the U.S.S.R., but the Royal Air Force bomber force is small and old. The V-bombers might never penetrate the modern Soviet defense screen.

Before 1962 the British had planned to update their V-bombers with the long-range air-to-ground Skybolt nuclear missile which we were developing in the United States. In fact, the British had themselves been planning to build a similar bomber-launched nuclear missile called Blue Steel but we talked them out of it. We could sell them our 1000-mile range Sky-bolts instead, which would be a better missile at less cost than it would take to build the Blue Steel.

Such a deal was particularly fortunate for the United States. This big contract would help check the gold drain on Fort Knox which was (and still is) threatening our dollar. It would also give us some control over Britain's major nuclear weapon system since she has no ICBMs or IRBMs.

Our control over Britain's nuclear weapon system was exercised even before it became operational. The Kennedy-Johnson Administration canceled production on the Skybolt!

The United States Joint Chiefs of Staff were as surprised as the British when announcement of this cancellation was made at the Nassau summit conference with the British in December, 1962.

Mr. McNamara explained that the Skybolt was not working

out technically as a feasible weapon. Days later, and just before
the official word had percolated down through the channels to
stop work on the Skybolt, I had the Air Force launch one of
these revolutionary IRBMs and it performed rather well for a
first model. Little public notice was taken of this flight. A political decision had been made and we closed down the project
with heavy hearts.

Of course, OSD claimed that while money had been wasted,
the remaining money in the program had been "saved." Since
World War II we have spent almost $20 billion on missile
systems that were never completed or have since been gradually eliminated as obsolete. Of course, the knowledge gained in
these early or abortive missile developments contributed in
large measure to the success of many advanced and sophisticated missile systems now in use. Most research and development money is spent for new *knowledge* and is never wasted.

The abrupt cancellation of Skybolt set the tone for the
Nassau Conference because Britain had counted so heavily on
the missile. Since Britain had stopped Blue Steel production a
year earlier, she was left holding the proverbial bag. Skybolt
would have extended the life of the V-bombers, her only nuclear deterrent. Cancellation of Skybolt left her with the pro-
spect of soon losing her nuclear deterrent entirely. She would
then be wholly dependent upon the United States. The British
were stunned. It portended the end of the United Kingdom as a
world power. The friendly government of Prime Minister
Harold Macmillan barely escaped being overthrown.

To ameliorate the situation, we offered to sell the British
Polaris missiles. When this failed to quiet the furor in Britain,
the Americans came up with the idea of the Multi-Lateral
Nuclear Force, commonly referred to as the MLF.

There had been no military members assigned to the American delegation at Nassau, and the MLF scheme definitely did

not spring from military minds. Secretary of Defense Robert S. McNamara, who had been responsible for the Skybolt cancellation, readily recommended the MLF as an alternate nuclear deterrent for Great Britain. Included in the package was an offer to sell Polaris missiles for five British submarines, which were to be pledged to a multi-*national* force. Ambiguity over the two kinds of "multi" forces confused almost everyone.

As first conceived, the MLF was to be a force of NATO nuclear submarines manned by mixed crews from participating countries. Control of this force, however, would remain with the United States although any one of the participating countries would have a veto on firing the missiles. Still, only by ultimate United States command could the Polaris missiles be armed. This plan greatly pleased the arms controller for with fifteen fingers on the safety catch—*not* the trigger—there was not much chance of a Polaris missile ever firing. It soon became apparent, however, that such a submarine force would be prohibitively expensive. Additionally, a submarine MLF might reveal United States defense secrets which we could not afford to divulge and still keep secure our own national Polaris deterrent. So it was later decided to put the Polaris missiles in twenty-five merchant ships.

When the MLF was finally revealed to the JCS we evinced a marked lack of enthusiasm for the project. But we were overruled in no uncertain terms. We were told this was a political decision and we had to make it work. It has been said with no little accuracy that strategically the MLF is one of the most bizarre concoctions the nuclear strategists—perhaps better referred to as the "arms controllers" in this context—have come up with yet. After long arguments for making nuclear delivery systems invulnerable it was incredible that anyone would seriously advance the notion of mounting missiles on slow-moving surface ships. The United States JCS had long before considered and rejected the idea of mounting Polaris missiles in cruisers.

However, this did not discourage the policy-makers who saw this plan as the only possible way of controlling the proliferation of nuclear weapons and at the same time of maintaining a bipolar nuclear world so that disarmament might eventually be realized. The mixed-manning and vulnerability features of the scheme particularly disturbs the military. A picked American crew had enough difficulty operating a nuclear submarine let alone a crew composed of men from several countries. It took a visit to the White House by Vice Adm. Hyman G. Rickover to move MLF from submarines to surface ships.

Admiral Rickover pointed out to President Kennedy, according to one report, that a Polaris submarine had three major characteristics: first there was the submarine itself, a complicated nuclear-powered vessel developed at the cost of billions of dollars; second, there was the Polaris missile which was also an intricate secret weapon in which we had invested vast sums. Most of the money devoted to these two technological marvels was an investment not in hardware but in knowledge. Should the United States blithely give away this knowledge? Was this in the nation's best interest? There is a limit to what the United States should disclose to its allies, as relations with Russia demonstrate.

Admiral Rickover, so the story goes, said that we could probably risk revealing the technology of our submarine and of our missile but what about the rest? "The rest?" the President was reported to have asked. "What do you mean by 'the rest'?" "The rest," went the Admiral's response, "is all the control information. How the submarines get the word to fire, how they are deployed and maneuvered, how they are communicated with, what codes are used, what are their targets and a vast amount of equally sensitive information. Should we hazard our own survival by revealing these kinds of data?"

So the idea of a submarine MLF was dropped during the spring of 1963. Official sources then attempted to illustrate the military value of a surface-ship MLF. Only the civilian public was deceived.

The Supreme Allied Commander in Europe endorsed the idea of the MLF but with little enthusiasm. He was understandably concerned with the 750 Soviet IRBMs aimed at European targets. It was this threat which led to his request for medium range ballistic missiles for NATO. Since MRBMs were not forthcoming because of the presumed proliferation dangers of stationing nuclear missiles on European soil, and since United States IRBMs were removed from England, Italy, and Turkey by the Kennedy-Johnson Administration, SACEUR was willing to accept MLF as "better than nothing."

Presently the only counter to Soviet IRBM/MRBMs is the United States based ICBMs and the intermediate range sea-based Polaris missiles. This means that if the Soviet Union should fire IRBMs at Europe, the United States must fire its long-range missiles at the Soviet Union in retaliation and the logical counterattack to that would be the firing of Soviet ICBMs back at America. Thus the feared intercontinental nuclear holocaust would be started by a nuclear war in Europe.

Although the North Atlantic Treaty specifies that " an armed attack against one or more of them is to be considered as an attack against all of them" there is some reasonable doubt whether this pledge would be honored in case of nuclear war. In submitting this Treaty before the United States Senate on February 14, 1949, the then Senator Tom Connally of Texas explained that if such an attack on NATO occurred, "the United States can determine, legally, morally, and constitutionally, what our course will be under the given circumstances. That is reserved to us." In his speech the Senator flatly denied that the United States was bound to go to war by any terms of the Treaty.

It may not be forgotten by our NATO friends that there are definite reservations to American defense of Europe, and de Gaulle's question of whether the United States would sacrifice its life for Europe is a reasonable one. De Gaulle's withdrawal from NATO may not be the worst consequence of our myopic nuclear policy. It is not inconceivable for France and Russia to get together. Napoleon's Tilsit treaty in 1807 was repeated by the Franco-Russian military convention in 1893, which was an underlying cause of World War I. A somewhat less dire consequence but one which might cause considerable concern would be a Franco-Germany nuclear pact.

Great Britain is now building four submarines to be armed with Polaris missiles. Although Britain agreed to assign these submarines to a multi-*national* nuclear force at Nassau she was given the option to withdraw them if her national interests so dictated. As noted above, this appeared to be an appropriate substitute for the impending loss of her independent nuclear deterrent caused by Skybolt cancellation. Then when the United States came up with the MLF in addition, asking the British to bear their share of its cost, the expense became too great. Although the British had agreed to this at Nassau in paragraph seven of the communiqué, they had not understood the MLF to be either so expensive or so high on the American agenda.

After the Franco-German friendship pact was signed in January of 1963, the MLF took on even more importance in American eyes because of the possibility of a nuclear alliance between the two former enemies. But even when Britain was asked to bear only 10 per cent of the cost (estimated initially at $5 billion over a ten-year period) this appeared to be more than she could accept.

The problems of controlling the MLF never were resolved, although it seemed obvious, considering its fundamental anti-proliferation purpose, that the United States would never give up its veto for firing the missiles. Even so the United States held out the carrot of some vague mutual or allied control as then Vice-President Johnson noted at Brussels on November 8, 1963: "A united Europe may one day acquire control of the multi-lateral nuclear missile fleet." This thought not only frightened the Soviet Union but it was entirely incompatible with the nuclear philosophy and strategy of the United States. An allied MLF divorced from American control would have encouraged proliferation, not checked it.

It is interesting to note that the one situation, repeatedly alluded to, under which Europeans might control the MLF without United States interference, would be when Europe "united" and "integrated." The then President's assistant for National Security Affairs, McGeorge Bundy, said that the United States insisted on having the final word on the actual use of nuclear weapons by any joint allied nuclear force, but added: "If and when Europe is fully unified and has a political authority that could make an enormous decision of this kind, then the arrangement perhaps ought to be open to review." The vision of a United States of Europe still has powerful proponents as a basic American policy. But it is a far-off dream, and the United States continues to insist on exclusive control of nuclear firepower for the indefinite future.

Other than the United States and West Germany, only six countries tentatively committed themselves to the MLF, and the reception was lukewarm at best. The countries were Britain, Italy, Greece, Turkey, the Netherlands, and Belgium. Jokes were made about how the Greeks and Turks might get along on the same ship, but the experiment of a mixed crew from eight countries on the USS *Ricketts*, a guided missile destroyer, demonstrated that the normal technical problems of operating a ship with mixed crews were not insuperable. Operations in combat, unless all the countries represented were agreed on the courses of action, might be something else again.

Without Britain the MLF would have become essentially a United States/German activity. This would have defeated the quietly held purpose of the MLF to denuclearize either or both of the existing European nuclear powers, France and England. Most of the smaller countries felt that the present United States nuclear deterrent was adequate and that the MLF was superfluous anyway. The anti-proliferation argument did not seem to bear enough weight to evoke "enthusiasm," and many, like Norway and Denmark, refused to participate in any way.

After the lukewarm reception of the MLF at the NATO meetings in 1965, and after the Anglo-American summit meeting in December of that year, President Johnson took the heat off the MLF campaign. The drumbeat for the MLF in the press abruptly ceased. The problem was thrown back into the hands of the Europeans, much to the consternation of Germany. The British proposal for some kind of multi-national "Atlantic Nuclear Force" would give Germany even less part in the nuclear fortunes of Europe than she now enjoys.

The MLF campaign by American policy-makers is now as dead as the Third Reich. It was conceived in a quixotic dream of nuclear control, nurtured in political naïveté with the belief that NATO nations would satisfy their nuclear ambitions and calm their nuclear jitters with a farcical weapon system, which was spawned in abysmal military ignorance. Good riddance. But its short life further shook European confidence in United States support in the event of general nuclear war. The Kennedy-Johnson Administration had made giant strides in the breakup of NATO.

A word should be said here about France's nuclear deterrent, the so-called *force de frappe*. Most people think that this is de Gaulle's creation, but it began as early as 1951 when the

French government decided to build two atom piles for producing plutonium. Premier Mendes-France decided in 1954 to
build a nuclear bomb but the project stalled when his government fell. Two years later Mr. Guy Mollet notified the
Assembly that France was working on a bomb, and the Mirage
IV atom bomber was ordered that same year.

When General Maxwell Taylor published his book, *The
Uncertain Trumpet*, the French were alarmed over the new
concept of "flexible response." "Owing to the technical conditions," Taylor wrote, "now we must redefine general war. We
must call it a nuclear exchange between Russia and America.
All other forms of conflict will be called limited wars. To the
question of whether we should use atomic weapons in these
limited conflicts, the answer will be no, except in rare occasions
in which it will be in the interests of the U.S."

This doctrine, associated with John F. Kennedy's election in
1960 and his employment of General Taylor as a military
advisor, seemed to throw out the United States nuclear deterrent for protecting NATO. France accelerated her nuclear
weapon efforts accordingly.

The first generation weapons of the *force de frappe* consisted
of sixty two mach 2 Mirage IV bombers carrying atomic
weapons of about sixty-plus kilotons, a wallop about twice as
great as that of the Hiroshima bomb. This provided a deterrent
somewhat comparable and more advanced than the British
V-bomber force. The Mirage IV bombers can be refueled in
the air to give them unlimited range.

But France has not been contented with nuclear bombers,
and the second generation of weapons is now well along in development. These are seventy-five IRBMs to be deployed in
hardened silos. The third generation weapons, also nearing
completion, are nuclear missile submarines similar to our Polaris

vessels. One has been launched, *Le Redoutable,* and a total of five are planned.

We have done everything in our power to prevent the building of France's nuclear force. Our Government has stressed that the Atomic Energy Act of 1946 will not permit us to share nuclear information with other nations, even our allies, but this is a half truth. Careful reading of the law reveals that we can legally share nuclear secrets provided we deal with a country which has made substantial nuclear progress. This clause was written into the law to permit our sharing secrets with the United Kingdom. It obviously could apply to France as well by executive interpretation if our decision-makers chose to apply it. The fact is that they did not. The imagined dangers of nuclear proliferation haunted them even after France had actually developed her own nuclear force. Rather than accept this fact of life and learn to live with it, our Government still behaves as if by some international hocus pocus we can make the *force de frappe* disappear.

What would I do? I would go to President de Gaulle and say, "Let us let bygones be bygones. From now on, in fact, we shall help France with nuclear information as much as our law allows, and, in return, have some strategy talks to see how we can assist each other in some sort of nuclear collective security scheme. We do not want to dominate France, nor do we want to be dominated *by* France. But we do not want any Tilsit either. Our friendship is too old and cemented with too much blood for us to go separate ways."

Before going further in this analysis of limited war in the European context, we should examine the over-all enemy and friendly battle order. This may not reflect current strategic thinking but it will certainly reveal capabilities and leave us with little doubt about what must be done should war break out today. The communist threat facing NATO command was described briefly on April 24, 1967 to the House Committee on Foreign Affairs by Gen. Lyman L. Lemnitzer, Supreme Allied Commander, Europe (SACEUR) and Commander in Chief, United States European Command. He said:

The basis for the level and type of our military effort in NATO Europe is the military threat presented by the Soviet Union and other Warsaw Pact nations. This threat includes impressive forces of all types—land, sea and air; nuclear and non-nuclear.

Apart from maintaining and increasing its own great military strength, the Soviet Union has been providing the forces of the other Warsaw Pact nations with increasing amounts of modernized military equipment. This equipment has greatly improved their military capabilities.

Three Soviet Fleets, based in the Black, the Baltic, and the Barents Seas, constitute the naval threat to NATO.

Air support for an attack against Western Europe could be drawn from Soviet air units based in the Warsaw Pact countries and in the Western part of the Soviet Union. Soviet military assistance has permitted Algeria to improve its military capabilities beyond the level required for internal security—indeed, to a level which is causing concern for peace and stability on the southern littoral of the Mediterranean.

This, briefly, is the communist threat which faces my NATO command, Allied Command Europe, along its 3600 mile frontier, which extends from the northern tip of Norway to the eastern frontier of Turkey.

Weighing heavily on the side of the Soviet Union are its IRBMs. *The West has none.* The Soviet Union has at least 750 intermediate and medium range nuclear ballistic missiles in place mainly in western Russia. These have a range of between 1500 and 2500 miles. Many are mobile and difficult to spot. NATO assumes that these Soviet IRBMs are targeted on the major military installations in Western Europe, including London, Paris, Frankfurt, the Ruhr, Hamburg, Munich, and the NATO headquarters and bases. Because of this major threat to

NATO, the United States provided IRBMs to Europe: Thors and Jupiters in England, Italy, and Turkey. We deployed sixty in England, thirty in Italy, and fifteen in Turkey, for a total of a hundred and five. These IRBMs became operational just before the Cuban missile crisis in 1962, but after the crisis was resolved, the United States dismantled its entire IRBM operation in Europe, all 105 missiles. Nothing is left of the extremely expensive complex of Thors and Jupiters which were capable from their bases of countering to some extent the Soviet IRBMs. The reason for dismantling these sites given by OSD at the time was that United States IRBMs were obsolete and no longer necessary. Submarine-launched Polaris missiles could replace them.

The fact is, however, that our IRBMs in Europe had just become operational. I did not accept the explanation that the missiles had become obsolete so quickly, nor did any other military man I know. We should have left them in place. If President Kennedy had negotiated a *quid pro quo* with Chairman Khrushchev for getting Soviet missiles out of Cuba, I did not know about it.

The principal counters to the Soviet IRBMs today are the Polaris submarines operating in the Mediterranean and Atlantic waters and the NATO fighter bombers capable of carrying nuclear weapons. President Johnson has announced that we have seven thousand nuclear weapons in Europe, many of them capable of being loaded onto fighter bombers. These tactical weapons would be used only if the Soviets attacked with ground forces, and under "flexible response," maybe not even then.

Since the Western powers have no intention of launching a first strike, all our nuclear arms in Europe can be considered reaction weapons. How many friendly airfields would be left operational after a Soviet first strike with nuclear missiles? We can be sure that airfields are certainly a prime target for the 750 Soviet IRBMs. There is no missile warning system in Europe as with BMEWS in North America. Besides, short range IRBMs give little warning at best.

The United States nuclear-capable Pershing tactical missile with a range of perhaps 400 miles is available in Europe, but because of its short range could not be considered as a counter to Soviet missiles. It could not reach into the Soviet Union from European bases, no matter how close it is placed to the Iron Curtain.

Mr. Harlan Cleveland, the United States Permanent Representative on the NATO council in 1967, said in a talk to the American Club of Paris that "the Soviets are still aiming an enormous proportion of their actual military strength at targets in Western Europe." He also said:

Anybody who gets a peek at what our intelligence services know about Soviet military technology is instantly cured of any tendencies to euphoria. The Soviets are continuing to invest very large chunks of their own controlled economy in developing, producing, and deploying more intercontinental ballistic missiles in harder sites; they are working on an anti-missile defense; they are constructing an impressive fleet of submarines and other instruments of naval warfare; and they have aimed medium-range ballistic missiles at every relevant target they can find in Western Europe.

We cannot forget that this dynamic technology is at the service of Communist politics; that is, at the service of a party which thinks it has a monopoly of power. As long as this is true, the rest of us are compelled to maintain an effective deterrent at all levels of armed conflict which are in the range of Soviet capabilities. That does not require us to behave as though the Soviet Union were about to pounce. But we cannot know what the Soviets intend to do with their very large and modern armed forces. Aggressive intent without capability would not be particularly dangerous; but a known capability combined with ambitious intent is not to be trifled with. It takes years to make significant changes in military capabilities—but military intentions can be changed in a minute or days or hours. So with confidence and prudence we must maintain the strength to maintain the peace until alternative guarantees are available.

This is one of the most statesmanlike remarks I have heard from the State Department with respect to Western Europe security.

Europe's confidence in the United States pledge to defend it against Soviet nuclear attack has understandably been shaken by our failure to maintain an appropriate counter to the Soviet IRBMs. There has been a long give-and-take about supplying NATO with sea-based IRBMs, and our wholly national Polaris force is pledged to NATO defense. But many NATO powers believe the United States is no longer certain it would use its Polaris missiles and ICBMs if the Soviet Union launched its IRBMs against Europe.

The pull-out of Thors and Jupiters, the failure of the multilateral nuclear force, and the quibbling by American officials in various NATO discussions regarding the response to enemy attack have combined to raise doubts, first in France and more recently in Germany, about the creditability of the American deterrent.

Soviet writers have indicated repeatedly that Moscow policymakers consider Western Europe as the Soviet Union's hostage because of their intermediate and medium range ballistic missiles.

As Red China moves into a position where it has an intermediate range or medium range ballistic missile capability of its own, Peking may develop similar views toward Japan, Korea, Formosa, Southeast Asia, the Philippines, and India.

It has been reported that the United States moved three Polaris submarines, with sixteen nuclear missiles each, to the Western Pacific area. Presumably this is to counter the present

Chinese Communist threat. This raises the interesting question, however, of whether Asians consider the Polaris submarines a real threat. In two Asian wars the United States has not used available nuclear weapons. It is perhaps crucial to the free world in Asia that the Communist powers respect Western nuclear strength in the Pacific. But how can this be done when we show no resolve whatsoever to employ nuclear weapons. In fact President Johnson's Administration has publicly announced our purpose *not* to use them.

It is difficult to conceive of Russian IRBMs aimed at Western Europe as limited war weapons simply because they cannot strike the continental United States. But that is how they are regarded in Mr. McNamara's Posture Statement of 1967. At least they were not classified "strategic." Yet it is obvious that the Soviet IRBMs constitute the greatest threat to Western Europe. It was the knowledge of these weapons that caused Britain and France quickly to fold their tents on November 7, 1956, during the abortive Suez war. The Kremlin spoke pointedly about their "rockets" and we said nothing. Our NATO allies need positive reassurance that the United States still firmly intends to provide them with a nuclear umbrella against a possible Soviet attack.

It is widely assumed that United States Polaris-type submarines with their 16 missiles ready for underwater firing are invulnerable and well beyond the reach of a Soviet first strike. Any OSD calculation of the balance of power between the Soviet Union and the United States usually starts with an enumeration of the forty-one Polaris submarines, providing 656 IRBMs available for targeting on Soviet military objectives.

If our Polaris missiles balance off Soviet IRBMs what counterbalances the U.S.S.R. sea-launched ballistic missile force? The Soviets also have an effective submarine ballistic force and it is growing. The 1966 survey of the Institute for Strategic Studies in London shows the existence of 15 nuclear and 25 conventional Russian submarines capable of firing two to six storable liquid fuel ballistic missiles (Serb) from vertical tubes. The Serb, first displayed in Moscow in November, 1964, has a range of about 650 miles.

There is still another worry. The growing capability of the Soviet navy, as is well known, has been expanding at an impressive rate. One of its recent acquisitions has been a fleet of Bear bombers especially equipped with anti-submarine warfare (ASW) detection devices. Besides its submarine detection gear, the Bear is equipped with an air-to-surface missile.

Between the Bears, the Soviet navy surface fleet, and land-based radars, all watching for the launching of Polaris submarine missiles, it is now believed in some circles that the Soviet Union has a fairly effective system to track almost instantaneously the first Polaris missile fired. Polaris submarines, therefore, could be spotted after firing their first missiles and coordinates sent to the Soviet missile base command for retaliation measures.

It has been reported that Polaris missiles are fired serially on each submarine. Countering this, some 750 Soviet IRBMs may be fired simultaneously in salvo. It is quite possible then that only a few of the 16 missiles could be launched from each submarine on station before the retaliatory rain of Soviet IRBMs or ICBMs had been fired at the Polaris fleet.

It has been reported, furthermore, that at any given time one-third of the Polaris vessels are in transit, one-third in port, and but one-third on station. This means only fourteen vessels are actually in position to fire. Considering the great number of ready Soviet IRBMs and ICBMs, 224 (14×16) Polaris missiles are entirely inadequate.

In weighing this IRBM balance we must also take a look at the opposing ASW capabilities. The fact is that the United

States' anti-submarine capability has been decreasing in the past few years while the Soviet submarine threat has been expanding.

The then Secretary of the Navy, Paul Nitze, testified before the Appropriations Committee of the House in 1966, that the number of United States anti-submarine aircraft carriers had been reduced from nine to eight. Four anti-submarine carriers are now operating in each ocean. One balancing factor, he explained, was that sensor equipment and other weapons had been improved to make the remaining carriers more effective. The then Chief of Naval Operations, Admiral McDonald, testified that our ASW *capability* in the Atlantic has been reduced by two-fifths.

Could it be possible that we are reducing our anti-submarine force because *theoretically* we simply canot defend ourselves against Soviet fleet ballistic missiles? Are we behaving here in the same hopeless and despairing manner we show toward the Russian ICBM threat? The Texas towers, for example, radar stations which had been installed off the United States' East Coast to detect air-breathing missiles or aircraft approaching the United States, have all been taken out of commission. The EC-121 flying radar stations to extend the Distant Early Warning (DEW) line over the North Atlantic and North Pacific, have also stopped operating. At the present time, the possibility of detecting a missile launching from a Soviet submarine is slight indeed.

This leaves only the alternative of constantly tracking and searching out the submarine itself with the possibility of destroying it before it launches its missiles.

Many Soviet submarines and surface ships, it should be noted, carry air-breathing missiles with a range of about three hundred to five hundred miles; not all of the Soviet submarine-borne missiles are ballistic. According to unclassified sources, the

Soviet Union also operates cruise missiles launched from twenty-five *Kinda* class destroyers, eight per ship, and from forty submarines with four missiles each. Warhead yield is reputed to be something between one-half and one megaton (MT).

The United States, of course, is precluded from destroying Soviet submarines in peacetime. During the Cuban missile crisis we were aware of the Soviet submarines cruising near United States shores and around Cuba. The Navy announced in 1966 that several of the Kremlin missile-firing submarines now stand on station several hundred miles off the West and East Coasts of America. If they are bearing missiles, their mode of attack would probably be to surface at night, fire their missiles, and quickly submerge. By the laws of war they would not be subject to attack until after they had fired their missiles. Then it would be too late.

What is the non-nuclear potential of the fourteen NATO countries and the seven opposing Warsaw Pact countries? Let us start with the air defense of Western Europe. This is one aspect of SACEUR's responsibility with which France has continued to cooperate although many of the details are still undergoing negotiation. The tactical and technical nature of air defense would give France no other logical choice. Air defense warning will come from forward NATO radar stations from Norway to Turkey. Without the elaborate air defense control system France would be blind to an attack. This ACW system is being installed now at a cost of over $300 million.

France was "unified" wth SACEUR's system on May 1, 1961 ("unified" was the word used because de Gaulle objected to "integrated"). The British and French air defense systems were combined with the forces already under SACEUR, that is the Second and Fourth Allied Tactical Air Forces (ATAF) in Germany, the Fifth ATAF in northern Italy and the Sixth

ATAF in Greece and Turkey. Although these ATAFs are primarily designed for attack operations, they retain a secondary
air defense capability when controlled by the integrated warning and control system.

The Second and Fourth ATAFs together consist of about
3000 aircraft of which about 500 are USAF fighter bombers.
They are based primarily in West Germany. The Fifth ATAF
in northern Italy consists of about 400 aircraft, while the
Sixth with headquarters at Izmir, Turkey, totals some 750
aircraft.

On the other side of the Iron Curtain we find the Soviet
Union with about 10,000 aircraft in all, 4000 of these being
fighters, fighter bombers, and light bombers. Many of these
4000, however, are obsolescent MIG-15s, 17s and 19s. There
are even some Beagle IL-28 light bombers of ancient vintage.

Soviet tactical air power is augmented by that of its Warsaw
Pact partners: Bulgaria has 400, Czechoslovakia 750, East Germany 400, Hungary 150, Poland 950, and Rumania 300. These
figures are from the 1966–67 report of the London Institute of
Strategic Studies. The total comes to almost 3000. Combine
this with the number of Soviet tactical aircraft and we get
7000, which is almost twice the strength of the NATO tactical
air forces.

On the ground the Russian army continues to outnumber
American forces. In 1967 the United States Army mustered
eighteen divisions and the Marines added three more for a total
of twenty-one. The U.S.S.R. maintained 140 divisions although
only about 50 were at full strength. In terms of ground equipment and weapons the Russians were ahead of us in the 1950s,
but we have since rapidly built up our stocks, particularly
since the Vietnam war.

NATO plans called for thirty divisions in Central Europe
but this force level was never achieved. Some twenty-five divi-

sions were finally deployed in the European "crucial zone." This seemed adequate considering the rule of thumb that attacking forces should have a three to one superiority. It was estimated that if the Soviet Union tried to mount an attack with even a two to one superiority of fifty divisions there would be enough warning from this large assembly of troops to rob the operation of surprise. Since NATO strategy called for a nuclear retaliation to ground attack it appeared that a ground advance in a limited war context would not be a feasible Soviet option under the circumstances. This strategy has worked.

It is believed that the Soviet Union maintains about 300,000 troops in East Germany (twenty divisions), 70,000 in Hungary (four divisions), and 20,000 in Poland (two divisions). These twenty-six divisions are augmented by indigenous troops of the other Warsaw Pact countries: Bulgaria, Czechoslovakia, East Germany, Hungary, Poland, and Rumania, perhaps a total of sixty-three divisions. All told, the Warsaw Pact can count on eighty-nine divisions. Adding NATO's twenty-five divisions in Central Europe to those of Turkey, Greece, Italy, England, and Portugal (thirty), we get a NATO grand total in Europe of fifty-five divisions, which contrasts rather unfavorably with the eighty-nine Red divisions deployed in Eastern Europe.

Yet the Johnson Administration would have a European war fought on the ground. McNamara has pointed out correctly that NATO countries have a larger population than do Warsaw Pact countries and thus could mobilize more ground forces. The fact is they have not done so and probably never will. The democracy of the Free West just does not thrive in an armed camp. And I am not so sure that we would want it that way anyway.

On the basis of pure statistics, an exercise in which Mr. McNamara has been particularly adept, the Free World appears to have a demographic edge over its Communist rivals in

Europe. The West can muster 762 million people, while the Communist bloc, less China, numbers 465 million people. However, if we should lump Communist China's 686 million with this, the Communist total runs up to 1151 million. It is evident that with the opposing lines so vaguely drawn it would be unwise to rest our strategy on such population statistics.

The United States had an all-services total of 350,000 in Europe as of June, 1967. This reflected the withdrawal of 18,000 from France after de Gaulle told us to leave his country. Thirty thousand more United States troops are now being withdrawn from Germany; this will leave our force level at 320,000 approximately.

On paper we will still have six Army divisions in Europe but one division will consist of only one brigade with two of its brigades stationed back in the United States. The United States Army strength in Germany will then be just under 200,000.

The British Army of the Rhine has a strength of about 58,000, but this will also be reduced in 1968 to about 53,000.

The largest NATO ground force commitment is the twelve divisions provided by the German Federal Republic. Add these to the six American divisions, the three British and three from the low countries and Canada and we get the force of about twenty-five divisions in the crucial central zone. Directly opposed are perhaps twenty Soviet divisions and six East German divisions in for a total of twenty-six in the G.D.R. But there are six Soviet and fifty-seven indigenous divisions in other eastern European countries. Then consider the vast reserves in Soviet Russia proper. The standoff in conventional surface forces does not look very encouraging for NATO to say the least. This is why a tactical nuclear deterrent has been deemed necessary by military planners.

There were nine United States Air Force squadrons of F-4D jet fighters in Germany in 1967 but four squadrons are being withdrawn with the thought that they could be redeployed to

Germany in a very short time if danger threatened. A squadron contains about twenty-four aircraft. The same redeployment idea involves the two army brigades being brought home which I mentioned.

I favor these moves back to the United States as well as the fire brigade policy for expanding our NATO forces by airlift from the United States as need be. Huge jet transports such as the C-5A will make this strategy more feasible than ever.

I have long held that we have far too many ground forces in Europe. We need nothing like six divisions to show we are in earnest—just one division would do the trick adequately enough. Former President Dwight D. Eisenhower (the one who defended putting United States troops in Europe in the first place when he was CINCEUR) has also proposed that we now shrink our commitment to one division. And if we *must* use nuclear weapons from the outset, accepting an inferiority on the ground, why does NATO need very many army troops at all?

You may have noticed that I have disregarded the strength of France. Since France has virtually withdrawn from NATO we no longer can count on help from her five divisions and *force de frappe*. She may sit the next one out. Her nuclear deterrent is growing into formidable proportions, with a fleet of about 200 nuclear bombers and fighter bombers and a developing IRBM and submarine missile force which I have described.

It appears that the Soviets, too, are considering the use of tactical nuclear weapons from the beginning of a "limited" war in Central Europe. In 1966 the "ULTAVA" maneuvers held in Czechoslovakia were the largest yet and the exercise was begun by the simulated detonation of tactical nuclear weapons. Airlift of troops from Russia was also incorporated in this exercise along with highly sophisticated uses of helicopters, armor, and paratroops. It is interesting also to note that the Soviets have absolute control over their nuclear weapons in the Warsaw Pact countries, while we grant our allies a finger on the safety catch with a "two key" system. I doubt whether we would ever beat the Reds to the punch with this built-in delay.

When we count opposing tactical forces in Europe between NATO and the Warsaw Pact and weigh the balance, I think the Communist East has a distinct edge. What tips the scales so deeply are the 750 or more IRBMs which the Russians have pointed at the West. In any nuclear exchange confined to Europe these rockets would give the enemy overwhelming nuclear superiority.

The hopes of keeping a European war non-nuclear appear to be illusory. NATO cannot defend without them, yet if she employs them the Russians can out-gun her. The only way NATO could survive would be to draw in the American ICBM and Polaris forces—and a general war of ultimate proportions would then have been started. NATO expects us to do just this, yet the doubts that we would are tending to split up the Alliance.

It is disheartening to have lived through a period of history when the great United States has dwindled from the first power in the world to a questionable military entity. For so many years we held the biggest stick but through inattention and farout national defense philosophies we have let our big stick be whittled down to a lathe while our potential enemy has been busily carving out a huge club.

We could have held the communists in check during these years if we had wanted to. We probably could have made Russia pull out of Eastern Europe, but the sensible policies of "roll back" were never carried out. Our soft foreign policy kept us from making the most of our vast power advantage.

I am not crying about might-have-beens. I am mentioning

this because we can only correct a policy by recognizing past errors. How did we fail?

Our superior strength was not tied to our diplomacy. We seldom had our way in the diplomatic arena even when we were unquestionably superior militarily. Again and again we had opportunities to stabilize Europe and the Far East but we muffed them.

Although we have deployed about half a million uniformed men in Southeast Asia we have still not decided to use our muscle. Sometimes I think we are muscle-bound in a political sense, and I fear it is because we have allowed so many inept, inexperienced, and unrealistic people to determine our national strategy.

I often think of General de Gaulle's comment about diplomats: "Diplomats are useful only in fair weather. When it rains they dissolve in every drop." And there has been a lot of rain since World War II. Every time it has rained our great power has dissolved a little more in timidity and rationalizations. The whole concept of limited (non-nuclear) war is just one of those backward steps.

The approved JCS definition of limited war fills in the gap in the conflict spectrum between cold war and general war. It reads as follows:

Armed conflict short of general war, exclusive of incidents, involving the overt engagement of the military forces of two or more nations.

No nation, other than the U.S.S.R., has the current capability to apply its military force directly against the national survival of the United States. All other enemies have limited capabilities, and thus war between the United States and any of them would be limited war—limited by the assurance that the enemy could not, regardless of his intentions, threaten the over-all security of the United States. Even Communist China, with unlimited aggressive intentions, would nevertheless be a limited war enemy as viewed by the United States. Unless she could induce the Soviet Union to join in the conflict, Red China, with limited military machinery, could not pursue her unlimited objectives *vis-à-vis* the United States.

Since any overt conflict between the United States and a communist state involves the possibility of Soviet intervention, however, there is no permanent assurance that limited war will not expand to include a Soviet force and thus become general war. The best insurance against this is the threat of defeat to Soviet forces should they enter the conflict. If we remain prepared for such an intervention, it will be less likely to occur.

As a result of the possibility of intervention by the U.S.S.R. and the necessity to guard against it, we cannot regard limited war as a separate entity, with forces and strategies separable from those for general war. On the contrary, each segment of our force must be an integral part of one total force; our total strategy must take into account the full capabilities of the enemy, not merely those partial capabilities which they might commit to a limited war somewhere. Similarly, the enemy must not be permitted to assess their risks on the basis of just a portion of our total capabilities.

To say that each segment of our force is an integral part of one total force does not mean that all segments have a direct action role in all kinds of war, or that all forces are of approximately equal priority. Obviously Minuteman, Titan, and Polaris are not likely to be used in limited war, but the fact that we consider them interrelated with those forces which would be used in limited war emphasizes the potential which these most powerful weapon systems possess—and enhances their role in discouraging enemy-initiated escalation.

Not all engagements between the forces of the United States

and the Soviet Union would necessarily amount to general war. We have had confrontations and actual contact in the past and will probably have them again. Since World War II we have experienced numerous air encounters with the U.S.S.R. over international waters, but we think these encounters were not planned, nor did they involve sustained engagements. Important military objectives were not at stake, and because of these circumstances both sides had the option of withdrawing and breaking the contact in time to prevent the incident from expanding.

Literature on the subject lists many reasons for calling limited wars limited. For some, the war is limited because weapons limitations are observed (non-nuclear or non-chemical); for others, the limitations are imposed by geography (no bombing above the Yalu) or the observance of sanctuaries (Hanoi), or political objectives (bring Ho to the conference table), or the amounts of resources devoted to the war (tens or hundreds of billions). To be sure, a limited war involves some or most of these limitations, but the only guaranteed limitation is that it would be limited by the actual limited capacity of the enemy.

Having thus defined limited war, how do we intend to prevent such wars or to win them if they should occur?

Our primary objective is to deter all types of war. Because of the seriousness of the consequences, highest priority must be placed on deterring general war, but this does not mean that we are interested only in deterring general war. Our objective for deterrence extends across the spectrum of military conflict. It is not sufficient to deter general war and have the enemy erode our position wherever they find a vulnerable spot.

Even if we have an adequate general war force in being, we must not expect it to deter the enemy from initiating limited war under a variety of conditions, particularly when our policy is to sit on our nuclear arms until we suffer a direct nuclear attack. We can expect deterrence to fail any time the enemy concludes that he can best achieve his objectives through armed conflict and that the possible gains outweigh the risks. The gains will appear to outweigh the risks if the enemy thinks that the West will fail to respond with sufficient force, even though adequate military forces are available.

Deterrence can be made to work in the case of limited war just as in general war. The military base for successful deterrence at any level is over-all force superiority; that is, a capability to fight successfully *at whatever level of intensity necessary to win our objectives*. Over-all force superiority means maintaining control of the conflict by fighting on *our* terms, and its *sine qua non* is a war-winning ability to disarm the enemy even if the highest threshold of the war is crossed. There must be no opportunity for the enemy to increase the intensity of a war to the point where he possesses an advantage in the capacity to fight.

A realistic appraisal of the "highest threshold of war" probably never means thermonuclear holocaust. The proper concept of this stage of war is one of controlled and selective counterforce against the enemy's significant military targets—his air bases, missile complexes, military command centers, supply sources, POL, transportation, ports, air defense installations, nuclear weapons storage sites, and the like, but not necessarily his political or population centers unless they are truly meaningful military targets.

If we have a war-winning ability to disarm the enemy we can put such a high penalty on escalation that the enemy will seek other than military means to attain his objectives. No nation can afford to lose its military force entirely, especially a Communist state which depends on force for its internal control as well as the fulfillment of its external ambitions.

You may ask at this point, why do we not do this in Vietnam? In essence it is because our military power there has been placed under such rigid constraints. I will elaborate on this in a later chapter.

The clearer it becomes to the communists that their military aggressions will prompt firm and effective military counter-actions to whatever extent required, the less likely such conflict becomes. To this end the communists must be convinced that United States forces are capable of rapid and adequate response to any aggressive act and that we have both the will and the capability to fight if necessary at any intensity of conflict in the course of a limited war.

In the event of limited war it is important that we understand our primary objective, which is to attain the political ends for which the United States has entered the conflict. In the doctrine of limited war this will normally involve ending the conflict as soon as possible, on favorable terms, and at the lowest practicable level of intensity. This objective provides an insight to what is meant by "winning" in limited war. It is conceived to be the task of the military to establish the necessary preconditions for a successful outcome at the conference table, and to do this as quickly as possible and without applying any more force than is necessary to accomplish the task. "Winning" means attaining our political objectives, and in most cases this would not encompass complete destruction of the enemy.

The type of weapons employed would depend on the circumstances, but in no case should the enemy be assured of the conflict's taking any particular course. He should be certain of our response but uncertain of the means we might employ. He should not be permitted to control the conflict by determining either its extent or the type of weapons. By virtue of our superior over-all force capability, the United States should be able to control the conflict and thus pose to any limited war aggressor a risk too great to chance—the loss of his own military forces.

In spite of initial total force superiority, we could lose or stalemate a limited war through failure to understand the real capability which that superiority affords us. Even worse, the initial total superiority could be dissipated through heavy expenditures of resources and manpower to meet an adversary on his own terms. This is the kind of trap into which we have been led today by President Johnson.

It is my belief that our strategy and forces for limited war should not be separated from our over-all strategy and force structure. The artificial distinction of limited war forces for *this* war and general war forces for *that* war destroys the interacting strength of our military stance that will provide superiority and continued deterrence at any level of conflict. Our most potent limited war forces are those which contribute to our general war capability as well: our theater and quick reaction fighter bombers (F-100s, F-105s, F-4s and F-111s), our reconnaissance forces, our tactical missiles, and our carrier strike forces.

The United States alone cannot match the manpower of the Communist bloc, and to match the bloc's conventional armaments while maintaining an indispensable nuclear superiority would require budget expenditures far above reasonable levels. The Soviet Union and Communist China maintain the two largest standing armies in the world, and they enjoy this superioity by a wide margin. In view of this ground force superiority the United States Air Force must continue expansion and improvement of its tactical air power to provide unquestioned air superiority, interdiction, and close support for ground forces. It also must continue expansion of military air transportation for increasing the mobility of ground forces. In order to maintain over-all superiority at minimum cost, the added tactical air power should be dually capable, nuclear or non-nuclear. Nothing must be allowed to degrade our tactical nuclear or our strategic capabilities, which provide an umbrella under which all United States forces are able to operate. Those capabilities must be maintained as a matter of the highest priority.

Nuclear weapons constitute our greatest capability for military victory and we *must* consider them in our strategic thinking. Equally important, nuclear weapons provide our surest means of defense.

As the revolution in weapons technology advances, we can expect that the flexibility and accuracy of nuclear weapons will steadily increase. The spectrum of possible applications will expand in all directions—toward both larger and smaller yields, toward both dirtier and cleaner explosions, toward both larger and smaller targets, and toward new environments in space, water, and underground. Some of these new dimensions, especially those in the realm of smaller yields, smaller targets, and cleaner explosions, have important potential application in limited war.

At present there is a general fear that any use of nuclear weapons in limited war would have one of two inevitable results: at best, the area in which the conflict is joined would be reduced to rubble and any ally thus "rescued" would be worse off than before. At worst, the introduction of nuclear weapons —the distinction being one of "kind" rather than effect—would escalate the conflict into general nuclear war. "Thermonuclear holocaust" is the popular phrase. Neither of these positions stands up under scrutiny.

There is a vast but not widely understood distinction among various types of nuclear weapons. The distinction between an .01-kiloton weapon and a 100-megaton weapon is fantastic, and yet both carry the nuclear weapon title. The former is ten million times less powerful than the latter, and only twice as powerful as the conventional World War II blockbusters. In the popular image, however, the tactical nuclear weapon is equated with the super bomb.

It is not necessary or desirable to wreak indiscriminate havoc and destruction to neutralize or destroy military targets in limited war. Modern delivery systems make it possible to achieve great accuracy in placing weapons on target, and technology has made it possible to tailor the size of the nuclear yield to fit the situation. The basic target system for nuclear weapons, as in all conflict, is the enemy's military capability—his troop concentrations, logistics facilities, ports and transports, air bases, attack routes, and the like.

The introduction of appropriate-sized nuclear weapons should insure an early termination of hostilities, reduce casualties among American and friendly forces, and limit, not expand, the amount of economic disruption and destruction always associated with prolonged military campaigns.

In achieving our political objectives in limited war as soon as possible and without applying any more force than necessary the use of appropriate-sized low-yield nuclear weapons may in effect constitute *less* force and be *less* provocative and *less* difficult to control than non-nuclear forces used to do the same job. For example, a low yield nuclear weapon delivered by a single tactical fighter could produce a destructive force which would require 400 or more fighter sorties with TNT to duplicate. In either case the *same* amount of destructive force would be employed. In the case of the nuclear weapon it would be employed in a single instant and by a single airplane, while in the non-nuclear case the destruction process would occur over a sustained period and would involve hundreds of aircraft and their attendant logistical support. This cost-effectiveness increase is in hundreds of orders of magnitude.

Moreover, the concentration of forces represented by a single tactical nuclear weapon simplifies the control problem and insures the highest probability of target destruction. Against some targets there is virtually no limit to the number of aircraft sorties and the tonnage of conventional bombs that might be required, as evidenced by our attempts to knock out the Yalu bridges in the Korean war.

As to the question of escalation to general nuclear war, it would seem that this is a matter which should concern the Communists more than it does the United States, provided, of course, we maintain superior over-all fighting capability in the strategic nuclear area, and provided also that we express determination not to yield where the nation's vital interests are at stake. With United States superiority, the crossing of any threshold of escalation presents an outcome progressively worse for the Communists. Lacking a capability to fight and win a full-fledged war with the United States, they are obliged, in their own interests, to keep any war at a low level of intensity.

If we are determined to use it, our military strength gives us the means by which to control the course of any conflict. With that control we can establish the level of conflict at which we can achieve our objectives. And by a punishing retaliation we can inhibit the enemy from carrying the conflict to higher levels. With an over-all force superiority we can thus use escalation as a tool for achieving our own objectives, while denying it to the enemy.

The idea of controlled escalation is not valid when we are confronted by an irrational enemy. A country bent on suicide cannot be stopped short of that. Yet, the Communists, I believe, have demonstrated themselves to be rational and calculating. If they assess that their military capability will cause them to lose, they will not dare start a war. The record of the postwar years reflects Communist caution whenever they have been confronted with a firm stand backed by military superiority. The Berlin crisis of 1961 and the Cuban missile crisis of 1962 are such examples.

The policy we now follow, based on the fear that tactical nuclear weapons will automatically escalate to general war, negates the greatest single military advantage the United States has in limited war. By crossing the threshold of nuclear warfare through the introduction of tactical nuclear weapons in limited war, we would demonstrate the grave risks to the enemy of his continuing the conflict. However, we need not do this before exhausting every reasonable means of convincing the enemy that we are determined to deny him any fruits of military aggression.

And one must consider that in most limited war situations which we can postulate, the enemy would have *no* nuclear weapons with which to retaliate.

This concept for nuclear limited war does not hold that nuclear weapons are suitable for all occasions and all opponents. As I have noted, the amount of force applied in a limited war situation should be only as much as necessary to achieve our national objectives. But it must be *at least* that much force. Anything less is a cruel waste of American lives.

It would be as wrong to reject the advantages of nuclear technology as to use them indiscriminately. The side effects of nuclear warfare, which could spill over into cities, might be massive. So targeting must be handled with great skill. Regardless of this danger we cannot ignore either our capability or the enemy's for nuclear warfare. Even though we may intend to fight with non-nuclear weapons in order to exhibit our determination to resist aggression, we must be prepared to switch rapidly to nuclear means in the event we are unable to force the issue.

Our force posture and our policy must acknowledge that

nuclear weapons exist in both the Communist and Free World forces; that used with discrimination the advantages to the United States in some circumstances of limited conflict will far outweigh any disadvantages.

Based on the foregoing remarks, my concept on limited war may be synthesized into a set of maxims which are offered as a guide for our national strategies, military force postures, and planning in the real world of today. They are as follows:

1. Success in limited war is contingent upon maintaining a superior general war capability.

2. Escalation must be feared most by the power with the weaker general war capability.

3. A nation's resources for defense are not unlimited. Within these resources the required general war forces demand the highest priority; expenditures for forces capable of fighting less than general war must not infringe on the maintenance of a superior general war capability.

4. With general war superiority a nation should respond to limited war aggression with the timely application of whatever forces are necessary to achieve its objectives.

5. A nation with technological superiority would use this asset to produce the most effective weapons and delivery systems and thereby offset any deficiencies in defense resources such as total manpower, conventional armaments, etc.

6. In limited war, control of the course of the conflict is paramount. The conflict should be conducted to take advantage of our best capabilities, to provide us with maximum choices rather than have the choices forced upon us by the enemy.

7. Insofar as practicable, military forces should be designed with the range, mobility, flexibility, speed, penetrative ability, and fire power delivery that can perform in cold, limited, and general war situations.

8. The deterrence of war is directly proportional to the risk

assessed by the potential aggressor. Policies which appear to lower the risk in the eyes of the aggressor will encourage his aggressive acts.

9. One risk that is always unacceptable to any Communist state is the threatened loss or neutralization of its military capability.

10. If deterrence has failed and the United States is involved in a limited war, the primary objectives will be to attain the political ends for which the United States entered the conflict—normally involving the ending of hostilities as soon as possible on favorable terms.

The philosophy of limited war came about largely through the efforts of arms controllers to turn the clock back to the non-nuclear age. As long as the United States exercises a non-nuclear policy and fights against non-nuclear powers, this philosophy can be practiced. But its efficacy is in serious doubt when we consider the unsatisfactory and expensive stalemates we have suffered in Korea and Vietnam. Should the enemy be a nuclear power, as for example, Russia, in a war confined to Europe, there is considerable question as to whether such a conflict could remain non-nuclear for long.

Another feature of limited warfare is that national objectives are also limited, it being assumed that the enemy will call for a conference after a certain amount of punishment. As President Johnson has said, when the enemy realizes that the cost of aggression is too high a price for him to pay.

What is possibly overlooked is that a limited objective in our eyes may be tantamount to an irrevocable commitment in the eyes of our enemies with such overtones of passion and hatred as to cause them to fight to the bitter end. Another pitfall is that loss-of-face to a government in power may take on ultimate proportions. That elusive principle called "national honor" may become deeply involved even when the fighting is extremely limited.

In Europe the Western position and the NATO alliance continues to deteriorate. The cause of this is in part due to our concept of limited war which makes a nuclear response somewhat equivocal. We have launched several schemes such as the abortive MLF, to satisfy the nuclear fears of our NATO allies, but none has checked the disenchantment with America's guarantees.

France has gone her separate way, building her own nuclear force and in effect, cuting the geographical heart out of NATO. Our chance to rest the defense of NATO on superior air power has now been seriously reduced through lack of maneuver space, and backup airfields and depots.

We have seen that the order of battle in Europe, friendly versus potential enemy, is definitely not in our favor. Because of this it would seem that any armed clash across the Iron Curtain would escalate to general warfare with Russia and the United States exchanging megaton blows.

It seems to me that NATO can only protect itself with superior nuclear air power and missile power and that this is the only solution to the dilemma in which we find ourselves. The six divisions we have in Germany are of little value and all but one should be returned. This will have a salutory effect on our balance of payments as a desirable side effect. With nuclear air and missile power assigned to Supreme Headquarters Allied Powers Europe (SHAPE) it might not be necessary for Washington to confront Moscow directly or vice versa should war break out in Europe. In other words, a nuclear war in Europe might be isolated to Europe as a limited war.

The current official doctrine for limited war, however, rests upon one fundamental—and false—imperative: that the war must not escalate to nuclear proportions. Behind this is the

common belief that total nuclear war would follow and would
inevitably destroy Western civilization. This limited war imperative forces us to fight on enemy terms and at a sub-winning
level of conflict. Escalation by the enemy results in a reaction
philosophy for us, while true winning generalship must exercise
initiative at every level.

We are still fighting two limited wars. The one in Korea is
quiet for the moment but the armed truce may be broken at
any time. For seventeen years we have been guarding that frontier. The other limited war in Vietnam seems to be taking the
same unsatisfactory course.

I should think that with the evidence of Korea and Vietnam
we should begin to see the errors in the limited war doctrine
we now practice. Unless we start to win the wars we get into,
we may find ourselves overextended around the world on several frontiers, fighting equivocal wars. To maintain such vast
military forces America would become an armed camp with
all our sons being drafted for these endless foreign wars. God
forbid! The 1984 of George Orwell would be here. America
could then offer little more to its citizens than communism does
to its comrades.

VII. A European Solution

THERE ARE two major issues that influence our policies toward Europe. One is German reunification, which has gone unsolved for over two decades and which has boiled over several times in Berlin to menace hot war. The other is the problem of nuclear weapon proliferation, which I shall discuss in the next chapter.

The anomaly of Berlin, isolated within East Germany, is but part of the German problem. The total problem of Germany's division amplifies almost every other European problem. Statesmen are unanimous in agreeing that if the problem of Berlin and German reunification could be solved, East-West tensions would be considerably mitigated and a major threat of nuclear war removed.

It would be senseless to discuss a strategy for Europe unless we address ourselves to this central political problem. I propose here to suggest a solution to the German problem which was studied at length by the Joint Chiefs of Staff but which never was seriously considered because it appeared too radical. To my mind only a radical solution will solve this complicated issue.

The allied powers who twice in one generation fought Germany in two of history's most violent and costly wars understandably searched for some means of subduing Germany once and for all. Hitler's political excesses and the unconscionable horror of the concentration camps sickened the Allies. They were bound and determined that Germany should never again be permitted to threaten the world.

There are those who maintain that the German mentality, the same neurotic mind that sustained Hitler, is at large today, waiting in the wings for an opportunity to burst again on the stage of history and dominate Europe. Only this time America and France will be helping her.

One must appreciate the Russian anxiety about being overrun again. She probably suffered more from German guns and bombs in two wars than any other nation. Some historians estimate a Russian death toll of twenty-five million people in World War II alone. Until we understand the Russian attitude toward Germany we are not likely to find a solution to the German problem.

In 1945 the aims of America and Russia were quite similar with respect to Germany. It was dismemberment. Only by splitting Germany was it believed that she could be prevented from rising again.

Thus we ourselves created the problem of a divided Germany which has plagued us ever since and portends to bring World War III upon us, just as the shortsightedness at Versailles after the first World War contributed to the conflict of 1939 to 1945.

When Germany and Berlin were divided among the victorious Allies in 1945, it was believed that the Allied Control Council in Berlin could govern this hodge-podge. However, by 1948 it was obvious to all that because of Soviet intransigence, the Allied Control Council was a complete failure and the governing of Berlin and Germany broke into separate segments called sectors and zones respectively.

By reason of the anomalous geographical and political position of Berlin, over 110 miles inside Soviet-controlled East Germany, the U.S.S.R. has been able to threaten at any time the rights there of the Western powers. A slight turn of the thumbscrews on these occupation rights, a squeeze of the long lifeline to West Germany as was done as late as 1963, and another crisis is created. In July, 1963, Chairman Khrushchev boasted to Mr. W. Averell Harriman of this capability for "stepping on President Kennedy's corns." Continued deliberate irritation of this sort could well lead to open hostilities.

The political involvement of the United States in Berlin is not consistent with United States military capabilities in this situation. As we have seen, in a non-nuclear sense we are inferior. Locally we are inferior in a nuclear sense. Therefore, escalation to general war would appear to be a possible development from any armed clash. National prestige is at stake on both sides. The United States implied its willingness to go as far as general nuclear war in the summer crisis of 1961. And the Kremlin leaders are still being goaded by the internal Stalinists and Maoist Chinese to act tougher. Because of the combustibility created by Allied communications penetrating 110 miles through Soviet-controlled territory, the United States is committed far in excess of its true national interests, and the Western Allies are in a perilously inferior tactical position.

The symbolism of Berlin as a free city in a Communist sea has, ever since World War II, been of primary importance in the East-West struggle even though the loss of Berlin by either side would not directly affect the physical security of either the United States or the Soviet Union. In relation to the security of either power, Berlin is not worth a major war. But the symbolism has become so important to both sides that neither could afford to lose. It is now a matter of international face.

One type of solution the United States has adopted, albeit unwillingly, is to minimize military confrontations by relinquishing, one by one, small occupational rights by default in response to Soviet "salami tactics." One example is the *de facto* acceptance by the Western Allies of the Berlin Wall. Another example is Western Allies' acceptance of the elimination of the Soviet Berlin Commandant. A third example is the adoption by the United States (with France and the United Kingdom) of a formal and declared policy for dismounting personnel from convoys of a certain size for a head count. The end result of these little retreats is the continued erosion of our occupational rights. By thus abandoning our stated obligations to West Berlin, we weaken our alliance with West Germany and NATO, and strengthen the power and influence of the U.S.S.R. in Europe.

One means of coping with the Berlin, and German, problem —and that closest to current policy—is to maintain the *status quo*, making no more concessions, and by constant exercise of our remaining rights, leaving no chance for another salami slice. This is the policy we have attempted to follow but it presents many difficulties. The Soviet tactical position is just too good to permit our holding the hard line indefinitely. West Berlin is an island in East Germany. Trade with the surrounding Communist area is limited. Only heavy subsidies of government and industry, principally from the German Federal Republic, keep West Berlin alive. Almost all commercial traffic from the west travels over lines of communications controlled by East Germany. Toll rates are subject to East German control. The U.S.S.R. has repeatedly threatened the air corridors. In the final analysis, we are incapable of holding the *status quo*, and the *status quo* provides no promise for a final solution, but continues to aggravate the political scene. Such a result negates the very reason for the Western presence in Berlin.

Unilateral Western withdrawal from the Berlin commitments, however, would be a disastrous collapse of our policy. What then can be done?

There is one diplomatic tactic which might work: an equitable *quid pro quo*. There are many appropriate trading assets for both sides in the current European scene. Let me review what it is that we and the Soviets both desire and what might be bargained:

1. Each side has asserted its desire for a German settlement.

2. Neither side wants nuclear war. Therefore, a solution which lessens war dangers probably will be welcomed by both. Each side has subtly threatened war in order to achieve its Berlin objectives, yet each has hoped that war would not have to be joined.

3. Present United States commitments may not be inviolate. While Berlin is conceived to be the capital of an ultimately free and unified Germany, is the United States willing to fight for this? Not many years ago the United States desired to dismember Germany.* It is therefore relevant to inquire how the United States became so heavily committed.

The present United States policy for a unified Germany was initially established to permit better economic administration, thus reducing the expensive occupation while still preventing Germany from joining the Communist bloc. In other words the purpose was to promote administrative efficiency, not to accede to German aspirations. Failing this unification because of

---

* See Henry Morgenthau, Jr., *Germany Is Our Problem;* Sumner Welles, *The Time for Decision,* chap. 9; Robert Sherwood, *Roosevelt and Hopkins,* p. 711; and *Foreign Relations of the United States: Conferences at Malta and Yalta, 1945, Washington, 1955,* p. 614.

Soviet non-cooperation, the Western zones were consolidated, leaving Germany divided between East and West. The creation of NATO in 1949 brought a substantial increase in Allied troop strength in West Germany. Later, the Paris Agreements of May, 1955, permitted the Federal Republic of Germany (West Germany) to become a member of NATO. At the Foreign Ministers' Conference in October, 1955, the Soviets questioned the legality of this act just as we have since questioned the legality of the Soviet threat to negotiate a peace treaty with the German Democratic Republic (East Germany).

The abortive Soviet effort to eject the Western Allies from Berlin in 1948 strengthened our determination to remain there. As the Federal Republic grew in importance, its desire for German unification grew apace. The F.R.G. has attempted to incorporate West Berlin in every extra-legal sense, just as the Pankow regime of the G.D.R. has sought to incorporate East Berlin. The Federal Republic provides a lion's share of the subsidies running into the hundreds of millions annually which keep West Berlin viable.

There exists a strong Western commitment not to let West Berlin's 2.2 million people slip behind the Iron Curtain. For this reason, and in order to retain the symbol of German unification for our West German allies, the United States maintains its close ties to West Berlin. By pursuing this policy, the United States sustains world confidence and assures the loyalty of the Federal Republic to the West.

Getting back to the idea of a *quid pro quo*, it is possible that Soviet interests would permit negotiations. The Soviets are very chary of German reunification. They took such punishment from the Germans in two World Wars that they sincerely fear German *revanchism* and would prefer to see Germany forever divided. Thus the U.S.S.R. is anxious to legitimatize the German Democratic Republic, and one way to promote this cause would be to acquire the symbol of the capital city, Berlin.

To dismember Germany still further and to compensate Poland for the Eastern territories seized by the U.S.S.R., the Soviets would like the Western Powers, particularly the F.R.G., to recognize the Oder-Neisse line which places a good portion of pre-World War II Germany under Polish administration.

The Soviets might be willing to pay a price to have Western forces and the influence of the F.R.G. out of Berlin. This, they might reason, would cool Western unification hopes and keep Germany forever divided. Is there anything the West could ask for which would compensate for Berlin becoming a free city as the Soviets have proposed? Is there any way by which the West could bargain for such a move without antagonizing the Federal Republic? Without abandoning to Communism the people in West Berlin? Without appearing to retreat or surrender to Soviet pressure? Without weakening NATO or losing world prestige?

Because the United States is so heavily committed to Berlin, any change in that position would have to be compensated for by a most favorable and spectacular trade. Such a *quid pro quo* might be made possible by the Western Allies asking Russia for the return of territories which they conquered in World War II. The extreme limit of Allied advance in 1945 extended to the Elbe River, half the distance from the present East German border to Berlin. This extensive territory, conquered by the Western Allies, includes Thuringia, Saxony, parts of Mecklenburg and Anhalt—almost half of East Germany. (See map.)

Before Germany was conquered, a protocol was signed in London on September 12, 1944, between the United States, the United Kingdom, and the U.S.S.R. establishing the occupational zones in Germany and providing for the three-power

EXTENT OF ALLIED ADVANCE, 1945

EAST

Berlin

GERMANY

FEDERAL

REPUBLIC

OF

GERMANY

CZECHO-
SLOVAKIA

AUSTRIA

0   50   100 Miles

– – – – – Line of Furthest Advance by Western Allies, 1945

░░░ Area of Western Allied Withdrawal

occupation of Berlin. At the war's end, although no formal *quid pro quo* attended United States and British withdrawal to their zonal boundaries in Germany prior to their occupation of West Berlin, these moves amounted to as much.

On June 14, 1945, President Truman cabled Marshal Stalin regarding the withdrawal of American troops from the Elbe in East Germany back to the boundary established by the London Protocol. Soviet troops were then in possession of Berlin, including that area which was to be administered by the Western Allies. The President noted that he was "ready" to withdraw from the Elbe and then occupy the United States sector of Berlin. This cable was confirmed by Stalin and the movements carried out on July 1, thus consummating a trade in territory. It would not seem entirely impossible to reverse these moves. What has been done by agreement might be undone by agreement. The Soviets have already set the stage for this.

On November 27, 1958, the U.S.S.R. sent a note to the United States and the United Kingdom abrogating the London Protocol of 1944. We rejected this note in a reply of December 31, 1958, mentioning the fact that we had turned over the conquered territories of Thuringia, Saxony, etc., at the same time that the Soviets turned over West Berlin to us. Thus the way has been opened for a *quid pro quo* which could return to the boundaries which existed at the time of the cease-fire on V-E Day, 1945. This would be a *status quo ante* Potsdam.

A pure swap of territories would probably not appeal to the Federal Republic unless the territory which was conquered by the Western Allies were given to her. Certainly the U.S.S.R., already fearing the power of West Germany, would never agree to this expansion and strengthening of the Federal Republic. Our commitment to the people of West Berlin, moreover, would not be fulfilled by abandoning them to communism.

The Soviets proposed in their 1958 note that West Berlin be made a "free city," paralleling the "neutral status which was adopted by the Austrian Republic." The U.S.S.R. would have "no objection to the United Nations also sharing in one way or another." But no one was deceived by this gambit. Obviously, as soon as the troops of the Western powers were removed, Communist pressure for incorporating West Berlin into the German Democratic Republic would be intensified. Communist encroachment might be thwarted, however, if the Western powers had some leverage to apply in case the Soviets or East Germans moved to take over West Berlin or to deny free access. The necessary leverage can be found in the *quid pro quo* itself.

Let us refer to that part of East Germany which was conquered by the Western Allies during World War II as Middle Germany. The Soviets might entertain the idea of a Middle Germany governed in a similar manner to that which they proposed for West Berlin, as an independent, neutral, and disarmed country comparable to Austria. Thus the Soviet abrogation of the London Protocol might itself provide the new directions for negotiations. We could point out that a return to the pre-Potsdam position is essentially a Soviet idea (by their note of November 27, 1958) and to be entirely equitable, Middle Germany, which we conquered, should be considered in any proposal dealing with a Berlin solution.

So that the new country of Middle Germany would be completely neutral, it could be established as a United Nations trusteeship, initially under Austrian, or some other mutually acceptable neutral state's administration until its own freely elected government could be formed. Such an arrangement could also be made for all of Berlin as an initial bargaining position.

The lever to prevent the Soviets or the G.D.R. from taking

over Berlin could be incorporated in the treaty itself: any Communist encroachment on the independence and freedom of West Berlin—including failure to honor access rights which would also be specified—would be countered by allowing Middle Germany to align itself with the West. In other words, the neutrality articles of the treaty would become null and void if the freedom of Berlin were not maintained. This has worked with eminent success in Austria. There would be established an automatically operating lever based upon Allied analysis of the state of freedom in Berlin. Thus could United States commitments to the people of West Berlin and West Germany be upheld.

This leverage would be inadequate if the people of Middle Germany felt disinclined to align themselves with the West. All evidence, however, points in the other direction. The Soviets have not permitted a free election since 1946 when a Berlin election went strongly anti-Communist. The mass exodus of East German citizens before the Wall was built is another indication of the popular attitude. Finally, the ethnic ties and the desire of almost all Germans for reunification would undoubtedly cause a free Middle Germany to become closely associated with the F.R.G. unless constrained by the terms of the treaty. Any formal Western alignment with Middle Germany would, of course, be objectionable to the Soviets. Each side would have a hold on the other.

A form of mutual inspection could be established to police this treaty. An inspection body composed of the United States, the United Kingdom, France, and the Federal Republic of Germany could be located in Berlin to assure that treaty terms were upheld, with a comparable Soviet Union-German Democratic Republic body in Middle Germany.

It is conceded that this *quid pro quo* would legitimatize the Soviet hegemony over Eastern Europe and the truncated German Democratic Republic. The Oder-Neisse line would be accepted by the West, to attract the Soviets. However, with Eastern European countries now gaining more independence it might be wise for the United States to accept the *status quo* legally, as it has already done *de facto*.

It might also seem that the symbol of Berlin as the capital of a free and unified Germany would have been weakened by the removal of the Western military presence and by the Federal Republic's dissociation from it. But on closer examination, the chances of a reunified Germany would be markedly enhanced by an extensive rollback of Communism and Soviet power from Middle Germany, and the freeing of eight million Germans now behind the Iron Curtain. In addition, Berlin would still be free with the real possibility of becoming the capital city of a future, reunified Germany. Currently, the principal bar to German reunification is not its political divisions but the Soviet presence there.

At the very least, the creation of Middle Germany, unaligned, free, and disarmed, would provide a sound basis for a disengagement of Western and Soviet forces. The area of Middle Germany now contains most of the Soviet and East German divisions deployed in the G.D.R. These would be displaced to the east by fifty to a hundred miles. It would be the first rollback of Communist forces since the Austrian Treaty.

With the creation of a neutral Middle Germany, a *cordon sanitaire* of unaligned states would be created extending from the Arctic to the Mediterranean in this order: Sweden, Middle Germany, Austria, and Yugoslavia. Thus, at no place in Europe except western Czechoslovakia would NATO and Warsaw Pact military forces directly confront each other. Such a safety belt across Europe would undoubtedly lead to improved East-West stability. There would be little opportunity to look into each other's gun barrels as we do today.

This plan would seem to have more attraction for the West than for the East, and to get it off the ground other inducements to the Soviet Union might have to be offered. Removal of United States bases from Europe has long been a Soviet aim, and with a Germany solution this might become a possibility.

The regime of Walter Ulbricht, East Germany's dictator, would undoubtedly resist the Middle Germany proposal, since the gains of recognition and potential U.N. membership would not compensate for the great territorial loss. On the other hand, the *people* of East Germany might look upon the proposal with much favor if it included a means for removing the Soviet troops in what remained of the Democratic Republic. One should not forget the anti-Soviet riots there in 1953.

I think the Soviets might look with favor upon a phase-out of their armed forces in East Germany if a similar phase-out of non-German armed forces could be achieved in West Germany. A drastic reduction of United States troop strength in West Germany would be entirely feasible. And with the increasing technical capability of airlift it would be possible to return in a hurry if danger threatened or our allies so requested.

Since we are beginning a phase-out now in any event, it would seem appropriate to gain some political advantage from this redeployment. I would therefore recommend that the proposed treaty include an agreement whereby both non-German NATO and Soviet military forces phase out of their respective German zones over a period of two or three years.

Such a new political arrangement would have some obvious effects on the NATO military organization. The major military changes would be limited to those of the Allied Forces Central Europe located in West Germany. Since de Gaulle's withdrawal from NATO, the depth of this sector is so shallow now as to be a military liability in any event. The effect on

NATO would be minimal on the Northern, Southern, and Mediterranean components of Allied Command Europe. The Allied Command Atlantic and the Channel Command would remain unchanged. The major change would be in the substitution of a concept of national forces in central Europe in lieu of the concept of integrated international forces for that region.

This major political realignment and military disengagement would not be fatally damaging to the NATO concept of collective security and would have the political advantage of moving in the direction of the current tendencies of both France and West Germany. Greater European responsibility for the defense of its own territory would be encouraged. This reconstitution of NATO would be well worth the price for a settlement of the German and Berlin problems, for the withdrawal of Soviet troops from East Germany, and the consequent reduction in tension and risk along the central European front.

It seems to me that Federal Republic would look upon this scheme as a series of realistic and concrete steps leading toward eventual reunification of Germany:

1. Withdrawal of Soviet forces would leave the way clear for all-German conversations between East and West Germany.

2. Communications and trade between the various parts of Germany would be markedly enhanced.

3. Communist control over a large portion of East Germany would be removed, including control over approximately 8 million people now behind the Iron Curtain.

4. Access rights to Berlin which now apply only to the Western Allied powers would be formalized and guaranteed for all Western and Middle Germans.

5. If the Communists agreed to the inclusion of East Berlin

in the free city enclave, the Wall would be removed. The G.D.R. could restrict movement of East Germans into Berlin if they so desired but the city itself would not be truncated.

Although the proposed treaty would prohibit the alliance of either Middle Germany or Berlin with East or West Germany, it could be stipulated in terms of the treaty that the signatories would reconvene at some future time for the purpose of considering revision of the treaty to permit closer relationships among the four German governments. Such an article in the treaty would provide a clear possibility of eventual reunification west of the Oder-Niesse line. On the other hand, the U.S.S.R., being a signatory, would still be in a position to oppose such action if she chose to do so.

With all this, a World War II peace treaty could finally be written in such a way as to strengthen the security of both West and East, stabilize the political climate, reduce military expenditures, enhance the opportunities for trade, and create a détente with considerably more substance than the pseudo one now prevailing.

There are many possible variants to this *quid pro quo*. It is important to note that there are conditions associated with any withdrawals which would guard against West Berlin being taken over by Communism. The essential attraction of this scheme is that both United States and Soviet interests would be advanced by such a trade while the tensions which might lead to World War III would be greatly relaxed.

There is no assurance, of course, that the U.S.S.R. would find this *quid pro quo* sufficiently attractive to enter negotiations. But we shall never know until we try, and to anticipate failure with every initiative is to remain dormant, to drift with the perilous political winds.

I believe that this proposal need not weaken our resolve to defend the freedom of West Berlin. On the contrary, if the

Soviets openly refused to negotiate and rejected a *quid pro quo* guaranteeing the freedom of Berlin under adequate safeguards and reciprocal inspections there would be even more reason for the West to remain firmly in the city. At no point need the Western resolve to guarantee Berlin's freedom be lessened in any way.

The U.S.S.R. has suggested an Austrian type settlement for Germany, yet Western powers have feared the possible spread of Communism into a reunified neutral Germany. Also, we seem to think that NATO requires the strength of the twelve German army divisions. The solution proposed here might satisfy the goals of both East and West. The alignments of the F.R.G. and the G.D.R. with NATO and the Warsaw Pact respectively would not necessarily be disturbed. With foreign troops withdrawn from both East and West Germany, NATO strength would be no less adequate than it is today to meet the Soviet threat, whereas an Austrian-type solution with Middle Germany as a buffer zone would deter the spread of Communism westward.

In the final analysis, I believe that by proposing this action the West will have seized the initiative from the Soviets by making a legitimate proposal regarding an area which is presently in Communist hands. This would be a new and refreshing twist. For a change, negotiations could be conducted on the basis of what is theirs, not ours.

To construct a limited war strategy in Europe without taking into consideration the political situation would be an empty exercise. I have long advocated the disengagement of our ground forces because I frankly feel they have meager military value. We are outnumbered on the ground and in the air. We are woefully weak in the nuclear department. Geographically our dispositions are inherently inferior.

But the presence of our armed forces have been a political

asset. They are a symbol of our earnestness to live up to our treaty commitments to come to Europe's rescue. They have been responsible for bolstering the courage of our allies.

Removal of our forces from Europe would cause great consternation unless we could adjust the political climate to make such a disengagement acceptable to our friends.

I believe the Middle Germany idea would be a firm step in this direction. Win, lose, or draw, it would be an initiative which might lead to other feasible political adjustments. Nothing could be much worse than the political mish-mash and drift of Europe in which we find ourselves.*

Appendix

CERTAIN ARTICLES RELATIVE TO MIDDLE GERMANY AND BERLIN FOR INCLUSION IN A GERMAN PEACE TREATY

Article 1

Establishment of Middle Germany as an Independent State

The Allied and Associated Powers (the Soviet Union, the United States, the United Kingdom, and France), the Federal Republic of Germany, and the German Democratic Republic recognize the establishment of Middle Germany, consisting of Thuringia, Saxony, and parts of Mecklenburg and Anhalt, as a sovereign, independent, and democratic state.

---

* See the appendix to this chapter which outlines certain articles to be included in a German Peace Treaty that would establish a free Middle Germany and Berlin.

Article 2

Establishment of Berlin as a Free City

The Allied and Associated Powers, the Federal Republic of Germany, and the German Democratic Republic recognize the establishment of Greater Berlin, henceforth referred to as Berlin, as a sovereign, independent, and democatic free city.

Article 3

Frontiers of Middle Germany and Berlin

The boundaries of Middle Germany shall be, on the West, the January 1, 1964 Eastern boundary of the Federal Republic of Germany, and on the East, the line of the furthest advance by the Western Allies in 1945.

The boundaries of Berlin shall be those existing on January 1, 1938.

Article 4

Maintenance of Middle Germany's and Berlin's Independence

The Allied and Associated Powers, the Federal Republic of Germany, and the German Democratic Republic declare that they will respect the independence and territorial integrity of Middle Germany and Berlin as established under this Treaty.

Article 5

Method of Forming the New States

The Allied and Associated Powers, the Federal Republic of Gerbany, and the German Democratic Republic declare that Middle Germany and Berlin will be established as separate United Nations, Trusteeships, initially under Austrian administration, until their own freely elected and sovereign governments are formed.

Article 6

Neutrality of Middle Germany and Berlin

The Allied and Associated Powers, the Federal Republic of Germany, and the German Democratic Republic declare that political or economic union between Middle Germany and any other signatory of this Treaty, or between Berlin and any other signatory, is prohibited. Middle Germany and Berlin fully recognize their responsibilities in this matter and shall not enter into political or economic union with other countries in any form whatsoever.

Article 7

Inspection Provision

The Allied and Associated Powers, the Federal Republic of Germany, and the German Democratic Republic agree that mutual inspection teams in Berlin and Middle Germany will be established to ensure that these treaty terms are upheld. A team representing the United States, the United Kingdom, France, and the Federal Republic of Germany will inspect Berlin. A team representing the Soviet Union and the German Democratic Republic will inspect Middle Germany. These teams will report to their own governments.

Article 8

Enforcement of Neutrality

The Allied and Associated Powers, the Federal Republic of Germany, and the German Democratic Republic declare that they will not encroach upon the independence and freedom of Middle Germany or Berlin. They will respect the rights of free access to and from Berlin by autobahn, rail, and air. Access rights and tolls will be those in effect on January 1, 1964. Any foreign political or economic interference with the freely elected government of Berlin as determined by any of the Allied and Associated Powers will cause the neutrality provision of Article 6 to become null and void, and Middle Germany will be free to align itself with

other states. Similarly, any foreign political or economic interference with the freely elected government of Middle Germany
will cause the neutrality provision of Article 6 to become null and
void, and Berlin will be free to align itself with whatever states
it so desires.

Article 9

Military Withdrawal

The Soviet Union will phase-out its military forces from the
German Democratic Republic and East Berlin. The United Kingdom, the United States, and France will phase-out their military
forces from the Federal Republic of Germany and West Berlin.
These phase-outs will be made at no less than 35 per cent each
year of the force levels on the date this Treaty becomes effective.
All non-German military forces will be removed within three
years of this date.

Article 10

Recognition of the Federal Republic of Germany and the German Democratic Republic

The Soviet Union, the United Kingdom, the United States, and
France will, upon ratification of this Treaty, each establish formal
diplomatic recognition with the Federal Republic of Germany
and the German Democratic Republic as sovereign nations by ex-
ecuting separate peace treaties with each.

Article 11

Renouncing Claims to Middle Germany and Berlin

The Federal Republic of Germany and the German Democratic
Republic renounce all territorial and political claims in respect to
Middle Germany and Berlin and recognize their sovereignty and
independence.

VIII. The Proliferation of Nuclear Weapons

THE DRIVING force behind American foreign policy and national strategy is the movement for the anti-proliferation of nuclear weapons. This issue has assumed overwhelming proportions and one cannot comprehend American policy without understanding this issue.

I believe the nuclear weapon anti-proliferation issue involves the greatest fabrication of fallacies and misconceptions that has ever been foisted upon the American people and the Western world.

My voice and a very few others are isolated cries in the wilderness. The vast steamroller of a worldwide movement and its propaganda campaign is moving relentlessly forward crushing all sober analytical opposition to its singleminded conclusions.

The widespread concern that as more countries achieve a nuclear weapon capability nuclear war becomes more likely has become almost pathological. Writer after writer has associated the spread of nuclear weapons with an eventual nuclear holocaust, and now almost all governments believe a holocaust to be a natural and inevitable consequence of proliferation.

[186]

In his American University speech of June 10, 1963, which led to the test ban treaty, President John F. Kennedy called the spread of nuclear arms "one of the greatest hazards which man faces." A little more than a month later the President addressed the nation and enjoined the nuclear powers to prevent the spread of nuclear weapons by using "whatever time remains . . . to persuade other countries not to test, transfer, acquire, possess, or produce such weapons."

In a message of New Year's greeting to Soviet leaders on December 30, 1964, President Johnson placed non-proliferation at the topmost rank in urgency. "We can and should move to limit the spread of nuclear weapons," he said.

This issue has been referred to in numerous terms: as the "Nth Country Problem" as "nuclear weapon diffusion," or most often as "nuclear weapon proliferation." In an effort to prevent further nuclear weapon proliferation the United States proposed a treaty providing for "non-transfer" or "non-dissemination" of weapons, facilities, and knowledge from nuclear powers to non-nuclear powers. Those not in the nuclear club would pledge themselves not to build nuclear weapons. Other methods to halt nuclear weapon-spread would establish "nuclear free zones." Nuclear free zones are those geographical areas where by international agreement no nuclear weapons would be permitted. As we have noted, the Multi-Lateral Force (MLF) was also largely inspired by the concern over nuclear weapon proliferation.

The principal basis for the fears of nuclear weapon proliferation, or at least the reasoning most often expressed, was presented by General Maxwell D. Taylor in his book *The Uncertain Trumpet:* "The number of atomic weapons and atomic warheads in the hands of the opposing power blocs increases numerically each year, thereby enhancing the mathematical probability of disastrous accident." In other words, it is believed that the more nuclear weapons, the more likelihood of a nuclear explosion. Implicit in this reasoning is the belief that a nuclear explosion, even an accidental one, will cause war and that the war will inevitably expand in scope and intensity to a worldwide nuclear conflagration.

This issue had been given top ranking on the United States foreign policy agenda. On February 18, 1960, Secretary of State Christian Herter referred to nuclear weapon proliferation:

> The proliferating production of nuclear weapons might eventually enable almost any country, however irresponsible, to secure those weapons. We are not so concerned with regard to the free nations which might be the next to produce nuclear weapons. But we *are* concerned lest the spread becomes wholly unmanageable: The more nations that have the power to trigger off a nuclear war, the greater the chance that some nation might use this power in haste or blind folly.

Literature dealing with the subject of nuclear weapon proliferation has followed a rather common pattern. The analogy of a physical or materialistic environment in which an increase in numbers increases the chances of any isolated event occurring in a given population. For example, if a quart jar is filled with nickles and pennies, the chances of drawing a nickle at random would be based on the ratio of nickles to pennies. The more nickles to pennies, the more chance of drawing a nickle. It is thus argued analogously in an oversimplified way that many bombs in many hands increases the chance that a bomb will detonate. Then, by a kind of chain reaction or escalation, a nuclear war is bound to follow.

Among others issuing dire warnings about the nuclear problem have been Hugh Gaitskell, late Labor Party leader of the United Kingdom; Vice-President Hubert Humphrey who as a Senator was a leader in the creation of the United States Arms Control and Disarmament Agency; and Senator Robert F. Kennedy who extolled non-proliferation efforts in a 1965 Senate speech; and political scientist Hans Morgenthau of the University of Chicago who fears that "only a miracle will save mankind."

One of the principal concerns of the advocates of arms control and disarmament with respect to nuclear weapon proliferation is seldom stated directly. This is that the international environment is conceived to be more *controllable* and disarmament agreements more possible if the nuclear club is kept exclusive. "If we are chiefly interested in . . . disarmament —a multi-polar world may prove more intractable than a bipolar one . . ." wrote Karl W. Deutsch and David J. Singer in *World Politics*. This is one more major reason given for the urgency of measures to solve the problem; that is, to keep the number of bargaining nations few.* But since eight neutrals already have been included in the Eighteen Nation Disarmament Conference (ENDC) at Geneva (a United Nations compromise with the U.S.S.R. on the Troika idea) the danger of proliferating the negotiating *countries*, and hence the problems of arms control and disarmament, has already overtaken us. This is so even though the eight neutrals of the ENDC with

---

* This motive is most significantly revealed in the "not for quotation" *Collected Papers* of the Summer Study on Arms Control, 1960, sponsored by the American Academy of Arts and Science and the Twentieth Century Fund. This extensive Summer Study met for three months in Dedham, Massachusetts in 1960, and spawned a series of arms control and disarmament publications which provide the general philosophical guidance behind the current arms control and disarmament movement, including the problem of nuclear weapon proliferation. The principal publication is *Arms Control, Disarmament and National Security*, Donald G. Brennan, Editor (New York: George Braziller, 1961). Others are: *The Nation's Safety and Arms Control*, Arthur T. Hadley (New York: The Viking Press, 1961); *Arms Reduction Programs and Issues*, David H. Frisch, Editor (New York: The Twentieth Century Fund, 1961); *Strategy and Arms Control*, Thomas C. Schelling and Morton H. Halpern (New York: The Twentieth Century Fund, 1961).

the possible exception of India seem to have no intention of acquiring nuclear weapons.*

We might as well accept the fact that many non-nuclear countries will henceforth be in the middle of discussions to harness the atom and that no non-proliferation measure is likely to exclude them. The precedent set by the ENDC has assured this. In fact, it is the non-nuclear countries who create the most difficulties in negotiating the non-proliferation treaty.

The thesis of the bipolar nuclear world was clearly described by Harvard Professor Stanley Hoffman. In the Summer 1964 issue of the *Atlantic Community Quarterly*, he wrote:

. . . the United States currently favors the concentration of strategic nuclear weapons in the two great land masses of Russia and North America and in the oceans. The Americans are evacuating some of their thermonuclear bases in and near Europe (against the wishes of General Norstad) and (despite German uneasiness) they are tightening the control over the tactical nuclear weapons placed in Europe. The Nassau communique officially reversed the use of the terms "sword" and "shield" so that atomic forces now appear to be no longer conceived as preventive *deterrents* but as the ultimate defense, with doubtful deterrent value.

So the pattern of United States nuclear policy has taken shape. It clearly rests not just upon the almost-bipolar nuclear *status quo*, but upon the concept of turning back the clock to when there was no Nth country beyond the United States and the Soviet Union. The effort is, purely and simply, to bottle

---

* The eight neutral or "non-aligned" nations participating in the ENDC are: Sweden, Mexico, Brazil, the United Arab Republic, India, Nigeria, Ethiopia and Burma. The United Arab Republic and India have debated the advisability of joining the nuclear club and reports persist of a United Arab Republic nuclear program. Other members of the ENDC are the Soviet Union, Poland, Czechoslovakia, Rumania, and Bulgaria from the Communist bloc; the United States, Britain, Canada, Italy, and France from the West. France did not participate in the proceedings but maintained an observer at meetings.

the nuclear genie eventually through bilateral treaties with Russia after the nuclear clock has been turned back to the pure nuclear bipolar world of 1950.

A professional statistician would question the accuracy of the statistical hypothesis that the probability of a global thermo-nuclear war increases as the number of nuclear powers increases. For one thing, the statistical population, i.e., those countries likely to develop the bomb (ten to twenty), is too small to provide a mathematical probability of any validity or reliability. Statistics require much larger "populations" to achieve validity.

The statistical population, moreover, is not homogeneous in the international environment. The similarities between any two countries or governments are very slight, while the differences are great. Thus two conditions, a large population and a homogeneous population, both necessary for sound statistical analysis, are missing in the international environment.

The weakest feature of the statistical argument, however, is the lack of actual experience upon which to base the evidence. And experience is the root of statistical prediction. There has been some nuclear proliferation—from one nuclear power (the United States) to five (the United States, the Soviet Union, the United Kingdom, France, and Communist China)—but nuclear war has not occurred.*

Statistical analysis is based upon what *has* happened. It requires numerical data of past events. It is not a system of deductive reasoning, from principle to isolated facts, but rather of

---

* Some may argue that Canada, too, is now a nuclear power since she has accepted nuclear weapons from the United States for her air defense system. This is an example of how a country can become a nuclear power without testing or manufacturing its own nuclear weapons. A "non-transfer" treaty would have prevented this nuclear sharing for the air defense of North America.

inductive reasoning from a series of isolated facts to the inferred principle. It is a means of predicting the future by extrapolating past experience. Without any past experience, the prediction is purely conjectural—specious circular logic attempting to explain a phenomenon in terms of itself, such as "you can see through glass because it is transparent." But the error in logic is more subtle than this. The non-proliferation alarmists have made an analogy between the physical world and the social-political world, a trap which has led many social scientists and politicians into grievous errors in the past.

The technique of analogy itself is a weak reed upon which to base a conclusion unless a tremendous amount of relevant evidence is available. There is absolutely none in the nuclear proliferation analogy.

Many Cassandras have warned that within the next decade or so five to ten nations will join the nuclear club unless some international check is devised. Countries generally considered candidates include West Germany, India, Japan, Israel, the United Arab Republic, Switzerland, Sweden, Belgium, the Netherlands, East Germany, Czechoslovakia, Mexico, and Brazil. One or two crude weapons are estimated to cost less than a quarter of a million dollars initially and this cost will continue to decrease. The unhappy experiences France has had should raise some doubts about these low estimates. There is considerably more to the problem than producing a few bombs.

Fears have also been expressed that a new and much simpler method of extracting weapon-grade uranium—the gas centrifuge system—may put nuclear weapons in the hands of many less prosperous countries. The costly gaseous diffusion system which we use requires a highly developed technology which does not exist, even in France. It has, however, been reported that West Germany and the Netherlands have experimented with the new centrifuge system.

It is shortsighted to look upon the extraction of enriched U-235 as the prime requisite for becoming a nuclear power. Uranium must be fashioned into warheads and married to delivery vehicles. A highly complex weapon system is essential to assure even a small chance of delivering the nuclear warhead to its target. It must travel incredibly fast, under precision control at all times if it is to accomplish its purpose, whether the weapon system is a ballistic missile or an aircraft. Such a weapon system must also contain extremely advanced communications, thousands of skilled personnel, a great training program, and a vast national industry capable of maintaining the weapon system is operational readiness.

An historical analogy to the proliferation problem might be the production of battleships in the first decades of the twentieth century. Battleships were the status symbols of great powers then just as nuclear capabilities are today, yet few countries chose to build these great dreadnaughts. The major maritime powers during this period were Britain, the United States, and Japan. France could afford few capital ships while Germany after World War I was denied them by the Treaty of Versailles.

Proliferation of battleships in the pre-aircraft carrier age never occurred simply because of the great expense associated with building and maintaining them. Countries such as Russia, Sweden, Canada, Mexico, and Argentina had the resources to build capital ships but preferred other safeguards, rather than the expensive luxury of becoming maritime powers. It is indeed difficult to find an analogy in history which supports the fears of nuclear weapon proliferation today.

It must be borne in mind that a small nuclear force will cost up to $2 billion for the next decade at least.* The expensive

---

* By the end of 1962 France had invested $2.5 billion in her *force de frappe*.

feature is not the bomb, which will eventually decrease in cost, but the vehicles (bombers and missiles) to carry the warheads. This cost will probably increase as it has each year since 1945.* Entrance fees to the nuclear club will be prohibitively high for most countries for a long time to come.

There is some uneasiness that Red China, which first exploded a nuclear device in October, 1964, and a hydrogen weapon in June, 1967, may employ nuclear weapons in her obsolete Beagle bombers. These old bombers could not survive in a modern air defense environment, but many countries in the Far East do not have a sophisticated air defense. With any reasonable nuclear air defense preparation not a single Beagle could be expected to penetrate to its target. Yet nuclear-armed Beagles (or MIG-21s) could easily penetrate an undefended area such as might be found in India or Burma. Nuclear blackmail under such circumstances could be an expected strategy.

Should Communist China succeed in developing an operational missile delivery system, even the present nuclear powers would be outflanked since no fully effective anti-ballistic missile system has yet been developed. The chances are unlikely, however, that a country unable to manufacture a warplane or even a satisfactory modern automobile will be successful in fully developing a highly complicated ballistic missile system. Of course, a few missiles would be enough to blackmail Japan, Nationalist China, the Philippines, or Thailand. Still, this does not make the proliferation point. Chinese nuclear arms will be dangerous because of her belligerence, not because the nuclear arms exist.

Pursuing the argument by analogy, let us look at warplanes for a moment. The United States has proliferated military air-

---

* The cost of building a hundred B-58s, Atlas missiles, or submarine-launched Polaris missiles was three to five times the cost of building a hundred B-47s. This comparison was based on total development of the weapons systems and operating them over a five-year period.

craft throughout the world with its Military Assistance Programs (MAP) for over a decade. This warplane proliferation, by itself at least, has not seemed to cause any appreciable increase in war. Why would a proliferation of nuclear weapons do so?

Every North Atlantic Treaty Organization country except Iceland has been aided by the MAP program in one way or another. In addition, Japan, South Korea, Nationalist China, the Philippines, Thailand, and many other friendly governments now fly American military aircraft. Although not all are provided by the United States, at least fifty-six countries are equipped with some model of jet fighter aircraft. In fact, the purpose of the United States in equipping our friends and allies with air forces has been directed toward peace. This policy of proliferating conventional arms among our allies seems strangely inconsistent with our policy of anti-proliferation in the nuclear field among those same friends and allies.

At the meeting of the General Assembly of the United Nations in 1958, the Irish delegation proposed that a study be made specifically on the matter of nuclear dissemination, and suggested that a resolution on non-transfer of nuclear weapons from the "have" to the "have not" nations, together with a pledge from the "have nots" to refrain from developing nuclear weapon capabilities. This was the beginning of active efforts to halt the spread of nuclear weapons. The United States abstained because of the adverse influence this might have on the Atlantic Alliance, and the resolution was withdrawn.

However, the United States voted for a similar Irish resolution the following year. This resolution enjoined the Ten-Nation Disarmament Committee then in session at Geneva to consider the non-dissemination measure.

On December 20, 1960, a third Irish resolution called upon:

Powers producing [nuclear] weapons . . . to refrain from relinquishing control of such weapons to any nation not possessing
them and from transmitting to it the information necessary for
their manufacture. . . . Powers not possessing such weapons . . .
to refrain from manufacturing these weapons and from otherwise
attempting to acquire them.

This wording is essentially the same as that in the current
United States proposal for a non-proliferation treaty.

The United States abstained from the third Irish resolution
again because of its possible effect on NATO, whose sup-
porters still held the upper hand in the State Department. But
by 1961 the United States voted for the measure reworded so
as not to curtail NATO nuclear programs. Having been
adopted unanimously by the U.N., this resolution tends to
constitute a moral commitment by the United States which
militates against individual and collective self-defense. It is
unenforceable as an isolated declaratory measure and hence
undermines the principle of verification and inspection as an
arms control measure.

In 1961 a Swedish resolution, more restrictive than the Irish
resolution, was introduced in the General Assembly, pledging
non-nuclear countries not to accept nuclear weapons on their
territory. The measure, which included the concept of the
"nuclear free zone," was co-sponsored by Austria, Ceylon,
Ethiopia, Libya, and the Sudan. The United States voted
against this, as did all NATO countries except Canada, Iceland,
Norway, and Denmark.

Obviously such a resolution would prejudice the United
States defense arrangements with its NATO allies, whose strategy calls for tactical nuclear weapons on European soil. NATO
countries have nuclear capable weapons such as F-104 fighter-
bombers and Pershing missiles. And, of course, nuclear war-

heads for the weapons of non-nuclear allies are held by United States custodial units for use as directed by the President.

It is interesting to note that Canada's policy has changed since her vote for the Swedish resolution. The Canadian government has now accepted air-to-air and surface-to-air nuclear missiles for its air defense forces, although this is not generally construed as nuclear proliferation.

Before we fielded the non-proliferation treaty, the possibility of a non-transfer joint declaration of the United States and the Soviet Union was discussed in the press, but the Soviet Union showed no particular interest when this measure was associated with inspection. Although Andrei A. Gromyko mentioned the desirability of a "non-proliferation agreement" in his opening speech at the U.N. General Assembly on December 7, 1961, he was careful to link this with abandonment of the proposed NATO multi-lateral force which the Soviet Union opposed.

The Nth country problem seems primarily a Western fear. Not much anxiety has been expressed in Russia over Red China's acquisition of nuclear weapons. In fact, it was Russia who got China started. The Soviet fear of the MLF was related more to her paranoic concern over a *revanchist* Germany than to nuclear proliferation. Nor does the Soviet Union seem to be under any pressure to provide nuclear weapons to its Warsaw Pact allies.

Several kinds of "solutions" to proliferation have been sought through "nuclear free zone" declarations similar to the Swedish resolution. This could be achieved, it is claimed, if certain non-nuclear powers would neither acquire weapons nor permit them on their soil, thus creating nuclear sterile geographical zones. Poland's plan, put forth by Foreign Minister Adam Rapacki in October, 1957, to denuclearize Poland, the two Germanys, and Czechoslovakia was one of the first serious proposals of this sort. This "Rapacki Plan" has been debated at length, and in 1964, a later version referred to as the Gomulka plan called for a nuclear weapon freeze in the same area. The nuclear free zone in Europe may sometimes be referred to as "disengagement," although "disengagement" usually includes several additional arms control and disarmament measures. Other nuclear free zone proposals have included Africa, the Mediterranean, the Far East, and Latin America.

The nuclear free zone idea has not caught on because of strategic inequities and the disparity of objectives for different powers. For example, nuclear free zones would hamper the mobility of nuclear armed forces, which is more important to the United States than to the Soviet Union with its interior lines of communication. A nuclear free Mediterranean, proposed by the Soviet Union, would reduce the effectiveness of the Sixth Fleet and United States Polaris submarine deployments there, but would in no way interfere with Soviet capabilities.

The United Arab Republic objects to Africa as a nuclear free zone because Israel would not be included. The United States would also be wary of any Latin American agreement which might jeopardize our transit rights for nuclear weapons through the Panama Canal, or the deployment of nuclear weapons at bases such as Guantanamo in Cuba or Ramey Air Force Base in Puerto Rico.

Some talk has been heard, principally from Australian sources, of a Pacific Ocean area or an Asian mainland nuclear free zone. The United States could not accept the former and fulfill its bilateral defense commitments to Japan, South Korea, the Republic of China (Taiwan), etc.; while the Chinese Communists, struggling to become a nuclear power, could not accept the latter. Asian/Pacific nuclear free zone discussions have subsided now that Red China has the bomb. The possibility of keeping the Asian mainland free of nuclear weapons has been closed out and defense against this potential threat will require nuclear weapon deployments in the Pacific Ocean area.

Several Latin American countries have agreed to a nuclear free zone in their areas. Among them, and the first to sign, are Brazil, Mexico, Bolivia, Ecuador, and Chile. The United States supported these pacts in principle but noted that such zones have little meaning without a verification provision. Since then, Brazil, Chile, Peru, Argentina, and Uruguay have been negotiating with nuclear powers, principally France, for power reactors. Fuel from these, of course, can be used for weapons.

East Germany's Communist chief, Walter Ulbright, with Soviet leader Leonid Brezhnev standing at his elbow, called for an atom-free unified Germany in 1967. Soviet policy obviously has wavered very little in this regard, and the German solution, or something like it, presented in Chapter VII might strike some fertile ground.

The Atomic Energy Act of 1954 (P.L. 703) permits the United States to cooperate with other nations in developing and using nuclear energy for peaceful purposes. This "atoms for peace" program has resulted in atomic reactors being built all over the world, for scientific research or for electrical power. Other nuclear-club members have proliferated the "peaceful atom" until over forty small countries now operate reactors.

Many of these reactors are capable of producing high-grade nuclear fuel (plutonium), which could be used for making bombs. The United States plant at Rose, Massachusetts, for example, could produce 80 kilograms of plutonium annually, or enough to make ten small bombs of the Nagasaki type.

Reactors have been built by five countries: the United States,

Britain, Russia, France, and Canada. The United States has insisted that the reactors it installs abroad be inspected periodically to keep track of the nuclear fuel. It has also placed these reactors under the scrutiny of the International Atomic Energy Agency (IAEA) and would like the other nuclear powers who export reactors to do the same.

The strict restraints required by the United States are not practiced by the other nuclear powers. Canada, for example, has no provision for control of a reactor it has built in India. Britain's safeguards are superficial but are being improved, while France has no safeguards whatever. Russian-built reactors are equally unsupervised.

President Johnson appointed a task force in 1965 headed by former Deputy Secretary of Defense Roswell L. Gilpatric to see what could be done to bring all nuclear reactors under appropriate safeguards. It is believed that their recommendation for an agreed program of inspection of all reactors by IAEA will be incorporated in the proposed non-proliferation treaty sponsored by the United States, although at this writing the verification provisions (Article 3) are left blank for future negotiations.

Let me now address some of the common arguments against proliferation, such as the threat to world stability, the injection of incalculable factors into the equation of international politics, the possible irresponsibility of small nations, the hazards of fallout caused by increased testing, and the inability to detect nuclear stockpiles of Nth countries after they have "proliferated."

The assumption that the world would become less politically stable as more countries join the nuclear club is frequently heard, but is subject to question on the basis of recent history. Even with the war in Vietnam the world is somewhat more stable today with five nuclear powers than it was in 1949 during the Berlin Blockade and the Communist conquest of China. In 1949 there was only one nuclear power, the United States.

History also seems to refute the proposition that a bipolar world is more stable than a multi-polar world. Historical bipolar confrontations have usually led to war, as with Greece versus Persia, Athens versus Sparta, Rome versus Carthage, Christendom versus Islam, the Triple Entente versus the Triple Alliance, and so on. On the other hand, the multi-polar system has tended to stabilize world politics with a shifting balance of power. The *Pax Britannica*, for example, was based upon a judicious manipulation of alliances to provide a dynamic balance among hostile international elements. Both in the short and long run the instability of competitive bipolar systems seems substantially greater.

One nuclear scientist who has had second thoughts about the dangers of nuclear proliferation is Dr. Edward Teller, the inventor of the H-bomb. "The interests of the free democracies," he wrote, "are quite similar. . . . The sharing of nuclear explosives may well be the catalyst which will make the establishment of common institutions and common loyalties both necessary and possible."

One could also question the basic premise that stability itself is always desirable. When the United States confronted the Soviet Union over missiles in Cuba in the autumn of 1962, it destabilized the international environment. Had the United States not presented a credible threat, the Soviet Union would not have backed down. Similarly, it was necessary to destabilize the environment in 1961 when Khrushchev threatened to negotiate a peace treaty with East Germany. President Kennedy's mobilization program was perhaps destabilizing, but it preserved the peace. It is inconceivable how these crises could have been overcome with a purely defensive strategy. What might have happened to Israel in June, 1967, had she remained on the defensive?

Sometimes it is absolutely necessary to risk offensive war in order to achieve peace. Much has been said of the evils of "brinkmanship," but it probably will always be a practical and necessary feature of life on earth.

Let us now examine how proliferation of nuclear weapons might inject "incalculable factors" into the international environment. This argument makes the implicit assumption that the international environment is "calculable." Few scholars of international affairs or few experienced diplomats would claim that the world scene is very predictable, although efforts at prophecy abound. Most of these experts would agree that the international environment is inherently *in*calculable and each day brings surprises which were never predicted or foreseen. There is always "some damn fool thing in the Balkans," as Bismark said, to upset our predictions. The Arab-Israeli war of June, 1967, caught the whole world by surprise, as did the Cuban missile crisis in 1962.

It is true that proliferation of nuclear weapons might inject incalculable factors into the international environment, but so too might the *non*-proliferation of such weapons. A case can be made that the drastic disarming of Germany following World War I contributed to resurgent Nazi Germany; so, too, that the 5-5-3 naval ratio agreed to at the London and Washington disarmament conferences of the 1920s among the United States, Britain, and Japan led to Japan's embarking on her aggressive adventures in the 1930s. An excellent case is made for this thesis by David J. Lu in *From the Marco Polo Bridge to Pearl Harbor*.

It can only be said with certainty that incalculable factors will always be at work in international relations and that political and ideological differences will continue to dominate the action on the international scene.

What, then, about the irresponsible action of small nations who might gain control of nuclear weapons? The first point to be made is that responsibility in no way correlates with the size of a country. We need only reflect on Hitler, Stalin, Mussolini, Mao Tse-tung, and other irresponsible leaders of large and populous nations to recognize the truth of this. It is just as likely that small countries capable of gaining a nuclear delivery force will be as prudent as large ones. The presence of nuclear weapons may even have a sobering influence on diplomacy. Certainly small countries are as concerned about survival as are large ones.

Some writers have termed a war which might be started by an ambitious or desperate third nation a "catalytic" war. As for small third countries sparking catastrophic war with mischievous acts, it seems just as likely—perhaps more likely—that they would take such risks when *not* possessing nuclear weapons. Without nuclear weapons a country risks less by a military adventure because it would be less subject to nuclear retaliation. A small non-nuclear war could always escalate into nuclear war if the nuclear powers became involved. In other words, "catalytic" action can occur whether or not a small country possesses nuclear weapons. The 1967 crisis in the Gulf of Aqaba with the two big nuclear powers on opposite sides is a case in point. Non-nuclear Egypt and Israel were the catalysts. Fortunately, the nuclear powers were slow to act, and Israel won the war in a matter of days with an air victory.

The nuclear umbrella demanded by most non-nuclear countries before signing a non-proliferation treaty may be the very cause for a nuclear war. To me this nuclear guarantee to a number of small countries would be the most dangerous and shortsighted piece of American diplomacy yet devised. It would almost assure a general nuclear war should any limited nuclear exchange occur.

Every large war, of course, is sparked by some relatively minor event, as the murder at Sarajevo in 1914 or the Nazi march into Poland in 1939. Yet in hindsight a whole string of events could be identified with war cause. Before World War I, for example, one might point to the Austria-Hungarian ultimatum to Serbia, to Russia's defense arrangements with Serbia and Rumania, to Russian mobilization, or to the Schlieffen plan. Little Serbia's refusal of Austria's ultimatum has never been described as "irresponsible" simply because the terms of the ultimatum were unreasonable. Large Austria-Hungary was the less responsible country for submitting the ultimatum in the first place.

If one wished to choose a *casus belli* of World War II, one might start with Hitler's rise to power and his rearming Germany in 1933, or with his march into the Rhineland in 1936, or with the *Anschluss* of 1938, or with the Munich meeting between Hitler and Prime Minister Chamberlain that same year. The small countries of Austria, Czechoslovakia, or Poland most certainly cannot be accused of "catalytic" behavior during these tense times. Should Poland have succumbed for the sake of world peace?

The small country argument is sometimes related to the "statistical" theory. As more countries get the bomb, goes the reasoning, *something* is likely to happen that will cause a bomb to go off. Accident, miscalculation, or madness are fashionable hypotheses which have been repeated so often that some individuals—C. P. Snow, for one—look upon nuclear war as a "certainty."

This fear should be laid to rest. The number of nuclear bombs and warheads have already proliferated to the thousands and the first accidental nuclear explosion has yet to occur.

Spokesmen for the United States Department of Defense have mentioned "tens of thousands" of warheads in United States forces. The Soviet Union has thousands more. A bomb is handled by people and, being inert, is not concerned whether the people are nationals of one, two, or a hundred countries. Accident, miscalculation, or madness can occur in two countries or a hundred countries with equal frequency or infrequency. We have no idea whether Soviet controls over their bombs and warheads are, like ours, designed to safeguard against accident, miscalculation, or madness. Chances are against this since their literature seldom mentions the problem. Yet no serious Soviet nuclear accidents have come to the world's attention.

Even if we accept the "statistical" argument, which rests on pure speculation, it makes little sense to say that bombs in the hands of more countries are more likely to result in an unplanned explosion.

It is another fallacy to postulate that physical accidents present a danger which might cause a nuclear explosion. The probability of an accidental nuclear detonation is as remote as the collapse of the Golden Gate Bridge or the Empire State Building—something within the realm of possibility but highly improbable.

For example, on December 8, 1964, a B-58 Hustler bomber with a "nuclear device" in its bomb bay caught fire at Bunker Hill Air Force Base, Indiana. Although the airplane was consumed, the "nuclear device" did not explode and no radioactive contamination occurred. Of the four bombs dropped from a B-52 off Palomares, Spain, as a result of a refueling collision in 1966, none exploded, although there was some relatively harmless contamination caused by two which broke up.

A nuclear bomb is a highly complicated device and many sequential steps must be taken to light it off. Accidents simply do not occur in this manner. At worst, the chemical high explosive components of a bomb might detonate from fire and scatter some nuclear material which could cause a small area to become mildly and harmlessly radioactive, as in Spain. Nothing of this sort is liable to lead to a nuclear war.

The old concern over increased radioactive fallout resulting from increased testing is groundless as long as the present test ban is in effect. It is unlikely that the test programs of France and Red China, neither of which signed the test ban treaty, will ever reach major proportions. Even if atmospheric testing should be resumed by the United States and the Soviet Union, the danger of fallout from these sources has been proved to be so minor as to be insignificant. As Earl H. Voss has written in *Nuclear Ambush*, "the hazards of nuclear test fallout are trifling . . . compared to the background radiation hazards the world accepts without question."

To illustrate the absurdity of the public fear of fallout caused from nuclear testing, Voss has noted experts' findings that those living in frame houses as opposed to brick houses receive twenty times the radiation dosage one gets from fallout; that luminous dial wrist watches give off as much as ten times the radiation dose that fallout produces; that the background radiation in Denver is twice that of East Coast cities, yet nuclear test fallout would only increase background radiation by 3 to 5 per cent. These figures are based upon the fallout detected up to 1962, the year of greatest nuclear testing and the year when the Soviet Union conducted the most extensive test program in nuclear history, which included a 58-megaton bomb.

No one would presume that radiation from whatever source is harmless, but the degree of harm caused by radiation resulting from nuclear testing has been grossly exaggerated. Many arms control and disarmament advocates thus are open to the charge that they have helped to inflate the fear of fallout in their drive to achieve a nuclear test ban as a "first step" to more comprehensive disarmament measures.

It is unlikely that Nth country nuclear testing will produce a fallout hazard simply because the level of testing would at worst be quite low. Only with very extensive and indiscriminate testing, which would have to include the great powers, could the fallout hazard become real.

With respect to the inspection difficulties, it is true, as often mentioned, that stockpiles of nuclear weapons would be difficult to find. The proposed United States non-proliferation treaty would confine weapons to present nuclear club members, at least. But here again the horse has already been stolen from the barn, and locking the door at this late date will solve little. The stockpiles of nuclear weapons which concern us most are in the Soviet Union, and no non-proliferation agreement has any promise of opening Russia for inspection. Yet the have-not nations are to be inspected by IAEA to see that they do not cheat. Germany has protested, noting the possibility of Soviet industrial espionage. Other non-nuclear nations have objected. A strong undercurrent of hostility is found in Western Europe to the idea of a fundamental United States-Anglo-Soviet agreement. This attitude has even spread to Asia. Japan, for example, would like to see the "haves" cut back on nuclear weapons and be included in the inspection. Although the United States and the United Kingdom have permitted some IAEA token inspections of nuclear plants, Russia remains tightly closed. India is debating the need to become a "have" and is dragging its feet.

It is sometimes claimed that verification and inspection are not feasible in connection with a non-proliferation agreement simply because of the extreme difficulty of locating finished nuclear weapons which might have been hidden. Police of the proposed treaty by the inadequate and underfinanced IAEA illustrates how the United States has relaxed its former insistence on effective inspection as concomitant of a sound arms control agreement of this kind. We are quick to forget President Kennedy's caution in 1961 that the "indispensable condition of disarmament [is] true inspection" and that "disarmament without checks is but a shadow."

It is easier to inspect during the manufacturing period of nuclear development than it might be later. Gaseous diffusion plants for the manufacture of U-235 or breeders for producing plutonium are large and easily identified. These plants emit waste into the atmosphere which is detectable and measurable, permitting deductions concerning the amount and kind of fissionable material produced. Although inspection has its limitations and difficulties, it should not be abandoned simply for the sake of an agreement which, without open inspection, may be hollow and deceitful.

It must always be kept in mind that if the United States position on inspection weakens, the Soviet Union may enter into a treaty with the basic purpose of improving its relative military posture. This is more in keeping with past Soviet international policies than the "mutual self-interest" on non-proliferation which is frequently voiced as an argument for an uninspected agreement.

"Have-not" nations are demanding that the nuclear powers agree to provide them with a nuclear umbrella in case of a local nuclear attack. Since the major nuclear powers are in opposing camps, this means that a small nuclear war would automatically escalate to general war. It would be the surest blueprint to disaster. The Egyptian-Israeli crisis over the Gulf of Aqaba is a case in point.

American nuclear weapons have deterred the Soviet Union from overrunning Europe. The belief that the United States is superior in nuclear weapons has continued to deter the Soviet Union even after she achieved a nuclear capability. This was dramatically demonstrated during both the Berlin and the Cuban crises. There seems to be no reason why continued nuclear superiority will not still be effective in deterring major aggressive moves of the Soviet Union as well as of Communist China. Nuclear weapons in the hands of our friends might contribute even more to this deterrence.

As noted earlier, there is a great fear that the Communist Chinese might employ their new nuclear capability aggressively and irresponsibly. This conclusion has been reached after frequent bellicose remarks of Chinese Communists leaders, whose concern for the lives of their millions of subjects is apparently minor.

Certain Western enthusiasts for disarmament have shown such concern over the Communist Chinese nuclear program that they have even suggested bombing Chinese nuclear plants. Such a move would be nothing short of preventive war. This shows to what lengths the questionable fear of nuclear proliferation has taken us. Have we artificially generated a phobia which can in itself be the real cause of future nuclear war?

One might think that a poverty-stricken country such as mainland China, barely able to feed itself, with a mushrooming population and meager industrial capacity, can hardly be expected to become a significant nuclear power in any short order, although that is what we said about Russia in 1945. Through an intense concentration of energy and wealth over a period of several years (over 1 per cent of the gross national product and some early help from Russia) the Peoples' Republic of China has constructed and exploded seven nuclear devices: one each in 1964 and 1965, three in 1966, an H-bomb in 1967, and perhaps another on Christmas day, 1967.

It may be comforting to recall that even though China was

first to invent gunpowder, she utilized this new force in harmless firecrackers to frighten her enemies. It would be imprudent, however, to underrate China's nuclear capability. Her nuclear test in October, 1966, demonstrated the use of a domestically manufactured medium range missile. The warhead was twenty kilotons and accuracy was reported to be good. Although a few of these can be used to threaten her non-nuclear neighbors, the United States need not fear a direct attack just now. However, the Chinese nuclear threat should not be evaluated simply in terms of what it might do to the United States mainland. Nuclear blackmail in Asia seems inevitable.

Within five to ten years, assuming no national catastrophe (and catastrophes are more the rule than the exception in China, as witness the Red Guard madness), China may develop a number of intercontinental ballistic missiles. By then I hope the United States will have the protection of an ABM system.

The way to curb China from nuclear blackmail is to assist our allies in the Far East to develop a countering nuclear capability. This is far better than that the United States feel compelled to come to the nuclear rescue of every threatened free country. But such a suggestion would proliferate the nuclear powers and run counter to our basic policy.

Non-proliferation advocates are prone to refer to the dangers of escalation. They assert that if even one nuclear weapon anywhere in the world should explode the chances would be high for this incident to escalate into wild exchanges of multimegaton strategic weapons. Such warnings have been repeated so often without challenge that many regard escalation as a sort of automatic chain reaction. This is not so at all.

Escalation of this sort works both ways; it works up and it works down. Conflicts intensify and conflicts cool down. War grows more widespread and war subsides and terminates.

Wise, timely, and judicious statesmanship coupled with capable and alert military forces can *de*-escalate a conflict quite readily. Escalation usually occurs when one side believes it can achieve success by intensifying the conflict. If the other side is unable or unwilling to respond in kind it will *de*-escalate, as the Red Chinese did during the 1958 Taiwan Straits crisis, and as the Soviet Union did during the Cuban crisis of 1962.

As the countries of Western Europe became more prosperous and hence more independent after World War II, it seemed only reasonable that they would some day seek their own nuclear deterrent forces. Great Britain, of course, has been a partner with the United States in nuclear developments from the outset, and the Atomic Energy Act is so worded as to permit the United States and Great Britain to exchange nuclear information and equipment. On the other hand, the United States has done everything possible to deter France from acquiring a nuclear capability, all in the interest of non-proliferation of nuclear weapons. As we have seen, this has understandably annoyed France, which has gone ahead alone at great expense to develop the nuclear *force de frappe*. It also seemed that Western Germany, which had denied itself nuclear weapons under the Paris Protocols of 1955, might eventually develop nuclear ambitions, although there had been no outward indication of this sentiment. Other NATO countries were capable of building nuclear forces. How was this possible proliferation to be prevented?

The idea of the MLF emerged in American arms control circles. Harvard Professor Robert R. Bowie is frequently credited with the initial idea. It remained for the Summer Study on Arms Control of 1960 to bring this proposal into the light. Arthur Barber, formerly with the Air Force Cambridge Research Laboratories, but more recently the Deputy Assistant

Secretary of Defense for Arms Control, wrote a significant paper for the Summer Study dealing with European proliferation. This paper described, as it was titled, "A NATO Military Program for the Future." Barber accurately predicted that since Europeans would find the American nuclear commitment less credible with the growth of Soviet ICBMs, they would seek their own European deterrent. Therefore, he reasoned, NATO should have "an invulnerable deterrent of ballistic missile submarines or aircraft on airborne alert," and that "*the United States must provide the atomic deterrent for NATO*" ... [and] ... *persuade its allies to abandon nuclear weapons.*" He admitted that the greatest obstacle was President Charles de Gaulle and his concept of an independent French deterrent. But Mr. Barber contended that de Gaulle might be persuaded "to reappraise his dreams." Mr. Barber thought that if Britain and Germany relinquished nuclear weapons the pride of France might no longer be at stake.

Once having removed nuclear weapons from the soil of Europe, Mr. Barber then proposed "agreement on an atom-free zone," suggesting that a version of the Rapacki plan might serve this measure. There, then, was the outline for the grand design that evolved (and devolved) step-by-step into the mixed-manned MLF of 1963, the Atlantic nuclear force (ANF) proposed by Britain in 1964, and the consolidated committee of NATO countries for determining nuclear policy proposed by Secretary of Defense McNamara in 1965.

One of the first objections to Mr. Barber's plan was that the United States should pay for it, particularly when the United States was suffering from a balance of payments deficit. This drawback could be overcome by asking all participants to pick up their share of the bill, but with this they would certainly ask for and deserve more direct participation. The whole purpose of European de-nuclearization would be vitiated if the

Allies provided their own individual nuclear forces to the NATO force. Certainly this would never do because even if the NATO nuclear force were the only such force in Western Europe, the separate countries could withdraw their contingents and negate the concept of non-proliferation. From this apparent dilemma the concept of mixed-manning was born. Each vessel of the MLF would be crewed by personnel from each country. This would make national withdrawal virtually impossible. Here would be a truly integrated European force, even more integrated than the formerly proposed European Defense Community (EDC) which had been pushed so hard by the United States until it was finally killed by the French National Assembly at the end of 1954. No doubt Robert Bowie, an enthusiastic advocate of EDC and, at that time, the Assistant Secretary of State for Policy Planning, had visions of the new MLF becoming a nucleus for a politically integrated Europe, as was conceived when the EDC was a hot issue in the early 1950s.

The State Department claimed that the MLF was the only system ever designed with a "built-in arms control opportunity." This seems to be the fundamental rationale which drove United States foreign policy in support of the MLF and subsequent anti-proliferation schemes.

Both East and West fear the possibility of a resurgent Germany gaining nuclear weapons. The demonstrated industrial ability and scientific attainments of the Federal Republic leave no doubt of Germany's capability to construct and operate an effective nuclear force. The danger of a *revanchist* Germany, considering the history of this century, cannot be ignored by either side. But the U.S.S.R., which suffered most at the hands of Germany in World War II, has an almost paranoic anxiety about Germany's getting control of nuclear weapons. Knowing this, the West would be shortsighted indeed not to extract some concessions from the Soviets in return for any agreement to bar nuclear weapons from Germany. There should be sufficient leverage in this situation to solve the Berlin problem, as I have proposed.

Of course the Germans, who provide NATO with more infantry divisions than any other member of the alliance, do not appreciate the attempts of her allies to negotiate away the nuclear weapons which Germany might need for her own survival. Nor does Germany enjoy the second-class status which defeat in World War II imposed on her. Over twenty years of war-guilt is hard to carry with grace. Therefore, measures to denuclearize German territory, or any similar plan which might set her apart from the Alliance, would probably be bitterly opposed.

Even though German interest in joining the nuclear club is not immediate, there is reasonable concern that her sentiments may change. Regardless of United States efforts to hold her in check, she may some day opt for first-class nuclear status. With this possibility in mind, the United States should make certain that Germany remains bound to the Atlantic Alliance— and that the Alliance itself remains strong. Any divisive antiproliferation measure hardly seems the appropriate approach at this time.

When on August 17, 1965, the United States proposed a nonproliferation treaty to the Eighteen Nation Disarmament Committee at Geneva, the U.S.S.R. dismissed it as a "joke." It was also criticized by several of our NATO allies because it provided that nuclear states would not transfer nuclear weapons to non-nuclear states even indirectly through a military alliance. Russia, of course, wanted some explicit provision that would prevent West Germany from acquiring even indirect access to nuclear weapons through NATO. In September, 1965, the Soviet Union's Foreign Minister Andrei Gromyko, presented a non-proliferation treaty proposal to the U.N. General Assembly. This version would prohibit transfer of nuclear weapons to "units of armed forces of states which do not possess nuclear arms even if these forces are under command of a military alliance." This would obviously do away with the two-key system of nuclear sharing in NATO.

In October, 1966, President Johnson indicated that he would abandon the concept of alliance sharing in return for progress on a non-proliferation treaty. The United States was weakening its position at the expense of NATO. This position came out of a meeting between the Soviet Union, the United Kingdom, and the United States, indicating a high degree of agreement.

Several of the have-not nations are now having second thoughts about signing. Most of them regard the treaty as a means for undermining the solidarity of NATO while the United States-Soviet Union "bridge building" seems to weaken the credibility of the American nuclear deterrent.

France and China will have nothing to do with a non-proliferation treaty, of course, which leaves big holes through which nuclear weapons can spread. The anti-proliferation dreamers conceive of a contented France with a minimum nuclear deterrent, of a Red China brought into the international fold of "responsible" nations, and of the security problems of countries like India and Israel solved so that they will not need nuclear arms. But if that nirvana should ever come, there would be other equally serious problems on the international horizon. Certainly the big problem now and probably in the future which we *must* contend with is the great proliferation of nuclear weapons in Russia itself.

President Charles de Gaulle will hardly discard his nuclear force, which cost 21.8 per cent of the French budget in 1966, simply because the United States will not help him develop it.

By not helping with nuclear know-how, the United States only slows his progress and makes it more expensive; it does not halt it. It is understandable why President de Gaulle opposes our non-proliferation treaty.

Is it not a fallacy to assume that the United States slows proliferation by refusing nuclear help to France? What the United States does by denying help at this late stage (after aiding Britain in her nuclear program) is to goad France into seeking an all-European deterrent. The Johnson Administration in Washington is thus abetting the breakup of NATO.

France is now a nuclear power and the United States might as well accept this fact of life.

From the foregoing discussion I can only draw the conclusion that the greatest danger from nuclear weapon proliferation lies with the Soviet Union itself. Not only are there thousands of high yield nuclear weapons in Soviet arsenals, but these weapons are controlled by a government which has no orderly system of succession and which has been marked by irresponsibility and violence in the recent past. We have no conception of what nuclear controls or command restraints the Kremlin may have placed on the handling and employment of its awesome weapons. Why has this *greatest* danger not been treated in more detail by the President Johnson's arms controllers?

The assumption seems to be that the Soviet Union will simply not play this kind of game. Soviet policy-makers look upon nuclear weapons in the traditional way insofar as their *own* are concerned, but are delighted to see the United States and the free world allies put nuclear restraints upon themselves.

As long as this Soviet philosophy prevails—and interminable negotiations have revealed no crack in the Soviet armor against inspection—there is very little that can be done about proliferation of nuclear weapons inside Russia. Consequently, advocates of arms control turn their attention from this paramount concern to more soluble features of the problem, even though they are of less moment. As in the mathematical theory of least squares, these disarmament specialists may be refining only minor factors of an equation which contains dominating inaccurate and uncorrectable factors.

The hope is always held out, however, that the Soviet Union will someday see the light of the arms control philosophy. The periodic Pugwash conferences between Western and Eastern scientists are pointed toward this end as, to a great extent, are the various international conferences at Geneva, and of course at the United Nations. Let us hope that these exchanges do not lead us to drop our inspection guard and accept the Soviet view. There may come a day when the proliferation of nuclear weapons in the two opposing blocs can be halted and shrunk, but the United States cannot safely participate in such a pact until the Soviets accept the principle of mutual inspection to assure the world that anti-proliferation measures are, in fact, being carried out.

Red China will reap immediate psychological advantages in Asia by having demonstrated her nuclear ability. In a very few years, however, China will be able to invoke nuclear blackmail on her neighbors, and possibly on the United States itself. Some years will pass before Communist China can develop an ICBM system which might threaten United States survival, but by that time I sincerely hope we have developed nuclear protection. Time is running out. There has been too much delay in starting our ABM deployment.

As for deterring nuclear blackmail in Asia, I see no recourse other than helping free Asian nations gain their own nuclear deterrents. Otherwise we set ourselves up as the world's nuclear policeman and invite general nuclear warfare at every turn. The urge for free Asian countries to develop independent nuclear forces will be dampened as long as the United States promises them nuclear protection, as we seem to be doing now with Polaris submarines in the Pacific and B-52s on Guam. This is a very dangerous policy to which I do not subscribe. It means that if Red China, for example, should launch a nuclear missile at India, we would be obliged to retaliate against Red China, and the U.S.S.R. might then be obliged to launch missiles at us. The classic escalation pattern is built into the "nuclear guarantee."

The Soviet Union has not found it advisable to station nuclear forces in the Warsaw Pact countries of Europe. The explanation usually given is that these countries might not be trustworthy, and if at some future time they gained control of the weapons, they might point them in the wrong direction—at the Soviet Union. There seems no doubt, however, that Soviet control of Eastern European countries is still adequate to deter the development of independent nuclear forces and the chances of proliferation there in this manner appear to be unlikely.

Cuba provides one exception. Probably the only reason that Russia made this exception was that the nuclear-tipped IRBMs installed in Cuba did not have the range to strike Russia. The Soviet Union was safe no matter what happened to the Castro Government. The Kremlin had only the United States to contend with, and by installing the missiles in Cuba the Soviet leaders created enough bargaining points to profit even by backing down. As we have seen, United States IRBMs in England, Italy, and Turkey were subsequently removed, hardly before becoming operational.

It can be expected that more countries will gain possession of nuclear weapons either by manufacture, purchase, or gift. But the experience of France, where such vast sums have been required to create a small nuclear force, is enough to discourage most countries from nuclear pretensions. Even Great Britain has found her nuclear deterrent force of V-bombers and Polaris submarines so expensive that both Conservative and Labor governments have debated giving it up and relying exclusively on the United States for nuclear deterrence.

Former United States Under Secretary of State, George W. Ball, appealed to Britain in May of 1967 to renounce all nuclear arms in an effort to curb proliferation. This has been a recurrent theme of Mr. Johnson's arms controllers, but there is no evidence that a renunciation by Britain would do anything to hasten an anti-proliferation treaty. It certainly would reduce the Western deterrent. Yet the dangers of proliferation loom so forebodingly in the minds of policy-makers in the current Administration that they are willing to override the wishes and interests of our allies in order to get the treaty.

As for those countries which cannot be dissuaded from building their own independent nuclear forces, such as France, it would seem to be the prudent course to keep them firmly allied to the United States rather than to pursue a policy which could encourage the establishment of a third nuclear power bloc. Avoiding this might require considerable nuclear sharing and assistance on our part.

There is no reason to fear that every small country will develop nuclear forces. Although a few may wish to profit from the political prestige of becoming nuclear powers but they will soon find out that the maintenance and operation of a modern nuclear force is a constant and prohibitive drain on their treasuries. Moreover, a second-rate nuclear force will be found to be like everything else second rate—a questionable prestige factor. When these facts of life become well known, the benefits of collective nuclear security will appear in a more favorable light. A small country can enjoy booming prosperity by letting a big friendly ally assume much of the responsibility for its security. However, I hope that the United States does not feel that only *she* can provide the free world deterrent.

There is likely to be no relaxation in the United States effort, nonetheless, to bottle the nuclear genie as long as there appears to be any hope left in international negotiations. The fear of nuclear proliferation will continue to haunt American policymakers. This exaggerated worry will underpin United States foreign policy until more immediate critical issues take over. It is too much to expect that, as Walter Goldstein put it in *The Correspondent*, "*A* replacement [by the United States] of such nuclear obsessions with more traditional and non-military forms of diplomacy might improve the position of the United States in Europe as well as the long-term security of the European *detente*."

Speaking before the Center for Strategic Studies in 1964, George Ball praised the MLF as the best solution to NATO's nuclear problems, and challenged the audience to come up with something better. I would like to say here that the present practice for handling nuclear weapons in NATO seems far superior to any multi-lateral force arrangement. United States custodial units provide nuclear weapons as necessary and as authorized by the President to NATO nuclear-capable forces. In this manner the United States maintains its finger on the trigger but with the two-key system needs only to consider the finger of one other country at a time. In other words, within the Atlantic Alliance there is a series of bilateral nuclear arrangements. This provides the United States with far more positive control over NATO nuclear weapons than it would have in a multi-lateral arrangement.

And each ally, too, has more control now than he would have as a member of a multi-lateral force. More important, the present arrangement is militarily credible and tactically sound. All it lacks are more modern weapons such as mobile medium range ballistic missiles.

Some students of NATO have suggested that the United

States can trust its allies sufficiently to supply them with their own nuclear weapons. Others violently disagree. Until some less controversial plan for sharing is devised, it is probably better to keep on as at present. A multi-national force such as the ANF might provide the illusion of Allied nuclear control, but no more than that.

One of the most knowledgeable students in the United States Congress on the subject of nuclear proliferation is Representative Craig Hosmer of California. He has cogently pointed out that "the genie is out of the bottle—or so close to it that efforts to ram it back in seem increasingly futile," and he has called for an intelligent re-examination of the proliferation problem "as it actually is, rather than as so many close their minds and hopefully wish it to be." I can endorse this absolutely.

From a technical point of view the knowledge of nuclear fission and fusion is widespread. The manufacture of nuclear fuel is becoming increasingly easy. The relatively cheap gaseous centrifuge system of extracting enriched uranium U-235 is probably at the root of China's phenomenal success. From a political point of view, the world is not so tightly organized as to permit a global nuclear Volstead Act, and unrealistic and overzealous efforts in this direction can excite the very nuclear war that everyone wishes to avoid. From a military point of view, proliferation of nuclear *forces* seems less likely than might be expected because of the continuing heavy expenses involved. And from the point of view of national defense, it seems far more reasonable to pursue the traditional goals of strong alliances and basic military superiority than to be mesmerized and diverted from these goals by the exaggerated dangers of nuclear proliferation.

IX. Counterinsurgency and the War in Vietnam

UNTIL RECENT times the term "guerrilla warfare" described the hostile action of irregular armed bands against regular forces. This term did not encompass the rather sophisticated techniques of insurgency employed by communists to subvert the governments of developing countries—the "wars of national liberation" to which Chairman Khrushchev referred in 1961. Resistance to these insurgencies has also developed considerably more sophistication than former anti-guerrilla operations. Consequently, the somewhat awkward term "counterinsurgency" has been adopted to identify that kind of warfare undertaken by the United States in order to assist friendly countries when communist insurgency becomes overt guerrilla warfare.

Our early involvement in Vietnam at the invitation of the government of South Vietnam is a typical counterinsurgency activity. The war in Vietnam, however, has since grown to such proportions that the action is approaching limited warfare rather than counterinsurgency. What we call the conflict in Vietnam is immaterial, but it does illustrate the concept of a continuum of warfare: first, the sub-limited or counterinsurgency effort encompassing small-scale guerrilla actions; next, limited warfare in which large regular forces are engaged on both side but with the conflict constrained in several ways, whether in terms of weapons, geography, sanctuaries, legal declarations of war, or whatnot. Finally, as the tempo and ferocity of warfare rises, it approaches the "general" or "total" definitions.

Only since World War II have we felt the need to categorize warfare on the basis of tactical limitations, intensity, and scope. Before 1945 the United States forces sent to war were constrained only by the size of the forces available and their logistical capabilities. Objectives were usually quite clear: The United States went into Cuba in 1898 to destroy the Spanish Army there and permit Cuban independence. But we did not confine the war to Cuba. We tracked down and destroyed the Spanish fleet as far away as the Philippine Islands. We then stayed in the Philippines "to establish a government suitable to the wants and conditions of the inhabitants" according to a Senate resolution. This meant putting down the revolt of Emilio Aguinaldo in a successful counter-guerrilla war which ended after two years with Aguinaldo's capture.

To protect the lives and property of foreign residents and restore order, the Marines were sent to Nicaragua in 1912 and again in 1926.

Our rapid move into the Dominican Republic in 1965 was a similar decisive and successful operation even though there was little combat involved.

The same clear-cut policy of applying maximum military force to achieve positive national objectives was applied throughout the two World Wars. We were out to *win*, and the only constraints we recognized were financial pinches, manpower limits, availability of resources, and, of course, political influences.

As we noted earlier, the term "limited warfare" came into prominence as a consequence of the nuclear bomb. A school of thought arose which concluded that nuclear weapons threatened the very existence of civilization. Conceding that ambitions and animosities were at large which could lead to conflict, this school proposed to limit warfare to "conventional" or nonnuclear weapons. The Korean war from 1950 to 1953 was fought along these lines.

Gen. Douglas MacArthur explained and condemned the limited war strategy of Korea when he said, "Never before has this nation been engaged in mortal combat with a hostile power without military objective, without policy other than restrictions governing operations, or indeed without formally recognizing a state of war."

It is not inconsistent with MacArthur's remarks that in lesser conflicts military men have recognized certain limitations, whether they be physical or political, yet they have never before been denied the employment of their most effective weapons in the pursuit of military objectives. Military men would agree that an indiscriminate use of thermonuclear weapons might indeed create catastrophic postwar social problems—as, indeed, might the indiscriminate use of conventional weapons—but few military men would concede that *all* use of nuclear weapons should be renounced.

What is the logic in preferring to drop twenty thousand tons of explosive from one thousand aircraft, or in a thousand sorties of one aircraft, for example, when roughly the same effect could be gained by one aircraft with a small nuclear weapon? Military men talk of "tactical nuclear weapons" in the hope that political leaders will recognize the advantages of employing small nuclear weapons against purely military objectives such as invading armies, airfields, supply lines, and military storage areas. Such action would no more endanger civilian populations than the high explosive warfare of former years. Tacitly granting initiative to Soviet arms by fearing their aggression, and because the NATO countries were not disposed to deploy conventional forces against the Eastern threat on equal terms, the strategy of NATO has included the tactical employment of nuclear weapons. This strategy, however, has long been opposed by those who felt that any use whatever of nuclear weapons created an unacceptable risk of escalation to the dreaded thermonuclear holocaust. The nuclear fire-break, they affirmed, must never be breached under any circumstances.

Political leaders of this school thus faced a crisis in coping with expanding communism. The holocaust theory eliminated *general* war and descredited the "massive retaliation" policy of cold war. Yet deficiencies in Western conventional forces also discouraged us from becoming involved in *limited* war. What course of action, then, was open to us in the event our hand was forced? We had, of course, dispensed economic and military aid. But when these strategies failed, as they so frequently did, we became involved in sub-limited measures—counterinsurgency. Thus an emphasis was placed on counterinsurgency as a major combat pattern for American forces.

Counterinsurgency warfare has taken on increasing importance because of the effort to avoid employing nuclear weapons in a wider anti-communist context. Yet there is still another reason for highlighting this form of warfare today.

The doctrines and techniques of insurgency and guerrilla warfare have been brought to a high art under the leadership of Mao Tse-tung of China. His spectacular victory over Chiang Kai-shek in 1949 through guerrilla means, coupled with his scholarly writings on "peoples" warfare, left in their wake an aura of invincibility for this type of conflict. Successful followers have added to this image. Ho Chi Minh's principal general, Vo Nguyen Giap, vanquished the French colonialists in Vietnam in 1954 by following Mao's doctrines. Fidel Castro and Ché Guevara defeated the established Batista government through similar methods. These signal victories for the communist movement left little doubt that communism possessed a successful strategy and was still expanding. They called for some kind of Free World military response if the drive were to be checked.

Guerrilla warfare is by no means a new style of conflict. Americans cut their teeth on it. In the Revolutionary War, Francis Marion, the "Swamp Fox," made a significant contribution with his elusive irregulars. Napoleon's Peninsular Campaign was brought to a stop by the Spanish guerrillas. In fact, the word guerrilla is Spanish for "small war," and was first used in its present context in a dispatch by the Duke of Wellington in 1809.

The American Civil War saw guerrilla activity on both sides. Leaders such as Henry Morgan, Nathan Bedford Forrest, and John S. Mosby adapted cavalry tactics to irregular warfare. Lessons learned from two centuries of warfare against the American Indians were invaluable. Both the World Wars produced guerrilla leaders. T. E. Lawrence was instrumental in causing an Arab revolt against the Turks in 1916 which led to the destruction of Turkish communications. During World War II Yugoslav partisans, among others, were a thorn in the side of Germany and caused the diversion of seven full-scale offensives, each employing about ten divisions. In the end, the guerrillas, under Tito, inherited the country.

After Bataan fell in 1952, General MacArthur sent several groups of officers into the hinterland of Luzon to conduct guerrilla warfare until the reconquest of the Philippines could be achieved. Among our successful guerrillas harassing the

Japanese occupation troops was the famous Col. R. W. Volckmann of the United States Army, who operated from Northern Luzon and tied down sizeable Japanese forces. These highly successful operations permitted America to maintain the morale and loyalty of the Filipinos, and provided intelligence data which greatly aided the subsequent return of General MacArthur.

The "new" doctrines of Mao, Vo, and Ché are simply reinterpretations of the classic principles of guerrilla warfare. They follow the dictum of Maurice de Saxe that a war can be won without fighting battles. T. E. Lawrence wrote that irregular warfare could become an exact science if certain conditions were met.

First, he said, the guerrillas (or rebels) must have an unassailable base. Whether this be a sympathetic adjoining country as with North Vietnam and Cambodia, or impregnable mountains as in Yugoslavia and the Oriente Province of Cuba, or the desert sands of Arabia, there must be some area which is relatively safe against enemy attack.

Second, the rebels must have a burning cause which will provide the necessary determination to fight on in the face of grim hardships and possible death. This—the cause—is the substitute for the discipline of regular forces.

Third, a sophisticated enemy must oppose the guerrillas—an enemy whose forces are overextended and hence incapable of policing the area they occupy.

Fourth, a friendly, or at least sympathetic, population which will not betray the rebel movements is mandatory.

Fifth, the guerrilla actives must be capable of speed and endurance, and be independent of supply arteries—in other words, be able to live off the country.

Sixth, operations must be directed at enemy communications and weaknesses. Attack must be aimed where the enemy is not strong, utilizing maximum surprise, stealth, and mobility. Then, when the enemy recovers and counterattacks, the rebels break off and vanish into the countryside.

Varied local conditions require some adjustment of these rules of irregular warfare, but in general they apply universally. Mao began his conquest from his unassailable base in remote Sinkiang Province far inside western China. There he drilled his forces not only in tactics but in the ideologies of communism until his men were wholly dedicated. Instead of subverting the city factory workers as Lenin had taught, Mao directed his attention to the countryside. Once he gained control of the rural areas he encircled the cities. The peasant farmers became the "sea" in which his rebel guerrilla forces could "swim." Here he found the sympathetic population which Lawrence considered the essence of guerrilla success.

Mao was up against the established government of Chiang Kai-shek, which had survived the long Sino-Japanese war with much American help. But after the unsuccessful mission of Gen. George C. Marshall in 1946, United States military and economic aid was largely withdrawn from Chiang. This facilitated Mao's rebellion.

Mao's forces, protected and hidden by the friendly farmers, with radio communications were able to assemble and strike with speed and mobility. Soon they secured large areas where more orthodox military units could be formed, trained, and eventually committed in pitched battles against the regulars. This was the final stage of Mao's strategy, but it was not resorted to until victory was almost inevitable.

Mao introduced a new element into the pattern of guerrilla warfare as described by Lawrence. He used terror to gain the required popular loyalty. Through torture and violent murder he blackmailed the peasants to his side. Loyalty to Mao was seldom a voluntary decision.

There are radical differences between guerrilla and classical warfare. Guerrillas are irregulars who cannot be distinguished from the civilian farmer or tradesman until they begin to shoot. They emerge from the countryside, accomplish their mission, and merge back into the terrain and general population. They do not seize and hold objectives. They destroy, kill, and strike terror. They do not stand and fight unless they are obviously winning. They do not take high ground because as a rule they have no commanding artillery nor do they intend to hold any military positions.

But even though guerrillas seem to break all the classical rules of warfare, they can and do gain military and civil power. Guerrillas can weaken and destroy established authority, can tie down large forces, and cause the enemy to use or lose vast quantities of supplies. Unchecked guerrilla tactics can secure an unquestioned military victory. In fact, the guerrilla tactics of the American Colonials wore thin the English patience and contributed immeasurably to our independence.

The highly organized and excessively violent nature of the people's guerrilla warfare today as practiced by Mao, Ho, Vo, and the late Ché has required us to regard it as a special problem. Terror tactics attempt to gain near universal support of the countryside to guerrilla objectives. Yet some of the guerrilla backing appears to be genuine.

We are confronted by a precisely formulated technique capitalizing on dissatisfactions with the process of modernization, to win the allegiance of the population, to challenge the incumbent regime militarily on a gradually expanding scale, and eventually to replace it with a communist autocracy. Though I shall address the military aspects of the problem, I do not intend to imply that communist insurgency is primarily a military matter. The root causes lie in the social, psychological, economic, and political weaknesses of the developing states. With the grandiose and cynical promises of the communists for a new and better life, suffering people can and do become hooked by the new doctrine.

The problems presented to the United States in helping friends and allies confronted by an insurgency are numerous and frustrating. The first stage of insurgency is almost entirely political: converts are gained, government and private institutions are infiltrated, cadres are trained, and caches of arms and other equipment are established. This period of preparation may last for years. The problems we recognize today in Vietnam, for example, began as early as 1925 when Ho was being trained in communism. However, because this first phase almost entirely excludes overt military action, I shall deal here with the succeeding phases.

In counterinsurgency warfare the guerrillas' advantages—dispersal, mobility, immersion in the population, excellent intelligence, tactical initiative, and frequently support from an ostensibly neutral state—make it particularly difficult for conventionally armed and trained forces to come to grips with them. The traditional tactical task of surface warfare has been to find, fix, and fight the enemy. In counterinsurgency the difficulties lie in finding the enemy and in fixing him if found. From the United States point of view, the problems are compounded by the fact that the insurgencies are developing in independent states which are free to accept, modify, or reject American advice. Obviously, direct participation gives credence to communist charges of neocolonialism. It is difficult to make the point in international circles that we have been invited into the country by the local government—particularly if that government no longer exists. States in the communist sights today usually do not possess well-developed infrastructures or industrial capacity and may often be characterized by rough or jungle terrain. All of these factors reduce the impact of our advanced military technology *when we feel constrained to employ counter-guerrilla tactics on enemy terms.*

Our experiences in Vietnam have revealed one major exception to this general proposition. Air forces offer important advantages against guerrillas as a result of the aircraft's inherent speed, range, flexibility, and firepower. Aircraft may be used without significantly widening the war from the tactical terms laid down by the enemy.

Perhaps least glamorous but of great importance, military transport aircraft can partially offset a lack of roads, railroads, and other civilian transportation means by supplying military outposts, strategic villages, and military patrols. Troops can be rushed to action when an enemy force is found or when a friendly unit is under attack. This occurred at Plei Me and turned defeat into victory. Active patrol time can be increased by aerial delivery of a combat unit to its assigned patrol area. Wounded can be evacuated by air to better medical facilities, thus not only saving lives but reducing the number of medical personnel which encumber the unit. This permits the military operation and the pressure to continue rather than having to break off because of casualties.

Whole tactical units can be rotated at an outpost under siege. The United States Marines held the isolated post of Con Thien two miles south of the demilitarized zone against heavy communist artillery attack over a protracted period while being resupplied by air. Ho had assembled several northern divisions in what appeared to be an effort at a great tactical success with international consequences on the order of Dien Bien Phu in 1954. This planned offensive failed because Con Thien was never truly isolated as was Dien Bien Phu where air support was inadequate.

Aircraft provide innumerable opportunities for psychological warfare operations such as leaflet drops and airborne propaganda broadcasts. A show of force with supersonic jets can sometimes have a sobering effect on the enemy as when we paraded supersonic F-104s over the Taiwan Straits during the 1958 crisis. Mach 2 speed tracked on Red Chinese radars was a surprising development.

Air power can contribute toward correcting conditions which may lead to guerrilla warfare. I refer to the corrective role of aerospace power as civic action. Our Special Air Warfare forces, or SAW forces, bear a major responsibility for this function. They are involved in training Air Force personnel of a number of the less developed nations of Asia, Africa, and Latin America to combat internal problems which could lead to insurrection, or which might create situations that could be exploited by communist agents. Often, in these countries, military forces are the only elements with the stability, discipline, training, and equipment needed for the difficult task of nation building. Air forces are especially suited to the task in relatively primitive areas where railroads and highways are few or entirely lacking.

In Ecuador, for example, two United States Air Force C-130 transport aircraft flew 159 tons of road construction equipment over the Andes to an isolated area from which the trip to market had required ten days on horseback. On completion of the new road, the Javaro Indians of that region will be able to get their farm products to market by truck in two hours. In Libya our Air Force has trained about a thousand Libyans in the mechanical skills needed on our air base in that country— skills that become part of the resources of the country.

Information from aerial reconnaissance, when gathered efficiently and acted upon promptly, can do much to overcome the guerrilla's intelligence advantage which he gains from a sympathetic, or at least helpful, population. Light Forward Air Controller (FAC) aircraft in Vietnam provide the best source of information on Viet Cong movements. So do the supersonic RF-101s for locating targets in North Vietnam.

Air attack operations can be devastating against a guerrilla force, especially when the insurgents have no air force or anti-aircraft weapons. In Vietnam there have been repeated instances of Viet Cong attacks being defeated solely by the intervention of aircraft as those in the dramatic Ia Drang Valley operation when over two thousand Viet Cong were killed from the air. In fact, as reported from Saigon, ground checks of Viet Cong casualties in one month showed that air-delivered weapons accounted for over 80 per cent of the Viet Cong killed in action. The main problem does not lie in the effectiveness of airborne weapons but, as in ground operations, in finding and fixing the enemy until fire is brought to bear upon him. Fortunately the speed of aircraft reduces this critical difficulty.

Attack of external base areas, of course, as against North Vietnam transportation, petroleum products and barracks, can reduce the flow of supplies and reinforcements to guerrillas. This is done, however, at the risk of widening the war to something more than a counterinsurgency action.

Still there are many things that air forces cannot do in guerrilla warfare. Air forces cannot by themselves eliminate the stresses attending the modernization process which make a state susceptible to communist insurgency in the first place. However, air-supported civic action programs—such as transportation activities for indigenous civilians and officials, aero-medical team assistance, and aerial television or radio transmissions to remote areas—all can make important contributions toward this basic goal.

In the military realm, air transport operations cannot offer a permanently acceptable substitute for an adequate and secure surface transportation network necessary to the economy of a country. Short and rough field takeoff and landing capabilities of newer aircraft reduce but do not remove this limitation. In the final analysis, air transport operations are far too expensive to be used for most normal commerce in a peaceful environment.

Similarly, aerial psychological warfare operations should be considered as only one portion of a necessary pervasive and continuing program close to the people, not a substitute for such a balanced program. The problem of changing peoples' attitudes, beliefs, and loyalties requires much more than aerial techniques.

Nor can reconnaissance aircraft, despite their many military advantages, provide the information that a loyal population can. If loyalty is gained and retained, guerrilla movements will be reported to government forces in advance. Aircraft can only spot what has already happened. However, in collaboration with a loyal population, aircraft may prove a speedy and efficient means of collection which protects the observers from retaliation. This method was used, for example, in the Philippines during the Huk insurrection where signals observed from the air, such as the position of a plow or opening of a window, indicated the direction and size of the guerrilla unit.

Major guerrilla campaigns probably cannot be defeated by air attack alone. As long as guerrilla forces control the general population and possess the tactical initiative, the enemy must be confronted by an overwhelmingly large force which combines all appropriate arms. Some experts have asserted that the ratio must be ten to one against the insurgents as was necessary to pacify Malay. An enlightened use of air power has reduced this ratio considerably in South Vietnam, but much of a true counterinsurgency still has to be waged on the ground.

It should be kept in mind, however, that this surface force need not necessarily be composed of Americans. People wishing to remain free must be willing to bleed for freedom.

As emphasized earlier in this chapter, no technical or military development alone can satisfactorily solve an insurgency problem, but military success is essential to provide the time required for the political, psychological, economic, and social remedies to take effect. And in achieving the prerequisite military success, there must be a broad application of air power. This is a new feature of counterinsurgency warfare which has not been universally recognized or understood.

The Air Force Chief of Staff, Gen. John P. McConnell, has stated that the increasing participation of air power in South Vietnam has led him to the conclusion that "air power today is a primary factor in limited and guerrilla warfare." Heretofore air power was erroneously considered to serve in a secondary role to ground power, yet the conduct of the war in South Vietnam has proved air power actually to be a primary factor in limited warfare just as it has long been acknowledged to be a primary factor in nuclear and general warfare.

In point of fact, the major burden of the fighting in South Vietnam has been shifted to air power. Ground combat forces are employed primarily to find and fix the enemy for the air forces to attack. In other words, the infantry flushes the enemy, and when they become engaged they call for air support to do the major fighting. The environment is largely "permissive" for air operations since the enemy has no air power and meager anti-aircraft armament in South Vietnam. Should stiffer opposition to air attack develop it would be necessary to fight for and maintain air superiority, as we have had to do to some degree in North Vietnam. It is for this reason that we cannot afford to become overequipped with specialized aircraft designed for the particular geographic and military conditions existing in Vietnam today. Such conditions could change. We must retain our versatility and flexibility for other contingencies. Aircraft are expensive to build and to operate and it would be wasteful to have a special aircraft for every specialized job. "Wars of any kind cannot be won without air power," General McConnell has said, "and without exploiting its almost limitless potentials to the fullest." Hence we must have highly versatile craft.

It is interesting to note, in the face of this air power primacy in limited conflict, that air power also becomes increasingly effective as the war escalates to higher levels of involvement. Conflict of greater intensity requires a greater expenditure of ammunition and supplies of all sorts. Thus logistical "tails" become longer, more evident, and more subject to attack from the air. The enemy infrastructure provides an increasing number of critical targets. Thus as the enemy spends more of its resources on the war, he risks them more to air attack.

From this it would seem that we ourselves could escalate the war to our military advantage. However, our national leaders have declared that it will be our policy to use the minimum military power in achieving our goals in Vietnam. This is somewhat in conflict with President Johnson's statement during the Gulf of Tonkin crisis of 1964 when he asked for, and received, Congressional support for whatever military power was necessary. Our civilian leaders had then, and still have, a variety of military alternatives to choose from, largely in the air power realm. But they have chosen to limit the levels of fighting out of political considerations—which boils down to the philosophy of graduated deterrence and limited war.

It follows from the limited war postulation that the United States stands ready like a fire department, fully equipped to put out a brush fire anywhere in the world. We can move troops by air in a matter of hours, or at most days, assuming there are airfields to receive our airborne fire brigade. But the logistical tail of division-size military units is something else again. The air-transported forces would have little to fight with—only a few tanks, artillery pieces, and trucks; no large ammunition stock or heavy repair equipment; few helicopters, and almost no fuel backup.

To solve this logistical problem in a limited war, the Office of the Secretary of Defense has proposed the construction of a fleet of revolutionary-style ocean-going cargo ships called by a jawbreaker term, "Fast Deployment Logistic Ships" or FDLs for short. These forty thousand-ton behemoths would stow thirty-eight loaded barges on three decks plus fifteen thousand tons of liquid—the cargo equivalent of five conventional freighters.

The five thousand vehicles of an armored brigade together with sixty thousand tons of fuel would be carried on four of these huge ships. Thirteen ships would be required to move the equipment of one division.

An ambitious program of thirty FDLs has been proposed by OSD to the tune of $2 billion. This program comes with the usual claptrap of "savings" we can expect—by spending $2 billion! It is reminiscent of the "savings" which were repeatedly boasted of by OSD for the TFX airplane which ended up costing the government twice as much as advertised and which is still of dubious tactical value. This colossal defense blunder has been swept under the rug by the Johnson Administration.

Prepositioning supplies to back up air movements is not a new idea. We did this in Strategic Air Command for years by maintaining large stocks of heavy equipment at forward deployment bases. We even had mobile depots afloat in World War II. But prepositioning supplies in peacetime is an expensive way to operate because unused equipment deteriorates rapidly. To guard against this, engines must be run periodically and batteries kept charged; in the tropics, warehouses become furnace hot and equipment dries out. In humid areas it rots and mildews. Stored dry foods spoil. The cost of humidity control or air-conditioning is usually prohibitive, but it is contemplated that the preloaded barges of the FDLs will get this plush humidity control.

The largest waste in prepositioned stocks is the need for *twice* the normal amount of equipment for each military unit. Wherever the Army division is stationed it will have to train with a full complement of arms and supplies. Men cannot be stored like equipment. Troops are a perishable military commodity who must be preserved by constant drill and exercise with equipment.

I have some serious doubts whether the FDL program is necessary at all. If we employ air power properly we could strike swiftly from the air in any brush fire situation and hold off the aggressor until surface forces could build up ashore, if necessary, in the normal manner. Certainly there was no need for rapid logistical reaction in South Vietnam. Our forces grew there in slow increments. A major factor in this growth of United States troop strength was not so much our lack of ability to deploy large forces in a hurry but rather the political permission necessary there and at home. We could not have moved in pell-mell. We have to be invited by the indigenous government. And the political climate at home had to be favorable. In any brush fire war this political factor will take unquestioned precedence over our logistical capability.

Proponents of the FDL concept have distorted history—or possibly have not examined history too carefully—by asserting that FDLs, had we had them, would have shortened World War II and Korea. This is patently absurd. In the opening days of World War II our fleet and air power was largely destroyed at Pearl Harbor and Clark Field. Had we had hundreds of FDLs then they either would have been destroyed similarly or else stayed right at home until we could have protected their passage with air and naval cover. Also, one must remember, we had few divisions ready for deployment. The governing factors early in the war were not the shortages of merchant shipping.

As for Korea, we had no intention of deploying a division across the Pacific until the Blair House Conference by President Harry Truman changed all our strategic plans overnight. Had we had FDLs they would not have been loaded. Thus it is inane to project such a logistical concept back into history when there was no corresponding strategy for its use at that time.

Today Congress has balked at building these expensive floating military warehouses. It may be true as the Defense Department maintains that these loaded FDLs would not be provocative considering our thousands of naval ships abroad in the Sixth and Seventh Fleets. But having them might be an encouragement to use them. These costly and massive supply dumps might themselves lend arguments to police the world again as we have in Vietnam. Such a policy could soon bankrupt the nation. For my money I would stay out of foreign fights unless America's national interests are directly at stake. And when this occurs, a judicious and rapid employment of air and naval action should be adequate to uphold our stake and commitments in the matter.

When it comes to spending $2 billion on ships which will sit dead in the water, never engaging in peacetime commerce, and loaded with possibly another $2 billion worth of military supplies which would rapidly deteriorate to worthlessness with disuse, then I think we are spending our money needlessly. We would be pursuing the same barren strategic philosophy which got us into Vietnam in the first place. Had we had the courage to use decisive weapons of air and sea power against telling targets in the beginning we would never have had to commit a half-million men to costly and futile ground warfare.

If America has $2 billion to spend for ships, those ships should be devoted to peacetime commerce, yet always available for war when needed. Or another investment of far greater need would be the upgrading of our aging SAC bombing force with an Advanced Manned Strategic Aircraft (AMSA) which would contain the flexibility of engaging in either general *or* limited wars as does the B-52 today.

The FDL plan is just another extremely costly and wasteful tribute laid at the feet of the false doctrines of flexible response, graduated deterrence, and limited war.

The rationale of this national strategy of counterinsurgency and limited war is sometimes referred to as "conflict management." This high sounding and wide-ranging concept has been reviewed by General McConnell in this way:

> *One*, and still foremost, deter nuclear war by maintaining a sufficient margin of strategic superiority to assure the destruction of any aggressor and to keep the potential damage to ourselves within acceptable limits. *Two*, endeavor to deter conflicts at all lower levels of intensity and, if deterrence should fail, *keep such conflicts at the lowest possible level* and help resolve them to our advantage. *Three*, assist in the resolution of local crises and help prevent them from expanding into armed conflict. . . .

Certainly the United States cannot engage in counterinsurgency or limited warfare without regard to its long-range objectives and over-all national strategies. However, the hypothesis that a dynamic communist movement can be brought to a halt by punishment below the level of surrender—that is, be induced to come to the conference table before the issues have been resolved on the battlefield—is a reflection of "conflict ignorance" on the part of our policy-makers.

The doctrine of counterinsurgency guerrilla warfare with a "flexible response," and even the doctrine of limited warfare is undergoing a crucial test in Vietnam. And in my judgment these doctrines are being found wanting. It is not that we cannot terminate the war in Vietnam in our favor: to win it is not our objective and would run counter to our present doctrine. We can and probably will achieve some sort of truce under the present ground rules as we did in Korea. But no matter how the politicians may hail such a truce as an American victory, it will have been gained at such a costly price as to be Pyrrhic. Additionally, the political gains will have been of dubious value to the free world. About all we shall be able to say is that we checked communism temporarily in South Vietnam. The virus of communism will continue to spread down through Southeast Asia because we failed to administer a sound and decisive defeat to its organized propagators.

There are those who look upon the war in Vietnam as somewhat of an opportunity to test the new doctrines of flexible response and limited war. Taking a long view of history and accepting the assumptions that general nuclear war will never be fought, they conclude that it is to our advantage to learn as much as we can about fighting under the new limited war doctrines while our national existence is not at stake. They point to the knowledge gained by German forces in the Spanish Civil War which proved out the successful blitzkrieg doctrine of ground-air operations and led to Hitler's rapid conquest of Poland and the Low Countries, Norway, and France. If we must fight only limited wars in the future, they reason, it is well that we develop the tactics and techniques in a war which does not threaten America directly.

This argument might make some partial sense to me if the doctrines of flexible response and limited war had been soundly conceived in the first place. But to engage in such a vast and costly training maneuver as Vietnam, merely to test ill-conceived doctrines based upon military fallacies, is to my mind a cruel and unnecessary way to develop our military might. In fairness, however, to those who regard Vietnam as a training ground, I am sure that none of them expected the war to reach the proportions it now has. In fact, those people were so confident of their limited war doctrine that they believed the war would have long since been terminated at a reasonable conference table. Yet with all the manifest failure of the new doctrine in practice its advocates cling to it with a blind and unreasoning faith.

Let us now take a three-part look at the Vietnam situation. First, let us recall how we got there. Then let us see what we are doing there, and why. Finally, and this is the big question, let us see how we can end it.

To begin with it is necessary to understand that Vietnam is part of a much larger and much longer war—a war between communism and the Free World.

This larger war was declared by the communists. It was declared by Marx and Engels before there was one communist country in the world. It was declared by Lenin. It was waged by Stalin. It has been pursued relentlessly by every communist leader. Communist conquest is the burning doctrine of Mao Tse-tung and Ho Chi Minh.

It is a war waged simultaneously on many fronts and in many forms. It is a cold war and a hot war, an economic war and a political war, a propaganda war and an ideological war. It is waged by the communists according to their own timetable and on battlefields of their own choosing. Although the war has many facets, it has but one objective: communist control of the entire world.

This is not my definition of their goal. It is the communists' definition. They have stated it over and over again in many different ways and they believe it. I believe it, too.

Winston Churchill, one of the few world leaders who understood the ambitions of the communists, tried to head them off. To keep eastern Europe from falling unopposed under Russian domination, Churchill argued for the invasion of Europe from the southeast. Through the "soft and vulnerable underbelly," Sir Winston called it. But in summit meetings he was outvoted. And the Russians alone moved against Germany from the east. The result twenty-three years later is a divided Germany, a sectored Berlin, and Russian occupation of eastern Europe.

By 1945 the United States was tired of war. The strongest nation in the world, we were optimistic about the future. We turned our strength and optimism to postwar problems: to the rehabilitation of war-ravaged countries, to the relocation of displaced persons, to the application of wartime scientific discoveries to peacetime uses which would advance the standards of living everywhere. We put together the United Nations. We were confident that we could maintain world peace through international cooperation and good will.

As an American, I am proud that we assumed that kind of enlightened world leadership.

However, while the ink was drying on the United Nations Charter, Soviet military forces barricaded the communist-occupied world. They stripped eastern Europe and northern China of industrial machinery. They set up communist puppet governments in most eastern European countries. The communists were carrying through their announced plan of world domination. But we somehow could not believe it. These people had been our allies. They were the heroes of Stalingrad.

It took Sir Winston Churchill with his famed Iron Curtain speech at Fulton, Missouri in 1946 to shock us out of our naïve complacency. He clearly explained the significance of Soviet actions. He warned of things to come. And America began to listen.

A year later when Greece was threatened by communist-supplied insurgents and Russia was pressuring Turkey for control of the Bosporus, our passive reaction to communist aggression ended. We offered the Greek and Turkish governments military and economic aid. President Harry S. Truman told the world of our determination "to help free people maintain their free institutions and their national integrity against aggressive movements that seek to impose upon them totalitarian regimes."

This Truman Doctrine marked a turning point for America. It announced our decision to defend the Free World against the expansion of communism. It set the stage for the Marshall Plan. It was the brave beginning of a new era.

During the later 1940s our practical education continued concerning the true nature of the communist threat and the policy of "socialist revolution." In the spring of 1948, Czechoslovakia, the last free nation in eastern Europe, fell to a communist coup. In June, the Soviet army blockaded Berlin. A year later, the Communist Chinese forced Chiang Kai-shek off the Asian mainland. Soviet veto after Soviet veto was hamstringing the United Nations. And in September, 1949, Russia detonated its first atomic bomb.

Within nine months, with Soviet blessing and support, Communist North Korea invaded South Korea. Our announced role as ally to the nations of the Free World was being pointedly put to the test.

In the meantime, however, our expanding strategic nuclear forces had been deployed to forward bases in England. Our commitment to European defense was further underscored with the creation of the NATO Alliance and the stationing of American forces on the continent.

United States' involvement in the Korean crisis was immediate. The Blair House Conference served unmistakable notice to the Communist world that we would not tolerate overt aggression wherever it might occur. Our strength, and our willingness to use it, formed a strategic deterrent against Soviet aggression, east and west.

By moving resolutely and risking a major war we actually prevented one. Time and again since then the Communists have tested us to determine if our policy has weakened. They engineered confrontations in Berlin, in Lebanon, in the Taiwan Straits, and in the Cuban missile crisis. Each time we demonstrated our willingness to respond to the threat of direct conflict.

Communist strategy was not working. It was time for an adjustment. In 1961 Khrushchev officially proclaimed the new, preferred method with his endorsement of so called "wars of national liberation." His pronouncement, with similar encouragement from the leaders of Red China, gave new impetus to the upheaval already in process in Southeast Asia.

As we have seen, these wars of liberation take a recognized form. They are low intensity conflicts fought by guerrillas against the established government using techniques perfected in China against the Japanese and later against the Nationalists. The tactics involve a wide variety of engagements, large and small. There are border incidents, hit-and-run raids, sudden terrorist massacres, blackmail, bloody ambushes, and a continuous flood of propaganda.

These tactics have worked. They were successful in China, in Algeria, and they brought Castro to power in Cuba. But nowhere were they more successful than when they forced the French to withdraw from Southeast Asia. This departure created a power vacuum and left political chaos.

Since we believed we could not deal with this growing threat by general or even limited war, we developed the new concept of the flexible response. We put together a package of land, sea, and air power carefully adjusted and limited to what we thought was the given level of provocation. Not too little and not too much, we thought. This package embodied global mobility. And because world tensions and international politics were involved, direct and specific control of all military action was retained by our national leadership in Washington.

It is this policy of flexible response that shapes our military activity in Vietnam today.

And why are we there? For one reason, because we were asked for help. First to advise, then to assist, and finally to fight. We were asked by the government of South Vietnam which was under heavy pressure in a "war of liberation" conducted by the Viet Cong who were inspired, directed, and supplied by the Communists to the north. It is important that this basic fact be kept in mind.

The Vietnam conflict is to some minor extent a civil war, and to some small degree a local war evolving out of local issues. But it is not a true peasant revolt any more than the Red takeover of China was a peasant revolt. The war in Vietnam is a typical and clearly identifiable part of current communist strategy. It is a calculated act of aggression. Even though there are many South Vietnamese who seem loyal to communism it takes no exquisite discernment to see the difference between a loyalty coerced by torture and terror and a loyalty won through help and respect. It does not follow that the first kind of bitter loyalty is a representation of the popular will even though there is more of it. A lot of "loyalty" can be bought with the assassination, wounding, or kidnapping of over ten thousand civilians each year, particularly when most of these massacres are directed against village leaders.

As I have noted, the war in Vietnam began in the 1920s when the trio who presently lead the North launched a struggle for independence against the French. President Ho Chi Minh, the seventy-seven-year-old leader who studied in the Soviet Union, along with Prime Minister Pham Van Dong and the military hero of Dien Bien Phu, Defense Minister Vo Nguyen Giap, are convinced today that they will defeat America just as they defeated the French—by a relentless and protracted struggle. They believe that the United States will grow tired and withdraw as did the French after eight years of guerrilla warfare.

North Vietnam's commitment to seize control of the South is no less total than was the commitment of North Korea in 1950. The war in South Vietnam is not a true local rebellion because the hard corps of the Communist forces attacking South Vietnam are trained in the North and ordered into the South by Ho. The directing force behind the effort to conquer South Vietnam is the Communist Party in the North, the Lao Dong Party. According to Communist doctrine the party is an integral part of the regime itself. The Lao Dong Party directs the war through its Central Office for South Vietnam. In 1960 the National Liberation Front (NLF) for South Vietnam was set up to create the impression that the war is a popularly inspired revolt. In point of fact the South Vietnamese have nothing whatever to do with the NLF, yet many people and even many governments have been deceived into believing this. The NLF is Hanoi's creation; it is neither independent nor southern and it seeks not liberation, but subjugation.

This is all clearly spelled out and supported with abundant objective evidence in the State Department's White Paper of March 12, 1965. Even the International Control Commission, composed of Indian, Polish, and Canadian members and set up to police, without teeth, the Geneva accord of 1954, agreed in 1962 that Hanoi had violated the provisions of the protocol.

In a letter to the new South Vietnam government of Ngo Dinh Diem in 1954, President Dwight D. Eisenhower promised United States support to "assist the government of Vietnam in developing and maintaining a strong viable state, capable of resisting attempted subversion or aggression through military means" and basing the United States' efforts on "performance" by Diem "in undertaking needed reforms." Things went relatively well until the end of 1960 when North Vietnam stepped up guerrilla activity in the South and formed the National Liberation Front. In the next two years we expanded our military assistance group (MAG) from five hundred to nearly three thousand. By the end of 1963 it had grown to twenty-three thousand and still our counterinsurgency effort was failing.

The assassination of Ngo Dinh Diem on November 2, 1963, and the overthrow of his government by a military junta placed America in the embarrassing position of supporting a government which by no stretch of the imagination could be called popularly established. Moreover, in the following eighteen months, ten governments rose and fell in Saigon.

In August, 1964, when the destroyer U.S.S. *Maddox* was attacked by North Vietnam torpedo boats in the Gulf of Tonkin, President Lyndon B. Johnson decided to use American force directly and he gained an overwhelming mandate from Congress for doing so. This resolution gave the President authority to "take all necessary steps, including the use of armed force, to assist any member or protocol state in the Southeast Asia Collective Defense Treaty. . . ."

By 1965 we were bombing North Vietnam and landing combat troops to engage the Viet Cong. Yet the South Vietnamese army was shot with desertions and down to one-third of its strength. Equipment worth millions of dollars from the United States was finding its way into Viet Cong hands. The Communists were definitely winning. Our only recourse was to commit our own American troops to combat.

This is a new kind of war. It is a war of flexible response not designed to win but rather to punish, and to punish only enough to bring the Hanoi government to the conference table.

It is a war that gives sanctuary to the enemy in North Vietnam, Laos, and Cambodia.

It is a war that, in the words of Harold Brown, Secretary of the Air Force, uses "the minimum force available to attain those ends. We are trying to minimize our own casualties, the casualties of our allies. We are even trying to minimize the casualties of our adversaries. . . ."

It is a war fought irresolutely and equivocally and with few specific objectives. What precisely do we wish Ho to agree to at the conference table?

It is a war commanded by civilians in the Pentagon who have little military experience. As Gen. Ira C. Eaker has written, it is a paradox: "In all our past wars we had professional military leaders and amateur soldiers. Vietnam is our first war where we have professional soldiers and amateur leaders."

It is a war where our powerful Navy allows foreign ships to supply the enemy with war materials. As Raymond Moley has said, ". . . if the United States Navy no longer has a mission to control the sea lanes, we have been wasting billions of dollars on an anachronism."

It is a war where we allow the one principle harbor—the harbor through which the large majority of enemy supplies must flow—to remain undamaged.

It is a war in which the advantages of surprise and initiative are yielded to the enemy because we do not wish to shock the onlookers.

It is a war which lacks a plan to win and hence the necessary materials and training have not been geared to a conclusive strategy. Shortages of every description occur as the war drags on and we jury-rig one quick fix after another in a piecemeal fashion.

It is a war in which we promise the enemy's survival and nurture his means for fighting us.

It is a war in which we are attempting to win without winning, trying to destroy without destroying. It is an Alice-in-Wonderland war.

This is the war of flexible response and graduated deterrence applied for the first time. This is the war concocted by the arms controllers of the Kennedy-Johnson Administrations to prevent, they believed, the feared nuclear holocaust. The consequences of such a cruel non-war will be heartache, frustration, and death rather than a reasonable political settlement.

We *must* change our strategy.

General McConnell, our Air Force Chief, said in 1966, "It is true that we could achieve this objective [of bringing North Vietnam to the conference table] virtually overnight, by destroying North Vietnam and forcing its surrender; we certainly have the military capacity to do so. But President Johnson has emphasized that it is our national policy to keep this conflict at the lowest possible level of intensity, for humanitarian as well as for political reasons. In the words of President Johnson, we are in Vietnam "to prevent the aggression from succeeding without attempting either to conquer or invade or destroy North Vietnam."

General Eisenhower, who has had successful experience both in the White House *and* in war, has declared, "I do not believe in 'gradualism' in fighting a war. I believe in putting in the kind of military strength we need to win, and getting it over as soon as possible." To this I can only say, Amen.

The strategy of flexible response introduces several new approaches to the use of American military power. Traditionally, the ultimate goal of military action was the military defeat of the enemy. Then he would come to terms. Even in Korea, despite severe restriction on the use of our air arm above the Yalu River, there were no holds barred within the combat zone. The notion of flexible response changed this approach.

Under the new doctrine, military forces are still expected to eliminate their immediate adversaries. BUT only the precise increments of force believed needed to achieve limited objectives are committed to combat. The military objective is restricted to halting enemy aggression and punishing only enough to make the enemy willing to negotiate. Yet who can tell how much punishment this may take? So far we have not been able to gauge it at all.

The underlying idea is to make it plain to the enemy that we could indeed destroy him if we wanted to, and that therefore he would reasonably prefer to negotiate a settlement once our determination had been made clear. This makes common sense to us. But does it to him?

In attempting to apply military power according to this new concept our leaders in Washington design carefully controlled military campaigns with limited political objectives. They try to use our military resources in such a way as to apply subtle pressures—employing military power as a versatile and precise instrument, they claim, as a surgeon handles a scalpel. However, it makes no sense to excise an appendix when the patient is suffering a heart attack.

Our leaders in the Johnson Administration are unusually concerned with world opinion. They are most sensitive to criticism from the foreign press and attempt to present a benign and peaceful image of America while fighting a war. At the same time that we are bombing Soviet-made SAM missiles in North Vietnam we are trying to build bridges of accord to the Soviet Union and collaborate on a non-proliferation of nuclear weapons treaty. We are attempting to dress and undress at the same time. But this broader foreign policy is not directly related to the flexible response strategy which I wish to analyze here.

I must admit that there are some positive features of this strategy. In pursuing this philosophy of flexible response we have learned to fight guerrillas and to inflict heavy casualties on a capable, secret, and swift enemy. We have developed certain ways of employing our superior technical weapons to give us mobility and a deadly striking power against a jungle adversary. We have made it increasingly difficult and costly for the Communists to operate. But we have spent five years doing this at a prohibitive cost in lives and fortune.

Our objective has always been the same: to make it clear to the Communists that they cannot win. And from our vantage point of obviously superior strength we hope to force them to negotiate through frustration and exhaustion.

What is the score at the five-year mark? Basically, I think it would be fair to say that the Viet Cong have gained strength while we are the ones who have become frustrated. The long, drawn-out conflict has created dissension, disillusion, and dispute in America. It has seemed to foster a greater sense of determination and purpose in North Vietnam.

Every American instinct makes us want to jump in with both feet and get this unpleasant job over with as quickly as possible. We are impatient people. This is a quality that has helped to build a great nation. Conversely, Oriental stoicism and patience make North Vietnam willing to extend the struggle from generation to generation, or so they say, to have a "protracted war."

Another reason for ending the war is that we are fighting with the commodity most precious to us and that which is held rather cheaply by the enemy—the lives of men. And what is our objective? To negotiate. The objective of peace through negotiation seems to take on more significance than the substantive objective of halting the Communist overthrow of South Vietnam. Our continued pleas for peace and talks can only leave an impression of irresolution, which encourages North Vietnamese resistance.

I submit that it is not possible for us to lose this war unless we choose to do so. We are too strong. But it is more than possible for us to lose the negotiation. And the longer it is delayed, the more likely we are to lose it.

After all, what is there to negotiate? The terms of the National Liberation Front (NLF) dictated from Hanoi? They want us to withdraw all troops and dismantle our bases. Then we must recognize the bogus NLF as the "sole genuine representative of the South Vietnamese people." This is preposterous and would mean the complete surrender of South Vietnam to communism.

The separation of North Vietnam and South Vietnam and the boundary between them has already been established by negotiations at Geneva in 1954. Our position is to abide by this agreement. Why should we re-negotiate it? Any concession to the Communists and any abridgement of freedom for the people of South Vietnam will reward the Communists for their aggression. We cannot allow aggression to be politically profitable. This would encourage further aggression in every corner of the world. We must see to it that Communist aggression results in Communist disaster. This we cannot obtain at the negotiating table.

The world is watching us in Vietnam. Our national leaders are very right about this. We have announced ourselves to be the champions of free people everywhere; the ally of every country in the Free World that calls upon us for help against Communist aggression. And every country in the Free World is watching to see just what kind of an ally we might become when the chips are down.

Can we—and will we—join with those who seek our help to resist Communist aggression? To resist it and repel it? Will we truly live up to our numerous allied and bilateral commitments? The world is watching us in Vietnam to see if we will put our money where our mouth is. It is that simple.

We are not engaged in a worldwide popularity contest with the Communists. In all candor the strong and the rich are seldom popular. They are sometimes feared and sometimes resented. But they are usually respected. So I thank God that we are rich and I thank God that we are strong. Because I know that it is for those reasons we are free. And it is our freedom and our strength and our riches that offer hope and encouragement to people everywhere.

Let us examine the Geneva Convention of 1954. As we have seen, the trouble in Vietnam can be traced back to World War II and before. French colonial rule had been not entirely enlightened, and a popular resistance had grown which collaborated at first with the Japanese and later with the Communists to overthrow French rule. Following the war, in 1945, the French sent in 70,000 troops to reestablish their authority. By 1954 they had committed 272,000 men and we were largely footing the bill. They fought heroically but unsuccessfully. The disastrous defeat at Dien Bien Phu on May 7, 1954, where she lost 12,000 legionaries, caused France to give up. The contest was judged simply too much for French resources. She withdrew and the baby was then passed to the United States, who tacitly agreed to a division of Vietnam. We then sea-lifted a million Vietnamese who did not choose to live under the Communist rule of Ho Chi Minh from the north to the south.

This division of Vietnam was decided upon by the Geneva accord of 1954. Although we did not sign this protocol, we generally supported its provisions. By the words of the Final Declaration of July 21, 1954: "In their relations with Cambodia, Laos, and Vietnam, each member of the Geneva Conference undertakes to respect the sovereignty, the independence, the unity and the territorial integrity of the above mentioned states, and to refrain from any interference in their internal affairs." And as Adlai E. Stevenson, the United States representative to the United Nations said in 1964, ". . . the political settlement for Vietnam reached at Geneva in 1954 has been deliberately and flagrantly and systematically violated."

Many of those who question our motives in Vietnam like to point out that we, too, violated the 1954 agreement by not encouraging a plebiscite as the protocol directed after a period of two years (1956). We were not, of course, the policeman to this settlement which we did not sign. The impotent I.C.C. was to police the agreement. But because we were assisting the government of Ngo Dinh Diem in the southern half of the country some people erroneously held the United States responsible. It must be noted that neither did South Vietnam sign the Geneva agreement.

In truth, we did *not* encourage a plebiscite. The facts were that an honest and fair plebiscite could not have been conducted in the atmosphere of terror caused by the Communist infiltration. The simple plebiscite is a fraud unless taken in an atmosphere of freedom. Voting in the kind of closed and controlled society which existed in much of Vietnam at that time, dominated by Viet Cong terrorists in rural areas, would have been nothing more than a propaganda exercise to confuse the gullible sheltered people of the free and uncommitted world.

We generously supported the Diem government but as the Communists gained ground we became disenchanted with Diem who, we thought, was not providing the freedoms and prosperity that even the Communists had promised. It was not a proud chapter in our history when we turned our backs on Diem in 1963 and tacitly encouraged a coup. The succession of coups since that time has left us in the position of supporting governments which were far from stable and of doubtful popularity. However, the elections of 1967 have lent unquestioned popular support to the new government of Lt. Gen. Nguyen Van Thieu who was inaugurated as President on October 30, 1967. The Vice-President of the new government is Air Vice-Marshal Nguyen Cao Ky, the former premier. This team gained 34.8 per cent of the vote while its nearest rival captured only 17 per cent. From all accounts, it was an honest and fair election.

In 1954 we thought we could pick up France's responsibilities and stem the communist tide simply with large grants of economic and military aid. It did not work. Then just as soon as we put our American instructors into combat, we were caught in a shooting war. Next we dribbled in reinforcements, taking one half-measure after another in the "graduated" manner of flexible response, pursuing a peculiar strategy which said, in effect, "Fight the enemy on his own terms."

Our political leaders believed that should we employ more decisive tactics we might bring Red China into the war. They felt that if we bombed the more valuable target systems which I recommended it would probably bring down the Ho Chi Minh government of North Vietnam and this would not fit the doctrine of flexible response and limited war. The Mao Tse-tung government of China might then feel compelled to come to Ho's rescue regardless of China's own poor circumstances for waging war. Then, it was reasoned, we would be involved in a great land war against the Red Chinese hordes. None of our leaders wanted this. A conflict enlarged to this extent, too, would bring us nearer to the employment of nuclear weapons, or even to the involvement of Soviet Russia with its capacity for intercontinental nuclear attack. So went the reasoning.

I grant you that these ultimate possibilities were and still are frightening nightmares, but I am not prepared to suggest that they are anything more than nightmares. They rest upon a whole string of unlikely events. Suppose, for example, that we should progressively bomb petroleum facilities, electrical power generators, factories, irrigation systems, transportation centers, and the harbor facilities at Haiphong. There can be little question that either the Ho Chi Minh government would sue for peace, or another government would overthrow Ho and accept the conference table alternative. Leadership of the Viet Cong and the NLF would cease abruptly along with the Viet Cong reinforcement by regular North Vietnamese troops. Viet Cong supplies would dry up. American and South Vietnam troops would then be in a position to mop up whatever die-hard Viet Cong insisted on continuing the fight.

But I am getting ahead of myself.

Regardless of how we have backed into this war we must now recognize, unequivocally, that we *are* in it and our only exit with honor and world respect is to win it. How can we do this?

The first step is to reverse our objective. Instead of the negotiating table we must aspire to decisive victory. We must make the war so costly to North Vietnam that it will sue for peace. The Communists started this war. Let them wish they never had. Let the Communists end it.

Second, we must fight the war from our position of strength, not theirs. We must fight it at the lowest cost to ourselves and at the greatest cost to the enemy. We must change the currency in this contest, from men to materials.

America's greatest strength in this military situation is air and naval power. We must use it strategically. We must use it decisively. And we must use it now.

It is important that we tell the world about this change in objective so that the world can correctly interpret our motives and evaluate our results. And we also must tell the Communists.

We must tell them that we are going to bomb increasingly costly targets in North Vietnam. They can decide how much they want to pay for the privilege of invading their neighbor. First, we must destroy the ability of the North Vietnamese to wage war and then, if necessary, their entire productive capacity.

We can pinpoint the targets we will hit and warn the civilians in advance to evacuate. In modern warfare, with modern warning devices, there is little surprise in bombing raids. Hanoi, for example, is ringed with far more and far better anti-aircraft devices than were ever in Berlin during World War II.

You will recall that North Vietnam is a rather recent arrival to twentieth-century technology and industry. Her resources, by our standards, are meager and hard earned. They are more valuable to her, in many respects, than human life. And North Vietnam must be made to pay for this war with her dearest coins.

To do this we must return to the strategic bombing doctrine which was tried and proved in World War II. We must attack the *sources* of supply and the *sources* of power. We must not waste our bombs, our multi-million dollar aircraft, and our precious fighter pilots on bridges, trucks, barracks, and oil drums when major factories, supply dumps, power plants, port facilities, and merchant ships go unscathed.

We hear dissenters say today that the bombing of North Vietnam is ineffective and, in relation to the great effort we are expending, they are right. Probably the weirdest aspect of this Alice-in-Wonderland war is that we have dropped more explosives on Vietnam than we did on Germany in World War II. Our strikes against Germany devastated one of the world's most powerful and industrially advanced nations, yet an even greater destructive force seems to have hardly dented the military capacity of a backward, third-rate power. How can this be? It is not air power which is wanting. It is the wrong *employment* of air power.

Secretary of State Dean Rusk has assured us that Ho "is hurting very badly" and that we do not intend to suspend the bombing. Then why in Heaven's name do we not hurt him more when we so easily can? For we must hurt him enough to make him meet our terms if we are ever to terminate this war.

"It's a daffy war in lots of ways," said a pilot who had been bombing the North. "Many times as we come in over Haiphong we'll see a Russian tanker steaming in or tied up at a pier. Its crew will wave to us and we'll wave back. But then for the next six weeks we chase individual oil trucks down camouflaged roads with maybe $30 million worth of airplanes. We lose some of those planes. And we lose men, too."

The sanctuary we have granted to the port of Haiphong is one of the strangest anomalies in the history of warfare. During the past two years 827 ships have brought munitions and supplies to North Vietnam. Of these ships, 267 were Russian, 258 were Red Chinese, 94 were from Eastern European countries, *and 210 were ships of our alleged allies and foreign aid recipients.* Could this trade have something to do with our granting a King's X to the port? It is a nasty thought, but I have a very hard time rationalizing a strategy that encourages the flow of supplies to enemies who are shooting our servicemen.

There are so many ways we could close that port! We could blockade it. We could bomb it to rubble. We could mine it. We could sink a ship in the entrance channel. The port of Haiphong is the Achilles heel of North Vietnam. Seventy per cent of her war supplies enter here. A steady stream of freighters, at least one each day, is needed to keep the ammunition pipeline full. And if anyone thinks that such a volume of sophisticated materials can be carried from China by individuals with A-frame packs, he has no idea of the size and weight of an SA-2 missile. The defense of North Vietnam is highly technical and Ho could not continue it by reverting to foot transportation. Nor could he adequately support the Viet Cong in the south.

Our token bombing has merely given our enemies a chance to develop massive defenses around the most critical targets and at the same time shoot down our $2 million fighters as they attack targets which are sometimes not even worth the bombs themselves.

The bogey of escalation and the pathological fear of antagonizing Red China was found to be unwarranted when we lifted certain bombing restrictions in the past. It was argued in 1964 and 1965 that if we bombed petroleum targets it would pose an intolerable provocation to Red China. It did not. But we waited so long and debated the move so thoroughly in the press that Hanoi had time to disperse much of its oil storage in drums.

I sometimes wonder whether we or the enemy suffers most under our flexible response strategy. We have lost over seven hundred aircraft over North Vietnam at a cost of well over a billion dollars. Our fighter-bomber production is just barely keeping ahead of our losses according to the Pentagon. And the heartache of having three hundred or more of our fine young pilots suffering indignities if not torture at the hands of the Red Vietnamese is a high price to pay for so few military results.

Another anomaly of this war is that our strategic bombers, the B-52s, are being used tactically to carpet-bomb enemy troop concentrations while our tactical fighters undertake the strategic role. Reasons given for this are that the high-flying jet bombers would be easy marks for the SA-2 missiles. This may be the right decision as long as we are so sensitive about bombing accuracy in the North and have so few worthwhile targets in any event. But when the time comes to bomb out the port of Haiphong the B-52s could and should be risked. They would make short work of that Achilles heel.

General Westmoreland has applauded the work of the B-52s in the South. "We know," he said, "from talking with many prisoners and defectors, that the enemy troops fear B-52s, tactical air, artillery, and armor, in that order." At least the big sword is being kept sharp.

As restricted and relatively ineffective as our bombing is, North Vietnam is truly hurting. Over a half million men are mobilized to repair the damages to roads, bridges, etc., caused by our bombs. And the flow of supplies to the south is definitely constricted. So to call a bombing halt as has been proposed by many as a signal for talks would be an expression of weakness and indecision. We may get talks, but not on our terms. So why talk?

The thirty-seven day truce of 1965–66 was used by North Vietnam to rush supplies south rather than to ponder peace talks. Why should we expect anything more today?

Both Russia and Red China can be very happy the way the war is now going. It costs them very little compared to the drain on our economy; we are getting all the bad publicity, not they; and they are making no commitments in lives as we are. China has long coveted Vietnam and if the Ho government falls Red China would be in a very favorable position to assume control. The charge might well be made that Red China is fighting the war against the United States in Southeast Asia to the last Vietnamese. It is no secret that Red China exerts pressure on North Vietnam to continue the war as long as possible.

With the Soviets and the Communist Chinese fighting "wars of national liberation" by proxy, and with the Americans fighting them directly with their own blood and treasure, we invite the Communists to pursue this favorable strategy in other parts of the world. However, if we punish Ho sufficiently, other nationalist leaders will be more reluctant to be pushed into American guns by their Communist "allies." We would also indicate to Russia and China that our fear of escalation will not permit us to be bullied into interminable limited wars.

The way to fight the war in North Vietnam is to fight it. Pussyfooting with bombing pauses and exempting the vital targets is the way to lose it. I offer this simple plan of campaign:

The harbor at Haiphong and the entire capacity to receive outside supplies must be eliminated. Our selected bombing of nearby targets has increased ship turnaround time but this is not enough. We must close the port absolutely. Gen. Earle G. Wheeler said that Haiphong is the chief source of war goods used in the South.

So must be eliminated the power system that fuels every war-making facility.

So must be eliminated the transportation system—rails, rolling stock, bridges, and yards.

Every factory and every industrial installation, beginning with the biggest and best must be bombed and destroyed.

And if necessary the irrigation system on which food production largely depends should come under our bombsights. We can burst the dikes that make rice farming possible in the Red River Delta. This is one of the most heavily populated areas in the world. Without the dikes severe flooding would occur during the monsoons. I know of no war of this size when such an effort has been made to *preserve* the agricultural base of the enemy.

We must be willing to continue our bombing until we have

destroyed every work of man in North Vietnam if this is what it takes to win the war.

We can and should avoid the civilian population. It can be effectively warned. But we must destroy the capacity of that population to slaughter innocent people for political gain. Let us not ever forget that our own deaths in this war exceed seventeen thousand.

We should destroy every supply dump, even those placed in populated areas. Of course we should warn the people to leave these areas.

I do not think it will be necessary to use nuclear weapons to accomplish this task. Nevertheless, I would not rule out any strength that we have, if the situation demands it.

Soviet Russia has indicated more than once that she does not want to project herself into a showdown with the United States. Not now, anyway. I again call your attention to Berlin, Lebanon, the Taiwan Straits, and the Cuban crisis. And Red China today seems entirely preoccupied with her own internal turmoil.

Mr. McNamara believes that the enemy cannot "be bombed to the negotiating table." I can see no other sensible way of getting him there.

I believe that the course I suggest will end the war much sooner than will the policies we now pursue, with less loss of life on both sides. I am sure that it will cost fewer American lives. And those lives are my primary concern.

The policy I suggest will not result in a compromise at the peace table. And it will not reward the Communists for aggression. It will, instead, encourage our allies in all parts of the world. And it will decisively check communist expansion in Southeast Asia.

X. Military Superiority

WILL AMERICA'S next test be a major confrontation with our principal nuclear rival, the Soviet Union? Next time will we be able to stand up to her as we did in the 1962 Cuban missile crisis? Or will we look over our shoulders at our shrinking nuclear force, at our missing anti-ballistic missile system, and succumb to Kremlin demands?

If we cannot win a small war because of the fear we hold of nuclear conflict, how can we expect to face the always present, and very real possibility of a large war?

The deterrent philosophy we now pursue has drained away our red military blood. The deterrent philosophy will not permit us to threaten war when our vital interests are in peril. And it has progressively weakened our capability for waging nuclear war. A mad dog retaliatory second strike is not a flexible or usable strategy. Its only purpose is hopefully to deter nuclear war. It could not, for example, keep the Soviet Union from West Berlin or from the Mediterranean or from direct or indirect aggression anywhere in the world.

Why are we bogged down in such a cruel and apparently endless war in Vietnam? Why does the President not instruct the Joint Chiefs of Staff to go in and win using whatever strategy and weapons can best to do the job? If we enjoyed a true general war superiority, deterrence of any Soviet or Communist Chinese intervention would be assured.

However, with our strategic limitations and the growing Soviet strength, is it any wonder that the President fears expanding the war in Vietnam?

What does the President know about Soviet weaponry that we do not? It is obvious that we have allowed our own military blades to dull. It would require no dramatic Soviet advance in weaponry to tip the balance definitely against us. Present well-known trends are running in the Kremlin favor. Even Secretary McNamara's posture statements reveal this. Have we already fallen to second place? Is that why the President refuses to act decisively in our heartbreaking struggle in Vietnam? Are we doomed to a face-saving negotiated withdrawal because we dare not risk a general war which we could not win?

If this is not so now, it will be soon. We must return to our strategy of nuclear superiority before it is too late. And time may have already run out. We cannot delay a single day.

Historically, behind diplomacy has always been the possibility of war. When negotiations break down in a serious conflict, war may be the next step. There are, however, new military thinkers who believe we can do without war. Since war is universally maligned as the ultimate human evil, these new defense thinkers have gained great popular acclaim. Those who venture to suggest that war may have a place in human affairs, whether or not we like it, are condemned out of hand. If we would only divorce ourselves from the emotionalism associated with war we could regard it in a colder and more logical light.

The new thinkers about war have succeeded in upsetting the traditional concept of national defense which is that a country, to survive, must be capable of defeating its enemies. These new thinkers tell us that through deterrence we can achieve a warless world—or at least a world without nuclear war.

What we must remember is that the innovators of the warless world scheme are experimenting with our very existence. If they are proved wrong *just once*, we are dead; individually, collectively, and nationally.

If we stretch a point and consider the kind of limited war we are fighting in Vietnam today as a sort of violent diplomacy rather than war itself—we refuse to declar war, employ our most potent weapons, or even attack the opponents' most vulnerable resources—the dangers of a wholly deterrent philosophy become apparent. Why is it, that with all our vast military potential, we cannot subdue little North Vietnam? Is it not simply because we fear that by using the force necessary to win, this war may escalate into the nuclear war we are not prepared to fight?

Why is it that we fear to move resolutely forward with confidence in our decisions? Why do we hesitate and publicly debate every new move? We speak of a nuclear umbrella beneath which it is possible to engage in limited wars, neither side daring to escalate to nuclear proportions. However, if this umbrella is an illusion because we are unprepared actually to engage in a nuclear war—to initiate such a war—then might not the other side enjoy a significant advantage in a limited conflict? Because we so fear the nuclear option we are constrained to engage the enemy on his own terms, to his own advantage.

A man-to-man confrontation in the jungle hardly seems an appropriate strategy for a great industrial nation such as ours. Technical advantages we have exercised—such as the carefully restricted bombing of North Vietnam—have been initiated by our President with extreme trepidation for fear of arousing the displeasure of Red China or the Soviet Union. In fact, the long debates over each next step, as in the decision to bomb petroleum supplies, have telegraphed our moves so well as to permit the enemy to take effective defensive measures. Stores of oil and gasoline in drums were cached throughout the country in sanctuary villages, for example, and hundreds of flak guns and SAMs were emplaced around POL targets. Surprise, a prime factor of successful warfare, has been sacrificed because of the apparent need to test Communist reaction before initiating the cautious escalating step. In other words, the nuclear umbrella is not permitting us to engage in a limited war to our advantage. The holes in the umbrella—the weaknesses of our nuclear capability and philosophy—make it necessary for us to be absolutely sure that we are taking no nuclear risks before applying greater pressure on the enemy. It is indeed possible to lose a limited war when fought in this hesitant, equivocal, and unmilitary fashion. And it appears that we are well on the way to losing this one by pursuing these illogical policies.

Great as would be the catastrophe of losing the war in Vietnam at the vain cost of over seventeen thousand American lives and billions of dollars in national treasure, the consequences of irrevocably losing our strategic military superiority would be vastly greater. We would undoubtedly lose confidence, prestige, and allies by losing in Vietnam. But an unquestioned loss of our nuclear war superiority would most certainly end America as a nation, if not our lives as well. For once the Soviet Union or even Communist China became thoroughly convinced that we would not begin a nuclear war, that we had no defense against a nuclear attack, and that our so-called deterrent nuclear retaliatory force could be knocked out, our days would surely be numbered.

As we have seen, our nuclear capability has dwindled over

the past several years. The prophets of "overkill" have convinced our national leaders that we need only enough nuclear
power to survive a first strike and retaliate with such force as
to destroy the attacking country—presumably Russia. This will
effectively deter the first strike, goes the argument, and hence
nuclear war will never occur. But will it provide the umbrella
under which we might successfully engage in limited wars? As
the vivid and painful evidence of Vietnam or Korea reveals, a
nuclear deterrent philosophy, being wholly defensive in nature,
does not provide an adequate umbrella.

The far-out doctrines of the arms controllers have set the
pattern for current American strategic thought and national
policy. The *jeremiads* of the arms controllers concerning the
pollution of the atmosphere with fallout and the end of mankind in a nuclear holocaust have become household beliefs
since few people have the technical knowledge to question
them. The hot-eyed evangelical defense intellectuals in the
Johnson Administration are out to save mankind at the expense
of America, if necessary. The leaders are as dogmatic and inflexible in their beliefs as the fire-and-brimstone preachers of
the nineteenth century. To make their points they cynically
twist the facts of national defense to jibe with their elastic
doctrine of stable deterrence through parity and disarmament.
The fact that Soviet Russia will not accept their topsy-turvy
doctrines of weakness to achieve security does not disturb them
because they can achieve their ends by holding down the production of United States armaments until the Soviet Union has
caught up.

It has been the practice of arms controllers in the Johnson
Administration to stigmatize solid military experience and even
uniformed military leaders in order to gain credence for the
strange philosophy of weakness. This has excited the civilian-
military struggle which is an ancient bogey of little substance.
Nevertheless, hotly debated bombing policies in North Viet-

nam, for example, are more often decided on the "civilian control of the military" bias than upon their intrinsic merits. Mr. McNamara has been a master at this game.

It has been said that Mr. McNamara controlled American military thought like a mahout rides an elephant—with a jabbing warning here of millions of civilian casualties and a stab there with billions of dollars in industrial contracts. This is topped by a brilliant ability to roll off convincing statistics. But what should concern us most is what does he and the present Administration believe? What is their philosophy of national defense? Are they, for example, arms controllers who wish to achieve some sort of nuclear parity with the Russians?

To judge whether the Office of the Secretary of Defense, and the Administration as a whole, are arms controllers requires a study of their individual statements and actions. Secretary McNamara's frequent speeches "quantifying" our nuclear superiority in missiles and bombers is apt to throw one off the track. But as we have seen, increasing defense budgets do not necessarily reflect increasing capability for major war. By holding static our numbers of missiles while simultaneously letting our Strategic Air Command air fleet grow obsolete we are gradually losing our nuclear superiority. I pointed this out repeatedly when I was Chief of Staff of the Air Force, and on at least two occasions in testimony before the Senate Preparedness Subcommittee. This was refuted publicly by Mr. McNamara.

At his Ann Arbor speech on June 16, 1962, McNamara announced his endorsement of the counterforce doctrine which is in opposition to the parity concept. Counterforce, of course, conceives of a major nuclear war waged against purely military objectives such as opposing missile launching sites. For a short time I thought we had convinced Mr. McNamara, but I soon learned how wrong we were. To be successful, such a counterforce strategy requires a clear nuclear superiority because it takes more than one missile to destroy another one. A missile is a pinpoint target usually buried in a concrete silo, unlike cities, which cover a wide area. In a war, counterforce associated with parity would lead to no resolution whatever and very little deterrence. However, even after the Ann Arbor speech the Secretary's decisions still followed the parity principle.

In his *Saturday Evening Post* article of December 1, 1962, Stewart Alsop praised McNamara for "discovering" counterforce. Counterforce had been an Air Force doctrine for years before this and our SAC forces had been so disposed. In fact, before McNamara's Ann Arbor announcement, several thoreticians in OSD had been arguing rather strongly for the concept of parity. What could have caused the Secretary of Defense suddenly to accept the military view for counterforce with its necessary nuclear superiority?

The answer to this possibly can be found in the dialogue at that time with Charles de Gaulle over the efficacy of his small nuclear *force de frappe*. The United States had always discouraged an independent French nuclear force. One argument against it had been that a small nuclear force would be of little value, that only a large force such as ours was worthwhile. McNamara said that ". . . limited nuclear capabilities, operating independently, are dangerous, expensive, prone to obsolescence, and lacking in credibility as a deterrent. . . ." Since the parity argument calls for a small nuclear force, our own parity moves would hardly help our dialogue with de Gaulle. Moreover, the aim to reduce nuclear proliferation came sooner on the arms controllers' timetable than the aim of parity. For these reasons one might have suspected that Mr. McNamara's counterforce statement was a tactical maneuver to be changed later. This proved to be so.

Another reason for suspecting this was that so many other McNamara acts and statements were in accord with the arms control philosophy. The denouement of his strategic thinking appeared in the Steward Alsop interview noted above. McNamara was asked if the Soviets might not achieve a "sure second strike capability" similar to our hardened Minuteman, and the surprising part was that his answer boiled down to "the sooner the better."

This indicated that McNamara had no real faith in counterforce, which would be more effective if the Soviets failed to harden their missile sites but rather left them soft and more easily destroyed. Most revealing, however, is that this thought is the same one expressed by those arms controllers who espouse the parity concept.

In his syndicated column of January 13, 1963, Gen. Ira C. Eaker commented on Mr. Alsop's article. General Eaker suggested that to assist Russia in becoming as strong as we are—a condition McNamara indicated he would be happy to see in the intercontinental ballistic missile field—two courses of action were open to us. "One, under lend lease, to give the Russians Minuteman and Polaris missiles. The other was to reduce our own armaments by progressive stages until we have military parity with the Russians. It now appears, according to this reasoning, that our leaders in the Pentagon have determined to adopt the latter course."

McNamara surrounded himself with arms controllers. One was his immediate deputy, Roswell L. Gilpatric, who resigned while highly regarded by the Johnson Administration early in 1964. The model second strike military posture leading to nuclear parity was described by former Deputy Secretary of Defense Gilpatric in the April, 1964 issue of *Foreign Affairs*. He noted that we are ". . . approaching the point at which further increases in strategic delivery vehicles promise little meaningful military advantage," and proposed a military posture with "all manned bombers retired from active deployment," the phase-out of all manned interceptors and "all other bomber defense." Finally he stated, "There would be no production . . . of anti-ballistic missile systems." Since this article appeared so soon after Gilpatric's retirement, it is inconceivable that the thesis was at variance with McNamara's views.

Several key OSD staff members contributed in some measure to the famous 1960 Summer Study on Arms Control which Jerome Wiesner and Victor Weisskopff promoted. This study drew the battle lines for the arms control movement and established the inner circle. Among those involved was Harold Brown, the Secretary of the Air Force. Prior to that, he had held the powerful position of Director of Defense Research and Engineering, a position so high in the hierarchy that his deputy was an Assistant Secretary of Defense. Brown had assisted Arthur T. Hadley in producing a layman's version of the Summer Study experience *The Nation's Safety and Arms Control.*

A long time boss of the powerful OSD office of International Security Affairs (ISA), was Assistant Secretary of Defense John T. McNaughton, who was killed in an aircraft accident shortly after being appointed Secretary of the Navy in 1967. Secretary McNaughton was perhaps the most unabashed and dynamic arms controller in the Pentagon. He began his meteoric rise in OSD by accepting the post of Deputy Assistant Secretary of Defense for Arms Control in 1961 and performing admirably through assisting William C. Foster's new Arms Control and Disarmament Agency (ACDA). Mr. Foster attended one of McNaughton's several promotion ceremonies and praised McNaughton highly for his services to arms control.

Another key arms controller in the Pentagon is Paul Henry

Nitze, who, as Deputy Secretary of Defense, was the heir apparent to Secretary McNamara. Mr. Nitze, a Harvard graduate and former New York attorney, also came to military prominence through the arms controller ranks. Although serving in 1949 as director of the Department of State's policy planning staff, he later became associated with the men who developed the arms control philosophy. One of his most controversial speeches was given at Asilomar, California, on April 29, 1960, where he described the doctrine of security through weakness, which would allegedly halt the arms race. His plan was to reduce United States nuclear strength so as to enable the Soviets to pass us in the arms race. He argued that only "purely retaliatory" weapons were necessary, and he "hoped" that the Soviets would follow our example.

From a theoretician on arms control Mr. Nitze graduated to the administrative and management end of national defense when he was appointed Assistant Secretary of Defense for International Security Affairs in 1961. From this post he moved up to Secretary of the Navy and thence to his present powerful number two position in the civilian defense hierarchy.

The present Assistant Secretary of Defense for International Security Affairs, Paul C. Warnke, revealed his sentiments for arms control in a speech in Detroit on October 6, 1967. He mentioned the possibility of talks with the Russians to limit strategic offensive and defensive forces and added that should such talks occur "we may have to depend on our own unilateral capability for verification." In other words, he is ready to disarm without insisting on any mutual inspection whatsoever.

Some of the fundamental aims of arms control appeal to everyone. The desire to reduce the huge expenditure for armed forces and armaments is universal. Measures to reduce the risk of war or its destructive nature are crucial matters to all. Military men are no less concerned about this than are civilians.

But this must be done at no risk to our national security. Differences arise not so much with the ends but with the means to reach these ends and in the evaluation of the means in terms of national security.

It is interesting to note that very few historians, political scientists, or military men have been attracted to the new philosophy. One would think that those experienced in history, government, and warfare would have the greatest competence in this area of study. But with a few exceptions experts in the natural sciences such as Drs. Jerome B. Wiesner and Herbert F. York have taken over even though their training seems less fitting for the subject. What is behind this phenomenon? Why have physical scientists taken up arms control with such consummate zeal?

Some scientists have suggested that there is a guilt complex at work. The physical scientists unleashed the horrible genie of nuclear energy and now they feel morally responsible for putting the genie back in the bottle. *The Bulletin of the Atomic Scientists* has beat this drum for almost two decades. Activists, initially led by Dr. J. Robert Oppenheimer—also a Summer Study contributor—set out to change the national ethos by making nuclear war so horrible to contemplate that national defense with nuclear weapons would be considered immoral and unthinkable. Oppenheimer expressed the motivation of the scientists when he said, "the physicists have known sin, . . . and this is a knowledge they cannot lose."

This anti-nuclear movement is a highly charged, emotional "cause" which has attracted many other groups. The peace organizations have joined with vim. Yet so have many able and well-intentioned politicians, diplomats, and businessmen. Almost every walk of life is represented. These are all people with a crusading zeal to do away with nuclear weapons and save the world from nuclear war.

Of course, communists and fellow travelers find this movement fitting well with their aim for weakening America. When
testifying at the hearings for the Arms Control and Disarmament Agency (ACDA) bill in 1961, former Secretary of Defense Robert A. Lovett warned that ACDA might become a
haven for Reds and crackpots. Fortunately, I do not think this
has happened. ACDA allegedly pursues arms control and disarmament with the purpose of not reducing United States
national security. Yet the questions remain: which agency of
Government and which authorities provide the most qualified
advice about what constitutes adequate national security? And
how can we rectify the basic conflicts between defense and
disarmament? As Gen. Thomas S. Power puts it, "How can
we dress and undress at the same time?"

It is my firm belief that the arms control doctrine is unilaterally affecting almost every feature of our military posture, from
strategy to weapons. This influence, one of the most pervasive
of all the forces of the arms control doctrine, can help us find
reasons for many of the puzzling military decisions which have
been made by the Johnson Administration.

Most arms controllers believe that the risk of war can be reduced by making our forces, as they put it, "non-provocative." They conceive of this as a unilateral enterprise. As we
have seen, such a military establishment would be made up of
forces which can survive a first strike and react slowly and
deliberately. Hardened missiles and positive command and
control arrangements stem from this doctrine. Arms controllers
want to deny nuclear weapons to Nth countries, fearing that
proliferation will increase the chances of war. Thus, no
MRBMs have been built for deployment in NATO countries
while France has been denied our assistance in developing her
nuclear weapons capability. Of course, the new school of strategic thought considers bombers to be vulnerable weapons,

only good for first strikes, and thus extremely provocative and destabilizing.

A stable world environment is implicitly considered to be the ultimate national objective. Is this always our objective? During the Cuban missile crisis we went to great lengths to *de*stabilize the climate. Certainly we are destabilizing the climate in Vietnam.

Some arms controllers seem to want nuclear war to be as horrible as possible, for then, they reason, war will never occur. Thus we should target cities and avoid civil defense, even for ourselves. They have fought against ABM developments and the extension of the so-called arms race into space. The resulting strategic posture is sometimes referred to as the "balance of terror," an apt phrase indeed.

It may be hard for the ordinary citizen to understand how we can pursue a strategy which will make general war not only more dangerous but also one which places the United States in a position where it will be almost impossible to win. I might say parenthetically that the average military man is equally perplexed by this inverted strategy. The arms controllers assert that this posture of terror supposedly will better deter general war. Since there is no historical evidence to support this assertion, and an abundance of recent historical evidence to refute it—twenty years without a general war while we maintained massive nuclear superiority—we rest our national security on the intuition of this new breed of military intellectual. Mr. McNamara is the high priest of this cult. Considering how unusually error-prone have been his judgments over the years, I am appalled as to why Americans sit still for them.

If we unilaterally pursued these arms control avenues while the Soviets continued to arm without restraint of any kind, to develop an ABM system, civil defense, and quick strike capabilities with Minuteman-type weapons as McNamara would have it, our power position will become so weakened as to make agreement with Soviet objectives our only means of survival. I do not suggest that this is an arms control aim, but many arms controllers would prefer surrender to general war. Without the leavening of professional military judgment applied to arms control measures, there is real danger of unwittingly falling into a second-rate military posture, which would leave no recourse other than to accept Soviet proposals, such as a disarmament treaty without adequate inspection provisions. Then we would disarm while they would claim to be disarming. We need only recall the uninspected test ban moratorium of 1958–1961 to see what might happen if we were caught in such a trap. The Soviet Union cynically entered into this agreement with no intention whatever of abiding by it. While we innocently disbanded our testing organization they diligently planned a great testing exercise.

Arms controllers naturally want to reduce nuclear delivery weapons as a first step in disarmament. They leveled their sights on B-47s and B-52s because these armaments were considered provocative and destabilizing. They bitterly opposed the B-70 and RS-70 programs. The cancellation of Skybolt perfectly fit the new philosophy by reducing the useful life of our bombers. The Nike Zeus cancellation which slowed the development of anti-missile weapons, and Dyna Soar cancellation, which might have given us a military capability in space, also reflected the new philosophy. Many arms controllers would like to see nuclear parity with the Soviets involving perhaps a top limit of 500 or less nuclear missiles on each side as a "stable deterrent" step in "General and Complete Disarmament." This, they feel, would effectively cancel out the use of nuclear weapons altogether. All war could then be fought conventionally, they predict.

These strategists have overlooked the fact that even a conventional war cannot be won without air superiority. Has the nuclear bomb or warhead taken on such overwhelming significance in their thinking as to blot out other military considerations? They conceive of nuclear weapons to be the greatest evil in the world, and this thought seems to becloud all judgment, knowledge, and sometimes even loyalties.

Strangely, many believe that the United States is as apt to cause nuclear war as the Soviet Union. This might happen through "accident, miscalculation, or madness," and thus arms controllers recommend measures to deter our own ability to employ nuclear weapons. These measures are positive command and control arrangements sometimes referred to as "permissive action links," which will prevent the arming or launching of nuclear weapons without direct Presidential command.

The possibility of war being caused by military accident is harped on so much that the public may soon come to regard the military itself as a potential enemy. Can there truly be any other reason for such emphasis on positive controls and permissive action links over weapons than distrust of or at least lack of confidence in the military who handle these weapons? In pre-nuclear days, military forces were capable of starting war with gunpowder and TNT weapons, but this fear was rarely expressed. What has occurred to cause us now to question the integrity and loyalty of our military commanders?

The accidental war concept was popularly launched by the novel *Red Alert* by Peter Bryand, a horror story describing a war started by a crazed SAC commander. It became required reading for many arms controllers. Soon after the story was published in 1958, it was ordered that tactical pilots would be medically examined for possible mental abnormalities. The connection seems obvious.

Fail-Safe by Burdick and Wheeler was a later thriller of similar plot. This impossible yarn related how a condenser blew in communications equipment, causing a bomber force to fly past its fail-safe point and attack Moscow. Such a ridiculously inaccurate story, deliberately twisting the whole concept of fail-safe which simply meant that if any part of the system failed the system was safe, was passed off by the authors as an authentic possibility, even a probability. Said the authors, "it represents a competent estimate of the technical and scientific factors involved in the 'fail-safe' system." As to the chances of its happening, Burdick said, "I believe it to be inevitable. . . . We interviewed scores of physicists and scientists with the AEC, the Rand Corporation, and the Government. Almost all of them gave us the classical response: 'Of *course* war by accident not only could happen . . . *it* probably *will*.' "

It may be interesting to note that military opinion on this assumed probability was not sought.

What are the military alternatives to these arms control doctrines?

First of all, the military refuses to accept some of the basic premises, the principal one being that continued improvement of our military posture, referred to pejoratively as the "arms race," will lead to less security. This simply flies in the face of common sense.

Second, the military endorses mutual disarmament only with a thorough system of inspection and verification to ascertain that agreements are truly honored. The unilateral planned obsolescence approach to parity, with no agreements or inspection, is an invitation to Soviet aggression.

Third, the military believes that it can be trusted with nuclear weapons, that it can exercise prudence and follow orders, but that it must be permitted to use its own judgment when all contact is lost with higher authority. Otherwise we ask for a nuclear Pearl Harbor.

Fourth, the military contends that deterrence will only be

credible with a quantitative and qualitative superiority of the forces which are necessary to win a general war; that is, nuclear forces. Parity, even if arrived at through agreement and verified by inspection would provide tenuous security at best.

Fifth, if nuclear war presents such a horrible picture of destruction, it is high time that we develop our defenses to lessen this danger. The thin ABM defense is a start. A nuclear warhead penetrating the atmosphere from space is highly vulnerable and anti-missile missiles have real promise as a protective force. Civil defense and shelters can provide still more protection. Who knows what science will develop if we continue to search for positive, physical means to curb the atom? If our scientists approach this problem from the direction of their trained expertise, rather than from the political and military directions where they have questionable capabilities, a true solution might be discovered.

The arms control movement is gaining new converts daily and has sometimes taken on the fervor of a religion. To question certain features of it means that one is branded out of hand as blind, unreasoning, stupid, and possibly evil, with little regard for civilization or humanity. Yet unless an arms control doctrine is tempered with the practical, political, and military understanding of historians, politicians, diplomats, and military men, there is grave danger of our demise. Too many Americans today seem to be obsessed with the idea of saving humanity while neglecting to save themselves. Let us be sure that we save our own segment of humanity first.

The impression has been subtly fostered by the Johnson Administration, and particularly by Secretary of Defense McNamara, that the policy of deterrence is, in fact, a policy of military superiority. During the Presidential campaign of 1964, McNamara gave a television briefing to the public which left just such an impression, while numerous strategically timed news releases added to the picture. America was told that since January, 1961 (the month when the Democrats replaced the Republicans) the number of alert weapons had increased 150 per cent, while the number of megatons on alert had increased 200 per cent. This was in August during the heat of the Presidential campaign. Earlier, in April, an OSD release claimed that nuclear warheads in the strategic alert forces had increased 100 per cent while the number of combat-ready infantry divisions had increased 45 per cent.

This sounded very reassuring and since absolute numbers were not used—and remained classified—Republican campaigners had no effective way to refute the statistics. Of course, this left the general impression, as have subsequent press releases from the Pentagon, that United States strategic forces were steadily growing stronger and certainly retaining their superiority over comparable Soviet forces.

Although the percentages released by OSD were undoubtedly accurate, they were nonetheless misleading. Unquestionably we were growing stronger in the ICBM department. Our planned deployment of a thousand Minuteman ICBMs—I had recommended seventeen hundred—was moving ahead and since we had started from scratch, the percentage figures showing our increase since January, 1961 (when we had but a few relatively crude Atlas and Titan missiles) looked very good indeed.

Similarly, our Polaris submarine fleet was growing. Of course, OSD did not state that these two excellent programs, Minuteman and Polaris, had been started by President Eisenhower.

However, the sleight of hand became evident to the sophisticated observer when the percentage increase of bombers on the alert was announced. Actually, our strategic bomber fleet was dwindling. We were rapidly phasing out the B-47 six-jet medium bomber fleet at the time. How, then, could an increase of weapons on the alert be possible?

A bomber (or missile) on alert is one that meets the arbitrary definition of the term "alert." Usually "alert" means that a certain percentage of our strategic bombers are ready for immediate takeoff, with crews in nearby ready rooms. The concept of maintaining an alert force was one which I had encouraged in order to guard against the chance of being attacked by surprise as we had been at Pearl Harbor. An air force is vulnerable on the ground but relatively safe in the air. In the event of trouble, I wanted at least a certain portion of our bombers ready for immediate launch. This was the alert force.

We started this kind of force deployment with just a few bombers on alert but as we learned more about it—and the Russians kept building and improving their own strategic forces—we added more alert bombers until by 1964 the SAC kept about 50 per cent of its force on the alert pad with crews nearby. These alert craft could become airborne in less than fifteen minutes.

Now in a crisis situation, or even in the event of some intelligence anomaly which would lend suspicion of increased Soviet military activity, we would begin putting more and more of our bombers on alert, increasing the percentage. Normally, we would have over 80 per cent of our fleet ready to fly, although not in combat configuration. By loading bombs and readying them in other ways for combat, and by bringing crews together near the airplanes, we would be prepared to launch most of our aircraft on a moment's notice. Thus they would be put on an alert status.

A high state of alert, however, would tie up the force so much that training would have to stop. After a very few days crews would have to be relieved from the alert pad. Even as much as twenty-four hours in a ready room while wearing flying suits is enough to cause considerable fatigue. Therefore, too large a percentage of aircraft on alert would, in the long run, be counterproductive from the standpoint of crew effectiveness and training.

Thus we see that the number of weapons on alert can fluctuate markedly, depending upon arbitrary orders or strategic conditions. It is not a fixed measure of strength at all, but a rubber yardstick which can be stretched to fit almost any measure desired.

The measure of "alert" is flexible in still another dimension. It is flexible with respect to definition, and there are many definitions.

There are usually various stages of alert. Defensive fighter squadrons, for example, might have a small number of aircraft on five minute alert, a larger number on ten minute alert, and a still larger number on one hour alert. So when speaking of aircraft on alert, as Mr. McNamara frequently has done, it is meaningless unless the particular alert definition is included. The casual reader or television viewer seldom thinks of asking the question, "What do you mean by 'alert'?"

There can be no question that at the same time Mr. McNamara was boasting of an increased number of bombers on alert, our total bomber force was actually lessening. And no provisions were being made to replace the old bombers we were sending to the scrap heap. Yet the impression was left with the public that our total force was growing in strength because OSD referred to bombers "on alert" rather than simply to bombers *in the inventory*. This would have shown a far different picture.

At the time of this sanguine statement by McNamara in 1964, to show how misleading such statements can be, I made

TABLE I
Percentage of Strategic Weapons on Alert

AIRCRAFT

Weapon	1960	alert	1964	alert	1974	alert
B-47s	1200	25%	400	50%	0	
B-52s	370	"	630	"	0	
B-58s	30	"	70	"	60	50%
FB-111	0	"	0	"	210	"
Strategic Aircraft Total	1600	(400)	1100	(550)	270	(135)

MISSILES

	1960	alert	1964	alert	1974	alert
MINUTEMAN	0		600	90%**	1000	90%
ATLAS	5	90%	100	"	0	
TITAN	0		100	"	0	
POLARIS	2	(2)***	256	(16)	656	(41)
Total Missiles	7	(6)	1056	(736)	1656	(941)

MEGATONS (in thousands)

	1960	alert	1964	alert	1974	alert
B-47s (15M ea)*	18	25%	6	50%	0	
B-52s (24M ea)*	8.9	"	15	"	0	
B-58s (15M ea)*	.4	"	1	"	1	50%
FB-111 15M ea)*	0		0		3.1	"
Megatonnage Deliverable by Aircraft	27.3	(7)	22	(11)	4.1	(2.1)
MINUTEMAN (1M ea)*			.6	90%	1	90%
ATLAS (3M ea)*			.3	"	0	
TITAN (9M ea)*			1.0	"	0	
POLARIS (1M ea)*			.2	(.016)	.7	(.041)
Megatonnage Deliverable by Missiles			2.1	(1.7)	1.7	(.9)

TOTAL WARHEADS (Aircraft and Missiles)

Actual	1607	2156	1926	
On Alert	406	1286	1076	

TOTAL MEGATONS (in thousands)

Actual	27.3	24.1	5.8
On Alert	7.0	12.7	3.0

* from unofficial public sources.
** 90% missile alert estimated.
*** only one missile on each POLARIS submarine is considered on alert; entire inventory is "on station."

a little table, which I shall present here. At that time the FB-111 (the bomber version of the General Dynamics swing-wing F-111 or TFX) had not been considered as a part of our strategic inventory. As you can see from the table, the addition of the 210 FB-111s would not materially affect my own statistical conclusion—that our strategic force is rapidly decreasing.

From the table it is evident that McNamara may have understated his case. There was actually a greater increase in the number of strategic weapons (or warheads) on alert. The increase was 300 per cent (406 to 1286). This increase came from the growing inventory of missiles as well as the increase in the alert status from 25 to 50 per cent of the bomber force. The total megatons of nuclear yield available in those alert weapons had increased from 7,000 to 12,700 or about 70 per cent. What was wrong with this? Weren't we growing stronger? Where, then was the catch?

Under the weapons policies then in effect, our *actual* capability to deliver destructive power upon the enemy had decreased from 27,300 megatons in 1960 to 24,100 in 1964. And under the policies then in effect, would have dropped to 2700 megatons by 1974. Even by adding the 210 FB-111s, which McNamara announced in early 1966 would be included in the strategic bomber inventory, the drastic reduction in our strategic strength would not be checked. The 210 fighter bombers would raise the 1974 total to only 5800 megatons as opposed to the 27,300 megatons we could deliver in 1960.

I am well aware of the statement made by the Secretary of Defense that the measure of strategic effectiveness is not megatons, but deliverability. In other words, an accurate one-megaton bomb, with adequate penetrating aids to get through enemy defenses and hit its target is a far better weapon than a ten- or twenty-megaton warhead which misses. To this I agree. But how do we get such accuracy and penetrability in a warhead?

We build into it the sophisticated gadgetry necessary to navigate to the target and to confuse or evade enemy defenses en route. This gadgetry musts displace a portion of the actual nuclear warhead itself. In other words, there is a weight trade-off. With a lower yield warhead we can carry more penetration aids. Payload will always remain constant with each kind of vehicle, be it a B-52 or a Minuteman II. And the megatons I have listed in Table I are for warheads *without* penetration aids. Therefore, they reflect the total payload of the weapons to which they are mated.

A portion of the payload can be converted to navigating gear or to penetration aids, but the nuclear yield will have to be correspondingly decreased.

An airplane or a missile can lift just so much weight. It can be configured to carry bombs or cargo, or some of each, but its gross payload will remain the same for a fixed range. So when I speak of megaton yield in the strategic vehicles listed in Table I, I am using an index which is almost directly related to payload. And this payload capability will, in fact, determine how much extra equipment a missile may carry to help it penetrate an ABM defense. The best index for measuring both destructive power and deliverability, then, is payload. And the policies of OSD are causing our strategic weapon payload—or megaton yield since the warheads we considered carried no penetration aids—to decrease from 27,300 megatons in 1960 to 24,100 megatons in 1964 to 5800 megatons by 1974. A *decrease* of over 500 per cent between 1960 and 1974.

This is a frightening degradation of our strategic forces and a condition which has been hidden from the American public by the legerdemain of statistics. OSD has played a con-man's shell game with us by managing to make a dwindling strategic nuclear force look stronger.

Let us work this shell game for a moment to further illustrate the point. If we decide to keep 50 per cent of 500 bombers on alert, we count 250 bombers. Then we compare this 250 with the number of bombers we maintained on the alert some years ago when we kept only 25 per cent so disposed. Even though we had 800 bombers then, we only had 200 on alert. Thus with a dwindling force we show an increase of alert forces. It has puzzled me why the American public will swallow this. It is an insult to everyone's intelligence.

In time of international tension the alert status of bombers can be increased to 80, 90, or even 100 per cent. Yet this index hardly reveals the true strength of our forces. An honest assessment of our strength can only be gained by counting the *actual number* of our strategic delivery vehicles and by considering the payload of each.

Counting alert forces is even a better trick in the missile field because there is no sure way of telling when a missile is truly on the alert and ready for firing. The only live missile ever fired by the United States was a Polaris, which missed its target. So Mr. McNamara conveniently considers that an unusually high percentage of our missiles are always on the alert, and as we increase this force it appears to outstrip the numbers of aircraft we are junking and wearing out. This again leaves the American public looking for the pea under the wrong shell.

As recently as July, 1966, OSD again resorted to this con game. It continues to be an effective argument to "prove" that our strategic strength is growing. The recitation of percentages of increases in various features of national defense is reminiscent of the story of three men, two of whom were teetotalers and one of whom was an alcoholic. Thus each teetotaler was 33 per cent an alcoholic and the alcoholic was 67 per cent a teetotaler. Use of percentages is meaningless and deceptive unless references are given. It can be a blatant exercise in demagoguery.

Let us look at another example: When former Assistant Secretary of Defense for Public Affairs Arthur Sylvester claimed a "200 per cent increase in number and total megatonnage of nuclear weapons in strategic alert forces in 1966," he failed to identify either "nuclear weapons" or "strategic alert forces." Actually he was equating one missile with one strategic bomber. A missile is a single shot. A bomber is a repeater weapon. A missile carries one warhead; a bomber carries several and of much greater explosive yield. A bomber can be reloaded and used again and again. Missiles are not the equal of bombers, and the two should not be added together any more than apples and oranges.

Secretary McNamara was letting our fleet of 650 B-52 strategic bombers wear out without appropriate replacements. We need ICBM missiles, but we need bombers too. We are in pretty good shape today, but like Louis XIV of France, Mr. McNamara has laid the groundwork for tomorrow's deluge when we shall have no true strategic bombers whatever.

At least let us not forget that strategic alert weapons are weapons as changeable as a definition or an order. These can be changed as often as one wishes to change the criteria. Since all missiles are in silos and not going anywhere, most of them are considered to be on strategic alert, cocked, and ready to fire. In 1961 when most of our strategic weapons were bombers, a small percentage of our total force was on continuous strategic alert. We had most of the bombers flying and being used to train crews. But in times of crisis, these bombers in training could be brought up to a strategic alert posture in short order. So the percentage of megatonnage on strategic alert is a highly variable figure and reference to it is just one more snow job.

A release on December 29, 1965, by Representative Craig

Hosmer of California revealed the machinations that went into the McNamara figures with respect to Army divisions:

He claimed to have increased by 45 per cent the number of "combat ready" Army divisions. The claim conveys the impression of an Army increase of nearly one-half, i.e., a boost of from 14 pre-McNamara divisions to 20 or 21 divisions, and a manpower increase of almost 400,000 over the Army's previous 900,000 level. In actuality, at the time of the claim he had added only 63,273 men—a 7 per cent boost. The arithmetic on division numbers is even more revealing. Under Eisenhower 3 of the Army's 14 divisions were considered "in training." McNamara subtracted these from the 14 to get 11 divisions against which to calculate his percentage of increase. He then produced 3 new "combat ready" divisions by the simple expedient of issuing the "in training" divisions additional equipment and relabeling them "combat ready." The two more divisions need to get 16 to reach the "magic 45 per cent increase" came out of thin air. They simply were created by reshuffling manpower from existing divisions to newly created ones and classifying them "combat ready," too. The final easy step was to divide 11 into 5 to produce the magic 45 per cent.

America's strength has been blown up unrealistically by OSD in other ways that hide the true state of our military posture. This deception is combined with a deliberate failure to mention known enemy strength. It serves no purpose, for example, to explain that we have increased such and such a weapon by so much per cent if we neglect to mention how many items we *and* the enemy had at the base point, and by what percentage *he* increased *his* supply. The game of war is not played like solitaire. We must ever consider our opponent; otherwise we have no sound method of analysis.

For some inexplicable reason OSD tries to sweep under the rug Russia's 750-plus nuclear-tipped intermediate and medium range ballistic missiles that are deployed against Europe. Perhaps this deployment draws attention to the fact that the West has no adequate countering force. Perhaps it is because of the secrecy surrounding our removal of comparable missiles from England, Italy, and Turkey after the Cuban missile crisis of 1962. This precipitous action smacked of a deal between Chairman Khrushchev and President Kennedy, the Soviet *quid* for the American *quo* being the removal of similar nuclear missiles from Cuba. If so, we definitely came out on the short end of the bargain in a confrontation which has been hailed as a great American diplomatic victory. Only the revelations of history will clear this up.

In any event, the U.S.S.R. looks down the throat of Europe with a great force of intermediate range nuclear rockets which are relatively invulnerable. A great number of them are mobile and very difficult to keep track of and to target. Our fleet of Polaris submarines in the North Atlantic would be far outgunned in any counterforce duel. With half our forty-one underseas ships on station, each with sixteen Polaris missiles, we can count on only 336 available missiles while somewhat less than this number would be in an alert condition for firing.

Another strength of Soviet Russia that is consistently swept under the rug is its thousand-plus Badgers. These medium range jet bombers are considered obsolete, and in any event incapable of two-way missions to the United States. Yet they can carry hydrogen bombs and can easily fly to North American targets on one-way missions. Why should they attempt to return since they can land in Cuba? Additionally, many Badgers have the capability of refueling in the air. They are indeed formidable intercontinental bombers and should be clearly recognized as such, but they are not.

A sober analysis of Soviet Union versus United States strategic bomber strength reveals that we have permitted the Soviet Union to overtake our lead. Obfuscation of the stark facts by

OSD has kept the American public in ignorance of the dangerous depletion of our relative strength.

However, comparing numbers of United States bombers with numbers of Soviet bombers makes little strategic sense. Bombers do not fight bombers. The missions of our bombers are not the same as the missions of theirs. We may, and I would hope, send our bombers to destroy their bomber bases and missile sites in a defensive counterforce attack. They may, with their much larger warheads, send their bombers directly against our cities. With this sort of an exchange we would need many more bombers than they would. Cities are easy to hit. It takes more than two weapons to destroy one weapon, however, since accuracy is something less than perfect and multiple strikes are necessary to be assured of a hit on a small target.

Even if both American and Russian strategic forces should target the other's cities, we would need a considerably larger force to achieve any sort of strategic parity. This is so because Russia is larger than the United States and Soviet cities are much more widely dispersed than ours. To achieve the same ratio of city damage we would require a larger strategic bomber force. Therefore, when we speak of parity in strategic weaponry we are actually talking about a factual strategic inferiority in this class of weapon.

We have scrapped all of our six-jet B-47s, while the Soviets have retained their similar aircraft, the Badger. In the last week of December, 1965, the Secretary of Defense announced a cutback of 425 B-52s and B-58s. Shortly thereafter Mr. McNamara announced the substitution of 210 FB-111s—the bomber version of the TFX bomber which the Secretary rammed down the throat of the Air Force and Navy. The uninformed public may be mollified by this entirely inadequate substitute, but it is unlikely that the Soviet Union will be impressed.

Less than three months after announcing the B-52 cutbacks,

Mr. McNamara was again reassuring the nation of our strength by quoting the increases of megatonnage in strategic alert forces. In a statement released on March 2, 1966, he said:

And, at the same time we were increasing our non-nuclear forces, we also increased our nuclear forces. For example, *the number of nuclear warheads in our strategic alert forces will have been inceased from 836 in June, 1961, to about 2600 in June, 1966,* and the total megatonnage of these weapons more than tripled. Moreover, by June 30, 1966 we will have doubled the number of tactical nuclear warheads on the soil of Western Europe, and large numbers of tactical nuclear weapons are available for use in other areas of the world, if required.

Of course, warheads are not deliverable weapons. It is as deceptive to count warheads as to count rounds of ammunition in an ordnance warehouse. Unless you have a gun to shoot the rounds they are worthless. And as we have seen, the strategic alert force is a variable and arbitrary figure which can be manipulated at will to make a favorable statistic.

As for the "tactical nuclear warheads on the soil of Europe," it was pointed out by Representative Craig Hosmer, Chairman of the Committee on Nuclear Affairs, in a release of December 29, 1965, that Mr. McNamara had redeployed tactical nuclear weapons in Europe away from points where they can be used immediately against surprise invaders. This is in line with the positive control and "permissive action link" philosophy of the Administration which would make it virtually impossible for Allied commanders to respond rapidly to a Soviet attack in Europe.

The tactical nuclear warheads in Europe may be as valueless as the ammunition locked up in the Wheeler Field warehouse during the attack on Pearl Harbor. Fighter pilots who were out of ammunition could not get into the warehouse until the action was over.

It is interesting to note that Mr. McNamara used a megatonnage criterion in 1966, and yet when a year later the American Security Council released a study indicating the rapid decline of American megatonnage superiority, McNamara was quick to point out that megatonnage of nuclear power was not an adequate measure. It appears that he chooses those criteria which suit his purposes and condemns those criteria which contradict those purposes even when the criteria in both cases are identical. In other words, when the megatonnage measurement is used to support an OSD policy it is a good measure. When it refutes OSD policy it is a poor measure—according to Mr. McNamara.

Assessing the relative strengths of two great nations like the United States and the Soviet Union is an extremely complicated exercise even when all the facts are known. It is impossible when we are teased and confused with irrelevant statistics.

It is unfair to ask the reader to take anyone on faith. He should be advised of the philosophical beginnings of any rationale dealing with so important a subject as national survival. I have touched on the new evangelism of arms controllers who self-rightously have set out to mold the world in their own untested and impractical image. It is only fair that I attempt to describe what intrinsic beliefs underpin my own philosophy.

To begin with, I consider myself to be practical. I pretty much accept the world as it is with all its diversities, *when no harm is being done to my country*. And I wish to make my country as strong as necessary in the event any enemies should appear on the horizon. Since 1947 the enemy of communism has loomed there and it continues to grow. Anyone who opens his eyes can see this. On December 11, 1967, the Secretary General of NATO, Manilio Brosio, warned that Russia is rapidly building up her military power with the biggest budget on record.

I am devoutly attached to the Constitution of the United

States, to which I have given my sacred oath, and I believe implicitly in the human precepts of freedom with order which stand behind that Constitution.

As to my views on military strategy I might turn to a little volume which has recently been published by a Naval thinker as a springboard to my own beliefs.

In his short volume, *Military Strategy*, Rear Adm. J. C. Wylie has examined the subject of strategy in its broadest context—a general theory of power control. His criticism of most strategic doctrines is that they are specialized and parochial, and he analyzes four such schools of thought: 1. the continental theory of the Army, 2. the maritime theory of the Navy, 3. the air theory of the Air Force, and 4. the Mao theory of guerrilla warfare. Admiral Wylie argues that each one of these theories is applicable under certain conditions and objectives, but that none constitutes a general theory which might be applied to any set of circumstances. He notes with a good deal of perception that other mental disciplines such as those of political theory, economics, and sociology are held together with general theories, theories which are the synthesis of extensive and profound study. Unfortunately, no general theory of military strategy exists and there seems to be little interest in constructing one.

Admiral Wylie does not presume to present a general theory of strategy. However, he does advance some precepts or axioms upon which a general theory might be based. These axioms seem unassailable.

The first such axiom is that, "despite whatever effort there may be to prevent it, there may be war." In other words, there is no need for a general theory of strategy if one begins with the assumption that war is no longer possible. One cannot study the chemical structure of water by first postulating that there is no such thing as water. Yet many present-day strategists are

doing just that: postulating the "unthinkableness" of war and
devising ways to deter it without having the capability of
fighting it.

So, reasonable as Admiral Wylie's first axiom seems, it is
nonetheless being challenged by the more influential policy-
makers of our government. War, they assert—meaning nuclear
war in particular—will be too harmful to friend and foe alike.
Because of this it will resolve few political issues and will introduce so many new and inscrutable social problems that mankind itself may perish. Therefore these thinkers start with the
basic premise that nuclear war must be deterred or avoided at
all cost.

Certainly this objective is feasible, if not practical. If deterrence fails, surrender, not war, is the next logical step. To be
more palatable, surrender might be exercised incrementally
through small concessions and appeasements. This strategy
would be understandable to a clever aggressor who no doubt
has heard of the Vegetius' doctrine in one guise or another:
build a golden bridge for the escape of your enemy. In Oriental doctrine: let him save face.

I, for one, must subscribe to Wylie's first axiom: war is
possible, at whatever level of intensity. The history of man can
lead us to no other conclusion.

One cannot study either history, anthropology, or zoology
without coming to the inescapable conclusion that warfare is
somehow endemic to life. Call it by other names if you wish:
call it the struggle against a hostile environment, survival of
the fittest, social conflict, political turmoil, revolution, or even
some kinds of business competition. Whatever it is, it is the
other side of the coin to human cooperation, affection, trust,
and friendship. It is hate, malice, doubt, fear, and hurt. All are
real human emotions however undesirable. It seems to me that

we cannot have one side of the coin without the other. The "heads" of peace are an integral part of the "tails" of war.

This is, I know, a hard way to view life. To conceive of man as always having to fight runs contrary to much religious, and even communist, doctrine, which promises an ultimate world of love, peace, and cooperation. Yet we never seem to reach nirvana. Heaven on earth gets little nearer if at all. There has been not the slightest indication that the coin might not come up tails with war at any time in the future just as it has in the past.

As a practical man, therefore, I must accept the proposition that warfare at whatever intensity is a distinct possibility. This does not mean that I approve of it any more than I approve of cancer or murder. It does not mean that I am callous to the pain and tragedy of war. In fact, I think I have a keener appreciation of this than most people—and particularly most of today's military strategists, few of whom have suffered actual warfare. It simply means that I reluctantly accept a fact of life on this earth. And by accepting this fact, I believe I am in a far better position to cope with it than those ostrich-like people who refuse to see the obvious.

The second axiom advanced by Admiral Wylie is another I subscribe to: "The aim of war is some measure of control over the enemy." This, I feel, is a good general way of regarding the aim of all conflict. There is a whole continuum of control to which an enemy might be subjected, starting from some very limited political objectives such as a negotiated agreement to honor a certain border or territorial jurisdiction, up through unconditional surrender and physical annihilation. However, no matter how war is fought, whether offensive or defensive, whether sublimited, limited, or general, the end purpose of either side is to assert its authority over the other in some way.

Here we may get into a discussion of Clausewitz' much-quoted reference to war as a continuation of political policy. War is that, of course, but what Clausewitz failed to appreciate was the hyperbolic nature of war: war itself tends to create new policies which frequently swallow the older policies of the peaceful environment. The reason for this is that wars place people, individually and collectively, at an intenser emotional level. From the intense levels of violent hates, loves, and desires come entirely new goals which may incite further fighting. Then, when the fighting stops, some of these goals, such as unconditional surrender, seem to lose their significance because we drop to a less dramatic and intense emotional plane of existence.

The hyperbolic nature of war is a relatively new concept and requires much more study. War itself changes politics and national interests. It is not just a continuation of peaceful aims.

Even so, the second Wylie axiom is sound. The purpose of war, or of all conflicts, is somehow to control the enemy. If we lose sight of this—or of the specific controls we seek—we may pervert war into a senseless and revengeful slaughter.

The third axiom presented by Admiral Wylie is particularly apropos today: we cannot predict with certainty the pattern of the war for which we prepare ourselves. This axiom can again be defended by historical example, yet it is flouted every day in the Pentagon with the "cost-effectiveness" philosophy. This analytical school of thought starts with the premise that we can predict with great accuracy what our military ends are today and what they will be in the future. Then, we can analytically devise the weapon systems which will most effectively achieve those ends. This approach is pleasing to those minds which are set in logical processes to achieve clearly defined goals. Yet experience has taught practical leaders that both goals and processes change. To cast our military forces today in a fixed mold designed to fight a certain kind of imaginary war with preconceived goals—however logically derived—is the purest military folly.

Let me cite an example of this. Before World War II we thought bombers had become so far advanced over fighters in speed at high altitude that fighter escorts would not be necessary. Had we eliminated fighter development by absolutely subscribing to this "cost-effectiveness" doctrine we might well have lost the air war over Europe in 1944 by pushing ahead with unescorted bomber raids. Instead, we saw our error in time and put superior long-range fighters into production which eventually escorted B-17s and B-24s to the limit of their range. These fighters were an expensive ace-in-the-hole which we had not discarded for the sake of economy. With these escorts Germany's air defense force was defeated and the air war won.

Our strategy, as well as our military forces to back the strategy, must contain a high degree of flexibility. We must have room to maneuver; to correct mistaken assumptions; to conform to changing political objectives. Cost-effectiveness can be a steel trap, leaving us incapable of responding to a threat from an unexpected quarter. Cost-effectiveness is a case-hardened, rigid doctrine as dangerous as that which put all of the hopes of France in the armored knight who became helplessly bogged down and encumbered against the English longbowmen at Crécy and Agincourt. It is as dangerous as the absolute doctrine of defense which built the Chinese Wall and the Maginot Line, both of which were breached by troops fighting under a more flexible doctrine.

It is the ultimate of arrogance, if not of stupidity, to believe so implicitly in one's capability for predicting the future. True, we must try to look ahead, for who could plan anything without an effort at prophecy? But such plans must have built into them repeated escape routes and alternatives, because almost never is a combat plan executed exactly as it was originally conceived.

I fall short of complete agreement with the fourth and final axiom presented by Admiral Wylie. Perhaps he is making a concession to the principal axiom of the "continental warfare" theorists or perhaps he is being somewhat allegorical. In any event, his fourth position is that "the ultimate determinant in war is the man on the scene with a gun." He goes on to say that this final control means the exercise of direct force over the enemy country, which is, he says, the soldier.

Now one must admit that control of some degree, at least, can be exercised without reference to the soldier in any way. When Admiral Peary opened up Japan for trade he was exercising a degree of control without a man on the scene with a gun. The situation was similar when Japan sought to surrender in 1945. Under the circumstances control could have been exercised, although not as completely, by civilian administrators alone. Eventually this was all that was needed in any event. It is handy to have an army or police force, of course, to enforce the desired degree of control, but it is not always absolutely necessary. One must only retain the necessary force or threat of force which will bend the enemy's will to resist the controls we seek. This force may be a naval blockade, a gunboat in a river, a visible tactical air force, or credible offensive missiles. As long as the enemy is adequately impressed by this force he can be controlled without troops on the ground.

I am not a Clausewitz or a Mahan, but no one who had been charged by his government with commanding or overseeing military forces vital to the defense of the nation could do his job rationally without believing in certain principles, stated or not. The executive orders coming from the President, the statutes from Congress, the directives from the Secretary of Defense and JCS may originate from a variety of motives:

political, financial, psychological, or national defense. Since such guidance has even been known to be conflicting, the responsible man at the receiving end must often interpret what is meant. Also, the commander or staff officer is simply not a sponge to sop up guidance from his superiors. He must make countless independent judgments on his own initiative. He must also recommend to his superiors changes of policy, strategy, force structures, and equipment as the situation warrants.

In other words, the military leader must have a system of values and principles regarding the conduct of his job. And he must constantly be weighing every aspect of his manifold tasks against these values and principles. These are much more complex and comprehensive than the so-called "principles of war," which are taught at every American command and staff school in one way or another. These, like any other "principles," are subject to wide interpretation depending upon the circumstances, but they have been derived through centuries of military experience and interpretation, and are applicable to almost any form of human conflict or human interchange where the objective is to gain some sort of influence, advantage, or dominance over another. I refer to the "principles of war" in moments of decision and interpretations. The concepts of the offensive, surprise, concentration, economy of force, security, unity of command, etc., are my second nature. Not that I ever utilized them automatically or dogmatically, but they have provided me with mental check-lists to examine new ideas and plans.

At the national defense level, however, the principles of war are not enough. A commander must have more comprehensive beliefs on how his nation is to survive. I have long been convinced, for example, that simple, factual military superiority in weapons, equipment, numbers, doctrine plans, and training are fundamental to the deterrence of war and certainly to survival if war should occur. This practical and straightforward concept which has validity in the depths of history has now been challenged with the concept of "deterrence through assured destruction" which has been discussed at length in earlier chapters. Implicit in this concept is that if deterrence fails, all is lost anyway; therefore our force need not be designed to fight or initiate a war, but simply to deter one.

Let me attempt to reduce to written principle some of the values which I have used with confidence and some success throughout my military career. The superiority principle, of course, is related to many others. Only actual warfare will reveal whether features of our posture that we assume to be superior to like enemy features are in fact superior. Thus a commander must rely on experience and judgment to a large extent. Cost-effectiveness is of little value in this mental exercise. In fact, the results of such judgments produce the criteria with which cost-effectiveness is assessed. My complaint against the practice of cost-effectiveness is not with its technique as a tool of analysis but with the judgments that are made by amateurs to introduce governing criteria and assumptions—the "garbage in, garbage out" principle.

Associated with the concept of superiority is the philosophy of how a war should be fought in order to achieve our objectives. The principle of the offensive, for example, if believed, will determine what weapons are ordered and what strategies are devised to achieve superiority. I have long been a devoted believer in taking the offensive—in war or any other human conflict. I realize, however, that war can be concluded with a less direct strategy. A defensive posture, if a strong one, can cause the enemy to wear himself out and bleed to death. But a defensive strategy takes longer, it is more costly in both lives and treasure, and it does not seem to be compatible with the dynamics of American life.

The principle of the military offensive has been a basic American military doctrine since Gen. George Washington assumed command of the Colonial troops at Boston Commons on July 3, 1775. The Colonies were defenders, true, against an invading army. But whenever Washington could muster enough regiments to attack, he did so. Again and again he was defeated, but he managed to keep the Redcoats off balance and sometimes achieve signal victories as at Saratoga (with the brilliance of Daniel Morgan) and at Trenton and Princeton where the shock of the offensive combined with surprise reversed the effect of his inferior numbers.

Gen. Henry Halleck, the Civil War general wrote, "Offensive war is ordinarily most advantageous in its moral and political influence. It is waged on a foreign soil and therefore spares the country of the attacking force; it augments its own resources at the same time it diminishes those of the enemy; it adds to the moral courage of its own army, while it disheartens its opponents." General Halleck admitted some disadvantages, however, such as extended lines of communications, the overcoming of natural geographical barriers, and the pacification of the indigenous population.

The offensive doctrine gives the power of initiative to the attacker. He can plan and carry out his campaign with precision. The defender is never sure which way to turn until it may be too late. His reaction is fraught with indecision, quick fixes, and vacillation. In the confusion of improvisation he is usually defeated.

Now I speak here of *military* doctrine, not of national policy. Although there is a real difference in outlook, these two can be compatible despite the seeming contradiction. How can a country be peaceful, defensive in nature, unwarlike, friendly to its neighbors, laissez-faire in trade and politics, and yet have an offensive military doctrine? Is not this illogical? I submit that with *the declaration of war doctrine* it is not.

American legal doctrine, and for that matter Anglo-Saxon jurisprudence, starts with a basic trust of people—and thus, of countries. Until proved otherwise by their actions and speech, our neighbors are considered good and honorable. This is a basic assumption fundamental to our way of life. A man is innocent until proved guilty. Therefore we do not try to impose our will on friendly nations and we assume they will treat us the same way.

However, although Americans start with an attitude that all countries are inherently good, we are practical enough to understand that any of these countries may change and may covet what belongs to us. When overt acts of war are taken against us, we "declare war." *Then* and only then comes the time when we switch from the passive, defensive, diplomatic role to the dynamic, offensive military role. *Then*, we make a complete reversal of our attitude toward the neighbor who has threatened us. *Then* we become determined to conquer and to win.

At least that is the way America used to do it. The new strategic thinkers and defense intellectuals have changed all that. It is truly amazing to me that centuries of successful military doctrine can be overturned by an unproved philosophical movement. This campaign carried on both by pacifists and sincere scientists to denigrate the offensive military doctrine has had a success the likes of which Madison Avenue advertising could never duplicate.

Let me get back to my ideas on military values. I believe that we should return to the "declaration of war" principle and present an open hand to all countries with whom we are at peace. If they threaten us to the degree that we feel we must take up arms against them, then we should declare war and go all-out to defeat them as soon as possible. This is the most humane way in the long run. To drag on an equivocal war with fuzzy aims and hesitant military operations is cruel to the enemy as well as to our own suffering servicemen and their families.

And there are other advantages to be gained by declaring war. For one thing we would have a better legal leg to stand on in insisting that American prisoners be treated according to the rules of the Geneva Convention. It is true that the Convention for the Protection of War Victims, which was hammered out by sixty nations in 1949, applied to any kind of war, declared or not; *but* Ho Chi Minh who acceded to the treaty in 1957 entered a reservation. This reservation declared that "prisoners of war prosecuted and convicted for war crimes or for crimes against humanity in accordance with the principles laid down at the Nuremberg Court of Justice (Sins of our fathers!) shall not benefit from the present convention as specified in Article 85."

I do not pretend to be an international lawyer, but it looks to me as if we do not have a legal leg to stand on. Our boys in North Vietnam prisons are being tortured and humiliated with horrible indignities. So in not following the rules of war available to us, war becomes increasingly barbaric.

Mr. McNamara says: "To declare war would . . . increase the danger of misunderstanding of our true (limited) objectives in the conflict by the various Communist states, and increase the chances of their expanded involvement in it. . . ." This statement reflects the whole equivocal nature of our policy. We are afraid to win. Afraid of the reaction of Red China and Soviet Russia. And in noting that the Geneva Convention applies to undeclared wars, McNamara conveniently omitted the caveats placed on the protocol when it was adhered to by the Communist countries and by Ho Chi Minh. In the absence of a legal state of war, Ho can and has mistreated American prisoners as pirates and criminals.

Let me now propose some basic doctrines about war. These doctrines, which I have always found to be valid, have guided my thinking ever since I became a professional student of warfare.

First, war in any proportion, no matter how limited, is a very serious and dangerous business. War is *never* "cost-effective" in terms of dollars and blood. People are killed. To them the war is total. You cannot tell bereaved wives, children, and parents that today's war in Vietnam, for example, is a counter-insurgency exercise into which the United States is putting only a limited effort. Death is final, and drafted boys should not be asked to make this ultimate sacrifice unless the Government is behind them 100 per cent. If we pull our punches how can we explain it to their loved ones? Our objectives must be clearly enough defined to warrant the casualties we are taking.

The total number of Americans killed since 1961 in Vietnam exceeds the total of 4435 killed during the Revolutionary War when our objectives were much clearer. Our losses so far in Vietnam exceed those of the War of 1812, the Mexican War, and the Spanish-American War combined. Are we paying this price simply to help a friendly country stop outside aggression or are we actually fighting expanding communism? It might help if this were made more specific.

General Eisenhower has declared that "the war should have first priority over everything else. When we get to the stage that we are losing American lives, then we need to view the war as a far more serious problem than going to the moon, or any domestic welfare programs, or anything else."

Second, since even small wars are cruel, we must fight them in such a way as to win them *as quickly as possible*. Graduated response may be a good doctrine for diplomacy, but not for war. Once we decided to employ large forces in 1965 we should have jumped with both feet before the enemy could prepare his defenses. Sharp, swift air blows of maximum strength in 1965 could have ended the war in days.

If the political objective is to bring our enemy to the conference table, then his arm should be twisted enough for him to yell "uncle," and the sooner the better. He can fight indefinitely if we twist just below the threshold of his ultimate endurance. Meanwhile he can hustle up alliances and solidify them to his relatively safe side for what Mao Tse-tung termed the "protracted conflict."

In the meantime we store up doubts as to the worthiness of our cause and the effectiveness of our tactics. It is a losing game for the stronger side to drag out a conflict deliberately. I thought we learned this lesson in Korea where we sacrificed some thirty-three thousand Americans for a bogus peace. Military history makes this point abundantly clear. Frederick the Great's victory in the war of the Bavarian Succession is one classic example. His enemies, far more powerful than he, dawdled and eventually fell out with each other, permitting Frederick to win the war at the conference table. Another example may be found in our own American Revolution. Six long years of equivocal war were more than Britain could stand, since the war was not popular in the first place. It is strange that many modern strategists seem to ignore some of the applicable lessons of military history.

My third basic precept about warfare is never to point a gun at someone unless you are prepared to kill him. A bluff in warfare should never be attempted unless one fully intends to back it up, if need be. If you do not disarm your enemy he will most certainly kill you. And the odds are too great against you if that bluff fails. As Stonewall Jackson put it, "When war comes you must draw the sword and throw away the scabbard."

I do not subscribe to the neo-Clausewitzian doctrine so prevalent today that war should be made as violent as possible, because then, it is argued, it will not be waged at all. Here again history should teach us that the violence of warfare has never seemed to deter it. In the face of Tamerlane's near total violence, his enemies still chose to defend themselves. On the other hand, an immaculate war which attempts to limit casualties at the expense of swift attack against the most telling military objectives has proved equally infeasible. This fictional doctrine of immaculate war helped the British lose Suez in 1956. The Israelis demonstrated in 1967 that the closest war can come to being benign or merciful is when it is fought swiftly and effectively.

To a certain extent we are practicing immaculate war in Vietnam by limiting bombing in North Vietnam to protect civilians. Strangely, we seem less concerned about the lives of civilians in South Vietnam villages. I believe that necessary violence should not be rejected simply because it is violent. Instead we should warn civilians to evacuate target areas and take whatever reasonable means are indicated to bring the war to a rapid conclusion in our favor.

My fourth doctrine is that we should never engage in a small war *unless we are prepared to fight and win a large war*. This is fundamental. The popular philosophy that we can, by cautious and timid tactics, keep the war from escalating into a larger conflict is the ultimate in military blindness. The only way to win a war is to escalate it one way or another above what the enemy can endure. If we feel that we cannot win without unacceptable risk we have no business fighting in the first place.

There are just two checks on escalation. One is the waning

of motivation for fighting the war in the first place. A long grinding war of attrition on the ground might achieve this. An appeal for terms would follow with eventual surrender. But I doubt if our enemies in Asia will ever take such a surrender route as long as we make it possible for them to resist. Let us not forget the teeming millions they can commit to such a land war. The Viet Cong and the North Vietnamese are fully indoctrinated to carry on the struggle. And they have suffered so much already that they burn with hatred for us.

The second check on escalation is to so overwhelm your enemy with such heavy and rapid destruction that he loses all hope of winning. Then surrender is an attractive choice when compared with inevitable defeat or certain death. This, of course, is the way we brought Japan to terms in 1945. *It was unnecessary to invade with infantry and fight a ground war.* We seem to have forgotten this fact. Even though Japan had four million troops under arms with two million guarding her shores, not a shot was fired. We invaded with fourteen hundred military administrators, by air. Not a life was lost in this invasion.

The Japanese had been highly motivated to wage war against us. Kamikaze tactics and no-surrender policies were typical. Yet a realization that Japan simply could not win and the certainty that continued resistance meant mounting devastation caused her to toss in the sponge. Former Premier Kantaro Suzuki of Japan said that ". . . on the basis of the B-29s alone I was convinced that Japan should sue for peace." We had pointed the gun and we intended to shoot to kill. In the final analysis hundreds of thousands of lives were saved and dozens of cities spared, which might have been leveled by infantry, artillery, and tactical bombing after a land invasion.

It is sometimes more humane and moral to perform drastic surgery in order to save a victim from cancer. The same reasoning can often apply to the waging of war. In Korea where we also pulled our Sunday punch, there were three and a half million military casualties on both sides during three years of drawn-out war. Over a million civilians were killed and other millions left homeless in this protracted *land* struggle. I cannot believe that this is the most humane way to fight a war.

I submit that it is politically immoral to use less force than is necessary to achieve a military objective when adequate force is available. It is immoral because more of our young men are killed or wounded or submitted to a cruel captivity than would have been necessary if *more* than enough force were used. Also, in a protracted struggle our total losses are greatly increased over the losses sustained in a quick, decisive war.

In any event, we should not indulge in hot counterinsurgency campaigns which can escalate into general war proportions unless we are fully prepared and capable of waging that general war. Otherwise, we should stand aside and trust to cold war measures alone. Thus, whenever we commit our young men to mortal combat we should be equally prepared to commit our leaders, our cities, our families, and *civilians*—our own or the enemy's. Modern war is *that* serious and we should not forget it. In the words of ex-President Harry Truman, "If you can't stand the heat, get out of the kitchen." Senators J. William Fulbright and Wayne Morse say the kitchen is too hot now. The Administration fears to let the kitchen get much hotter in order to win. I tend to believe that more heat in the kitchen is our only reasonable course of action.

To those who accept these four doctrines for waging war, the course we should take in Vietnam becomes clear. First, war in any proportion is dangerous and should not be undertaken lightly or haphazardly. We should be most cautious before committing ourselves even to a seemingly mild counterinsurgency conflict, and it should not be forgotten that our political leaders were warned by the professional military men against a land war in Asia. When we are fully involved in a hot war, however, we have no choice but to go through with it. Backing out would be a great defeat for the cause of freedom to say nothing of American prestige and honor. We have, after all, pledged our support again and again. We should never pretend that this is a business-as-usual sideshow.

Second, once we have taken the fateful step into war we should wage the war in such a way as to end it as quickly as possible. This means, as I have often recommended, that we should use naval and air power against the most valuable targets. As early as the African campaign in World War II we found it impractical to stop the flow of supplies by interdiction of roads and rails alone. We had to move back on the enemy lines of communication and attack supply depots, marshaling yards, fuel storage, and even factories. This we called strategic bombing. This tested air power doctrine has been disregarded by the present leadership. If "history is a lantern," the lantern has gone out. The thumbscrews will need much tightening before "uncle" is called in North Vietnam. Strategic bombing does *not* mean the bombing of populations, but rather of important industrial, transportation, and agricultural objectives.

Third, we must not try to fight a benign war against an enemy who utilizes terror as a basic tactic. If we take up arms against an enemy we should hit him hard without equivocation or vacillation. This means that we should destroy his economy and his will to wage war. Again, let me say as I have often said, this does not mean mass slaughter.

Fourth, we must be prepared to risk and fight a large war if necessary. With respect to Vietnam, we must not let ourselves be subdued by Red China's threats and blusters. If we are not prepared to escalate, that is, apply more power, then we are not prepared to win and we should get out.

Now let me suggest some principles of national defense which are related to the doctrines of war that I have just enumerated.

Rich as America is, we obviously do not have unlimited resources and military planners must decide on certain trade-offs. There is always an either-or decision when considering important military hardware, force levels, or deployments. Do we invest our resources in quality or quantity? Do we go into production today or improve the product and produce it next year? Do we "harden" weapons in concrete and steel or do we make them light and mobile (both approaches are intended to make it difficult for the enemy to destroy the weapons)? Do we sacrifice fire power for mobility or vice-versa? How much fire power must we sacrifice in order to permit a more likely penetration of enemy defenses with decoys, deceptive devices, and hardening of the warhead? Should we devote six weeks, six months, or a year to training our men, or should we commit them to active operations with less training because we need to deploy the uniformed manpower in defense of national objectives? Such trade-offs are always present in any military planning. How well they are made will determine the outcome of either deterrence or combat.

Of course there is no hard and fast yardstick to measure what to do. And decisions of this sort must represent a compromise between a number of objectives. As I have noted, I lean toward the doctrine of the offensive although I fully admit that we must take many defensive measures. I also lean toward the doctrine of mobility versus "hardening" for the same reason. Because a mobile force is elusive, it is thus more secure than a well-known fortification. It can also employ much more flexibility in attack.

I lean toward quality as opposed to quantity. In the air, one superior fighter can dominate a whole squadron of inferior airplanes. On the ground the same principle applies with better guns, better training, or better strategy and tactics. I am not one who boasts that one American can take on a dozen foreigners just because he is American. We have no corner on courage or personal strength. But we can achieve a superiority man-for-man with better weapons, better tactics, and better training. This is what I mean by the principle of quality over quantity.

There is one overriding prinicple which has a major bearing on my military thinking and I might call this *the principle of the most serious threat*. The most serious threat to our country is one that might come by surprise, instantly, and which could destroy our whole social structure. It is a threat that could not only destroy our government and way of life, but a large portion of our population and its wherewithal for simple existence.

Lesser threats might be those which threaten our treaty commitments, our trade relations, portions of our sovereign territory such as Alaska or Puerto Rico, or limited warfare and its attendant costs.

It would stand to reason that when assessing the possible threats to the United States we should be most concerned with the most serious threat—that threat which could utterly destroy our society.

Yet we have not shown this common-sense concern. In fact, we have recently invested greater resources, attention, and energies into guarding against the limited-war threat rather than the general-war threat.

Since we have been told as a nation by our leaders that general nuclear war is simply unthinkable, we have written it off as a remote possibility. The only kind of warfare that our leaders will seriously consider is non-nuclear limited warfare.

This is as irresponsible as playing Russian roulette with the life of our country. We have no assurance, nor will we ever have, that other countries will regard general nuclear warfare as unthinkable.

Let me recapitulate for a moment to review these principles of national defense.

Every responsible military leader must have a system of military values with which to temper his judgment. These can begin with the widely taught principles of war, but other doctrines are necessary when dealing with national defense problems. One such doctrine is that of military superiority. This used to be axiomatic but now it is being subjected to such questioning that our actual superiority has been permitted to wither.

Of course, military superiority is itself subject to a great deal of judgment. How do we determine what superiority really means? We must first judge how a war is likely to be fought and, more important, how we can win that war. Then we can make valid judgments on superiority itself.

In this connection, I lean toward certain doctrines of warfare because my experience and study have taught me their validity. One such doctrine is that of the offensive. Victory far more often smiles on the side that attacks.

My partiality to the offensive leads me into other preferences, such as that of mobility over hardening, quality over quantity, and thorough training of personnel in techniques and tactics. This system of values causes me to believe strongly in research and development in order to stay ahead of enemy technical developments. It also causes me to advocate well-drilled and well-armed forces being ready to defend or attack on a moment's notice.

How do I reconcile an offensive military doctrine with our peaceful, defense-oriented national policy? Again I say that there is no conflict here if we revert to our "declaration of war" policy of earlier years. We are everyone's friend until our national interests are seriously threatened. Then we throw down the gauntlet to our challenger and swiftly switch gears to offensive military attack with a clear objective to conquer and subdue our enemy.

When the issue is joined there are five fighting doctrines I would suggest.

First, take the war seriously. No business-as-usual attitude is worthy of a country willing to expend the lives of drafted young men.

Second, fight to win as quickly as possible.

Third, be as rough as necessary in order to win. Immaculate war is an impractical dream.

Fourth, be prepared to escalate to a general war. If not, stay out of limited war.

A final overriding principle is that we must devote our major resources and attention to the most serious threat. To do otherwise is to gamble with our national and social existence.

These principles for national defense do not begin to encompass all of the value judgments I have made in a lifetime of military practice and study. But they illustrate the point that military judgment must have a matrix of values upon which to rest and that these interlocking values are tremendously significant in sound military decisions. For this reason it is not likely that any superficial study will lead to successful solutions of our major military problems.

We are told repeatedly by the political leaders of the country and by the civilian authorities of national defense that we cannot move deliberately and decisively against North Vietnam with an air campaign because it would risk bringing China into the war. The memory is vivid of China's surprise advance across the Yalu River in 1951 which threw General Mac-

Arthur's forces back in defeat from North Korea. We were caught by surprise then, not dreaming that China would risk a direct air attack, possibly nuclear, to assist her North Korean allies. *Deterrence did not work in this instance.* Somehow Red China was assured that we would not bomb its supply points north of the Yalu nor that we would use nuclear weapons.

If China was assured in 1951 that we would not retaliate against her massive invasion of North Korea except at the point of advance, she has no such assurance today. If she has we would be repeating the errors of history. Following the Panmunjon truce, Secretary of State John Foster Dulles announced in no uncertain terms that should hostilities be resumed, the fifteen allied nations would not feel constrained to limit the war to the Korean peninsula. In fact, the Chinese agreed to a truce only after President Eisenhower assured them that he was preparing to use atomic weapons against them.

Of course, Administrations and policies have changed in the years since that announcement was made, but there seems to be little reason to suspect that, should China again push south in Korea, we would feel obliged to provide her with a sanctuary north of the Yalu as before. By the same token, it seems highly unlikely that we would confine our efforts to South Vietnam should the Red Chinese come actively to the support of North Vietnam.

I must admit that the not infrequent no-win statements and anti-nuclear policies expressed by people of influence and authority in America might encourage Red China to risk another invasion against our forces. However, perhaps she has learned the paradox of democratic America: our statements and actions can be widely divergent. Just as we apparently deceived China in 1950 by defending South Korea after our then Secretary of State Dean Acheson had placed Korea outside of our "defensive perimeter," so we might react more violently than we now suggest should China move south into Vietnam.

Certainly statements that we have no intention of using nuclear weapons in Vietnam harm our cause and prolong the war. In our effort to show the world how pure at heart we are, how benign our motives, how noble our aims, we give the enemy encouragement to fight on. And we may even invite more Chinese assistance.

I am absolutely opposed to steps that would get us directly involved in a land war in Asia with our own ground forces. The measures we have now taken, resulting in the deployment of our half a million troops, are not to my liking. Our present involvement in Vietnam could be resolved by air and sea action alone—and so, in fact, could a war against Red China.

In devising a winning air-sea strategy against North Vietnam, we must of course take into account the possibility of a Chinese military intervention as in Korea. Although the JCS consider this unlikely—the situation is not comparable to Korea either politically or geographically—to ignore such a possibility no matter how remote would be foolhardy. What, then, are the chances of Red China's intervention? And should China intervene, what are her chances of success? To assess this requires an analysis of Red China's situation, which is no mean task when the Red Guard turmoil of the moment is considered.

I do not presume to be an expert on China, but I have read many of the more objective studies made of that country, its people, and its armed forces. For years I have studied quite detailed intelligence reports on China. And I have traveled and served extensively in the Far East. It is only natural that I have drawn certain conclusions about a possible war with Red China.

Despite Red China's remarkable achievement in developing nuclear weapons, China remains a sprawling, backward, weak country. To overreact to her newfound nuclear capability would be a serious error in judgment. China is involved in a vast domestic insurrection—possibly a revolution. Civic confusion is rampant and the backward, ill-equipped armed forces are divided in loyalty. A country of over seven hundred million people, perpetually on the border of starvation and tragedy, is now compounding her almost insoluble natural handicaps with others of her own making. The Mao Tse-tung cultural revolution set in motion in 1965 has torn the country asunder with one traumatic experience after another.

It is truly amazing that a culture so fraught with internal chaos and economic failure could still produce nuclear weapons. It can only mean that a small scientific and industrial segment of China's massive population is isolated and relatively immunized from the vast political madness, and that both factions of the struggle support this isolation. How long such an anachronistic truce can survive is a matter for conjecture. My guess is that it will be some time before China develops very effective delivery weapons—missiles or bombers. To do this will require a larger and more integrated industrial community than was required simply to build warheads and test missiles. This industrializing, which is the *sine qua non* of modern military forces, has always eluded China and nothing in the present scene leads me to believe that industrialization is underway or even possible in the near future. However, because we said the same things about Russia after she exploded her first nuclear weapon, Red China will bear careful watching.

Red China cannot expect much help from the outside world. She is in conflict with several peripheral states and has fallen out bitterly with her former Communist ally, Russia, even to the point of open hostilities across mutual borders in the west. While she still shares a certain ideological link which might draw Russia to her side in the event of a war with us, the chances of this happening appear less and less likely. On top

of these breaches, Red China has declared ideological war
against almost all the rest of the world. This has adversely
affected her trade and development. It is indeed a wonder of
the age that Red China, with so much going against her, has
not collapsed into even more political chaos than she has today.
This is the hope, of course, of Chiang Kai-shek on Taiwan.

The current cultural revolution was set in motion by Mao to
regain his dominant position in the governmental hierarchy
and to return the people to the hard-nosed Stalinist brand of
communism, shorn of worldly ambitions and devoted to the
ascetic doctrine of world revolution. His opponents, whom he
called "revisionists," reputedly believe that communism and
China might be better advanced through adopting more of the
Western practices in order to industrialize and modernize their
society. They consider Russia's success in industrialization and
her foreign policy doctrine of peaceful coexistence worthy of
emulation. Mao factions assert that Russia's new policies are a
backward step from the pure communist doctrine.

We should not underestimate the seriousness of this rift by
saying that both countries are Communist and therefore inevitable allies. Brothers who fall out can be the most bitter
enemies, as can factions professing the same ideology but who
have split ideological hairs. Let us not forget that the terrible
Thirty Years' War was fought among Christians over doctrinal
precepts that the average man hardly understood. Nor let us
forget that one of our own bitterest wars, the Civil War, was
fought among ourselves over an ideological issue. It is conceivable that two Communist states, such as Russia and China,
could become even more bitter enemies than two states of obviously different outlooks.

Mao Tse-tung is over seventy-four years old. The madness
he has turned loose, with young Red Guards marching hither
and yon across China to correct moral backsliders, may well

have been set in motion by a senile man who is himself quite mad. Mao rarely appears in public today and what pictures we have of him do not reveal an alert, thoughtful leader. If this is true, and Mao has turned the corner, China might conceivably decide to fight us in Vietnam as she did in Korea. It would be madness, of course, but China herself is fraught with madness.

Of course, Mao is not completely in charge. There is great internal disorder in eleven of the twenty-eight Chinese provinces where Red Guards have run amok, and Red China is still largely ruled by anti-Mao factions. The people with common sense are resisting the Red Guard rabble, the school closings, the unrealism of Mao's doctrine. Reputable reports inform us that about four-fifths of China's municipal and provincial governments remain anti-Mao.

Mao's first target appears to be President Liu Shao-chi who has managed to retain his office against repeated insults and threats. Liu's power lies in the loyalty to him of large factions of the Chinese army, even though the Defense Minister, Lin Piao, is Mao's man and heir apparent. However, since Lin does not have complete control over the army, Mao is reluctant to try to remove his arch rival, Liu.

Not only is Red China's army, the Peoples Liberation Army (PLA), shot with divided loyalties, but its equipment is antiquated and poorly maintained, and its status of training and discipline leaves much to be desired. Dissension within the army has been motivated by a reasonable desire to improve its military effectiveness along Western lines. Although Mao is fundamentally a military man who believes that "political power comes out of the barrel of a gun," he resists any strategic thinking beyond that style of provincial guerrilla warfare which he used to conquer China in 1949. As long as the Chinese army (and this includes all Red Chinese military forces) is so restricted in its doctrine and development, we have little to fear from them—*unless* we stupidly decide to play their game and fight a guerrilla-style ground war.

Mao's position as Chairman of the Communist Party has been non-administrative for some years according to his own request. He took a back seat after his "great leap forward" resulted in such a fiasco. Attempting to make an industrial nation out of China with backyard furnaces and peasant-soldiers threw her into chaos in the late 1950s. Liu put China back on her feet. But because Mao sees Liu and others as departing from his "pure" doctrine, he seems determined to regain full authority. Many lesser leaders than Liu have felt the wrath of Mao, and have been relieved or have resigned or committed suicide. Liu, supported by much of the army and a large proportion of the people, is proving a tougher nut to crack.

Should Liu prevail, Red China's chances of becoming a greater military threat to us will improve. However, with the usual catastrophes of nature and the political turmoil caused by the Red Guard havoc, this will not happen soon.

Mao envisions the PLA as a great revolutionary school such as he organized in Sinkiang during the 1930s when he trained his initial cadres. This revolutionary military school should put public works like farming or running factories ahead of military training, say the Maoists. His opponents on the other hand want to build a professional army in the traditional sense.

There are 2.8 million men in the PLA. It is the third largest army in the world, standing behind only the United States and Russia. The PLA is primarily a ground force, although it boasts of 30 submarines and 833 ships (nothing deadlier than destroyers). The air force has 2300 aircraft, which are largely old and ineffective. A few Soviet MIG 21s (perhaps twenty-five) comprise its only modern equipment. Parts and fuel have been hard to get for training. Not only is pilot proficiency low but so is the general status of training at all levels. Some claim China is too weak to fight a major war, but led by a madman I am not so sure. In any event her transportation facilities are so poor that she would be hardpressed to support an army of over 100,000 in South Vietnam.

Amid all this backwardness, strife, and turmoil, how could Red China move ahead so fast in her nuclear weapon development? Until 1960 the U.S.S.R. gave Communist China active assistance in building her nuclear manufacturing complex. Their falling out caused a setback, but China continued the project. It is interesting, or frightening, to note that a great spur came through indirect help from the United States.

Several Chinese trained in nuclear physics and engineering by American universities and industries were attracted back to China in one way or another. One of these, for example, was Chien Hsueh-shen, a China-born son of a Shanghai businessman who came to America on a scholarship. He won graduate degrees in engineering from both the Massachusetts Institute of Technology and California Institute of Technology and then taught at both institutions. Later he was taken under the wing of Theodor von Karmen, one of our most brilliant engineers, and made privy to all nuclear secrets. He is reputed to have been the author of von Karmen's famous prophesy "New Horizons," which stressed science as the key to air supremacy.

When Chien decided to return to China after Mao's revolution, he was intercepted in Honolulu with eight trunkloads of books and papers and forced to stay in the United States. However, after five years Chien was allowed to travel home to China where he joined the Communist Party and became director of China's nuclear research program. He then gathered a team of scientists and engineers largely trained outside of China. The results of his brilliant efforts have now been added to the history of nuclear proliferation. I wonder if this event has made any impression on those scientists who complained so bitterly about the constraints of military security.

The thermonuclear test on June 17, 1967, at the Lop Nor

nuclear test site was the sixth Red Chinese nuclear explosion. Considering that the first such explosion was on October 16, 1964, this spectacular scientific and engineering achievement is nothing short of phenomenal. The June 17, 1967, device was probably in the megaton range and dropped from an aircraft. Since an earlier shot in 1966 was delivered by a 400-mile range missile, the capability of Red China to employ a small number of nuclear weapons seems firmly established.

In a study made by the National Science Foundation, it was determined that of two hundred and twenty-eight leading figures in the Chinese Academy of Science in 1967, ninety-five were trained in the United States, fifty in Western Europe, four in Japan, three in the Soviet Union, thirteen in China, and sixty-three had undefinable backgrounds. From this it seems obvious that scientific and military secrets cannot be long preserved, but steadily melt like a cake of ice. Since knowledge, once gained, cannot be forgotten, little by little it spreads to every segment of the literate world's population.

The only way to stay ahead in the race for more scientific and military knowledge is to keep racing. The quest must continue apace. Should we lose our momentum, another country will forge ahead and surpass us in military capabilities. As Dr. Edward Teller has remarked, "We live in an Alice-in-Wonderland world. The faster we run the more we stay in the same place."

With all of Red China's spectacular nuclear advances, however, I cannot believe that she presents any major threat to our national survival at this time. Moreover, I feel that should the gauntlet be thrown down, the United States could soon subdue her, *provided*—and only provided—our military leaders were permitted to direct the war as they managed the conduct of World War II. Any amateurish experimentation with pacifistic concepts of limited ground warfare would doom us to indefinite killing and bloodletting without a satisfactory political settlement.

How would I fight such a war? I would attempt to aggravate the economic and political problems which have always kept China one short step from chaos. As a preliminary defensive measure, I would gain unquestioned air supremacy by bombing out Red China's air power and missile power. Concurrent with this would be the destruction of her nuclear plants, storage, and weapon sites. Depending on the urgency of the war, these tasks could be performed with tactical nuclear weapons; although if our national policy demanded it the same tasks could be performed with conventional bombs, but with higher losses and increased expense, over a protracted period. Once air supremacy had been achieved, the next step would be systematically to destroy Red China's economy. The economic hardships and political turmoil thus caused would result in either a suit for peace or an internal revolution. With the help of Nationalist Chinese forces on Formosa and of South Korean forces, revolutionary elements in China would be encouraged to overthrow the Communist regime. We should place more faith in the ground forces of our allies. When President Johnson declared in 1964 that we would not "supply American boys to do the job that Asian boys should do" he made good sense. But he failed to follow through.

To let a paper dragon dominate our foreign policy and military strategy in Vietnam is unworthy of a great country such as the United States—the greatest and strongest country the world has ever known.

What should America's foreign policy be? Should we attempt to defend every small country against communist aggressions disguised as "wars of national liberation?" Or should we overlook those crises which do not touch us deeply and stop trying to police the world?

Should we continue in the John Foster Dulles tradition of allying ourselves with every free nation, joining collective security groups, and writing mutual defense treaties? Or should we back off from firm defense commitments which might embroil us in wars where there may be slight involvement with our national interests?

A superficial analysis might conclude that this is a choice between collective security and isolationism, but such a conclusion would be an oversimplification of the issue. Isolationism has been a bad word since World War II, and even to use the word would be prejudicial in an argument of this sort. Actually, the American isolation of the nineteenth century in the George Washington tradition of "no entangling alliances" is dead and buried without question. Beginning with the Spanish-American War we have engaged in one foreign war after another. America's position as the first world power keeps her inextricably involved with the affairs of every country in the world. However, this does not mean that we must be so involved as to take an active military part in every small war or revolution.

The question I raise is: To what *degree* should we become involved in the world's problems? When should we feel obliged to fight? This has nothing to do with the old isolationism which conceived of the United States as being hermetically sealed from the world about it.

Those who would become actively involved in every bush conflict believe that only through force can communism be held in check. They view every conflict as a struggle between freedom and communism. This black and white view of the world can get us into trouble where we have no business and trouble which may have nothing to do with communism. The war between Israel and the United Arab Republic in the summer of 1967 provides an example of this. How lucky we were not to become embroiled in that! Even though the Soviet Union took the side of the Arabs, the issues had little to do with communism and certainly were not affecting our vital national interests. One happy consequence of our involvement in Southeast Asia was our reluctance to deploy forces to the Middle East.

If, however, we had vigorously taken the side of Israel and she had not been so phenomenally successful, it is conceivable that the big power confrontation could have led to nuclear war. What a tragedy of errors this would have been.

Even when communism is clearly involved in a conflict it may sometimes be better for us to stand back from a foreign tangle. It is just possible that those who aspire to freedom can handle their own affairs. It is even possible that they can solve their own problems better without our help. Take the overthrow of communism in Indonesia for example. Had we intruded there, as we have in Vietnam, a Red Sukarno might now be in charge. The natural play of political forces does not always promote communism. Besides Indonesia I can cite the examples of Algeria, Argentina, Brazil, Ghana, and Guinea where the United States had little influence.

Whether we like it or not, nuclear weapons will proliferate. Our noble efforts to hold down their spread by treaty is doomed to failure. Short of our governing the world, which would be a very mixed blessing at best, the non-proliferation treaty cannot be enforced. Those countries which can afford nuclear weapons and feel they must have them for protection will undoubtedly acquire them, as have France and Red China.

I do not expect every little jungle country to become a nuclear power. But I do expect that countries such as India, Japan, Australia, Israel, and Egypt will some day have nuclear arms.

They really have little choice unless we stand over them with a nuclear umbrella. And this kind of protection when stark national survival is at stake for the little country leaves something to be desired.

From our point of view the question boils down to this: Do we wish to become involved in nuclear wars all over the world in our efforts to stem communist aggression? Is not this too big a price to pay for an objective which might well be achieved without our direct involvement?

If we pursue this "nuclear umbrella" doctrine and offer nuclear assistance to every free country who asks for our help, we will be perpetually radioactive. Much worse, we will constantly be involved in nuclear confrontations with the Soviet Union. Surely we can devise a more sensible and less dangerous foreign policy than this.

The "nuclear umbrella" doctrine has received much favor because we are so concerned with nuclear proliferation. Since we have been led to believe that proliferation will lead to a nuclear holocaust, we consider that any measures whatever to halt it are acceptable. Yet to endorse a policy involving us in repeated nuclear wars and frequent confrontations with the Soviet Union seems far more dangerous than nuclear proliferation, which is inevitable anyway.

After pondering this paradox for many years and observing the vain efforts to gain a nuclear non-proliferation treaty—a treaty which would be worthless even if consummated—I have concluded that we should help our friends to become nuclear armed and then ease off on the umbrella policy.

If, for example, Japan were equipped with nuclear missiles she could deter any nuclear blackmail attempts by Red China. Should war occur she could protect herself without our direct military participation. Today, under the umbrella policy, should Red China and Japan tangle, we would be obliged to jump in with our assistance since China has nuclear arms while Japan does not.

True, friendships and alliances change. Some day Japan may again turn on us as she did in 1941. But this remote danger should not sway our judgment when we have an immediate danger threatening us today.

Through the collective security of NATO we have provided our allies with nuclear assistance. Yet we have hung so relentlessly to the control of these weapons that any nuclear involvement will inevitably put us right in the middle. To my mind it would be better to assist France or even West Germany to develop their own nuclear forces. This, then, would give us the option of withdrawing from a nuclear confrontation if it appeared that our vital national interests were unimpaired.

NATO is breaking up and I am saddened to witness the demise of the greatest of all peacetime alliances and one which I helped build. NATO performed a magnificent service for the world by halting communism in Europe. Because of the prosperity which the Marshall Plan and NATO induced, European countries are now relatively free from communist subversion. But the danger of invasion based on U.S.S.R. and Warsaw Pact military capabilities—which is the soundest measure—remains as threatening as before. Kremlin intentions, however, appear much less bellicose and so the collective security of NATO becomes less pressing. If this trend continues American forces in Europe will probably withdraw.

The United States and Europe are not indispensable partners, as some statesmen insist. America grew strong in spite of Europe and it was American strength and wealth that saved Europe in two world wars—not the other way around. America will stay strong without Europe. But since we seem to be emotionally identified with European crises, it would be in our interest if we could keep Europe at peace.

Without an effective collective security arrangement our only telling influence on Europe would be through a judicious use of the balance of power. By using her weight to balance the power scales America may help to keep peace in Europe as Britain did under the *Pax Britannica*. If the United States comes to believe that American safety and survival depend on Europe, Europe will begin to dominate American policy. There has been too much of this thinking already.

An international equilibrium brought about by the subtle and judicious shifting of our military weight under the confident hands of astute diplomats and statesmen is the key to our future foreign policy. Keeping the peace is a dynamic problem demanding constant attention and the utmost skill and courage. The calculus of military power is the cost of this diplomacy, and we need leaders who understand these mathematics.

"We are not trying to establish a 'pax Americana' but rather a general system of peace among nations," declared Secretary of State Dean Rusk in 1966. Yet by rushing around the world to defend Congo tribes or the South Vietnamese we are, in effect, pursuing a "pax Americana" policy. I do not think it is possible, or even necessary, to achieve the kind of "general system of peace" that Mr. Rusk had in mind. There will always be strife in this world, somewhere. I believe we will assure more real peace if we stand back with some detachment and restraint from most small wars, whether conventional or nuclear, and use our strength to deter a major nuclear war. In this way we would have more flexibility to achieve a balance of power in the "third world" of uncommitted nations.

Yet when the time comes to engage in a small war, we should declare it and go in to win in the shortest possible time with whatever weapons are necessary.

* * *

Although I have dealt separately with general, limited, and counterinsurgency warfare, it must not be forgotten that these divisions represent merely convenient terms of reference to portions of a continuous range of strategies designed to cope with a broad spectrum of possible enemy challenges. Thus the problem of strategy extends over the entire range of military, geographical, and technological threats. There is no panacea or cheap solution such as minimum deterrence which will protect us. Only a difficult, expensive, long-term policy of strategic superiority that confronts every threat to our vital national interests and survival offers an acceptable solution.

Whether we like it or not, it is necessary for us to prepare for general nuclear war. I am thoroughly convinced that such a war need not introduce an Armageddon of utter destruction. A general war could well be fought in such a way that every incentive is offered the enemy to avoid city attacks and to negotiate. By catching air and missile power on the ground as Israel did with Egypt in 1967, a large war could be terminated just as swiftly.

A major state can survive a general nuclear war if adequate offensive and defensive preparations are made. This will require extensive bomb shelters and an ABM system, but more important, *it will require a lightning destruction of the enemy's offensive forces.*

The capability for waging a general nuclear war will provide a more credible deterrence than any posture of minimum, finite, or parity deterrence. When a nation has the capacity for defensive *or* offensive action, it is twice armed. If it relies simply on defensive retaliation, any enemy is invited to overwhelm that capacity with a surprise attack. Thus the inverted arms control doctrines are actually destabilizing the international environment, since they make it feasible for an ambitious enemy to conquer any nation guided by the arms control ideas.

A truly credible deterrence is flexible and has wide applicability. It helps discourage challenges both in the sub-limited and the limited-war ranges. Of course, if we perpetually profess our aversion to general war, this credibility lessens proportionately. Deterrence, which is a state of mind, is tied to credibility. By shouting to the world that we do not intend to use our strength we effectively reduce the value of our strength.

Strategic superiority—throughout the range of counterinsurgency, limited war, and general nuclear war—is economically and politically feasible. The $2 billion a month we can devote to the Vietnam war should lead no one to believe that we cannot afford the cost of survival at any level of conflict. Moreover, a defense budget of over $70 billion is not turning us into a "warfare state" as some have feared, nor limiting our traditional freedoms. I fully admit that deterrence should remain the kingpin of our policy. But deterrence cannot be our total policy, and to regard it divorced from the will and the capability to fight is an unreal dream.

Of all the concepts of war discussed today, that of deterrence is least understood. Deterrence is not a positive, factual condition but a changeable factor of human judgment. It may change overnight and for reasons of which we may have no knowledge. Deterrence is based upon enemy emotions and self-interest, not upon some estimated adequate destruction level such as "X" per cent of Russian industry or some assumed enemy moral commitment to "Y" per cent of its population as the Johnson Administration would have us believe. We can therefore *never* be sure of our deterrent capability. So we must *always* be prepared to defend ourselves.

Strategic superiority requires an emphasis upon technical superiority in all fields. Contrary to minimum, finite, or parity deterrence which imply a relatively static technology, strategic superiority requires continued dynamic technical advancement.

This calls for a vigorous and continuous competition in the military technological race.

A broad and energetic military technical research and development program must be pursued by all services. No promising weapon system should be disregarded.

The military posture of the United States should also include:

1. A mixed strategic force of aircraft and missiles to meet present requirements, to insure against technological surprise, to maintain flexibility, and to complicate enemy defenses. Not only should this force include space reconnaissance, but it should have the ability to inspect and destroy, if need be, orbiting weapons of mass destruction.

2. Military superiority in space. Although we cannot foresee all the military uses of space, we must maintain an ability to exploit this new medium as opportunities appear. We should expand and refine the uses of space in the areas of weather observation, intelligence, communications, and defense.

3. Our military posture must, of course, include both nuclear and conventional capabilities. When similarity of mission and training permits, dual-capable forces—forces such as fighter-bombers which may employ either nuclear or "iron" bombs—may be feasible, but in other instances separate forces may be required. We must be sure that efforts at economizing through developing dual-capabilities do not degrade weapon effectiveness. The "commonality" of the TFX fiasco is a case in point. Sufficient general purpose forces must be maintained to cope successfully with at least two crises simultaneously as we did with Vietnam and the Dominican Republic.

4. All of our forces must be designed to survive surprise attack. This means that we must strive always to improve the quick reaction to command and control of combat forces. Great strides have been made in satellite communications and electronic devices of all sorts, but this should not lead one to

believe that forces in the field can be operated in detail directly from the White House. The mere volume of activity in the field of action should convince anyone that the delegation of authority is fundamental to successful military operations. Yet continued improvement in command and control arrangements will lead to more responsive activities in the field and warn us against surprise. An effective ABM system also contributes to this goal.

These common-sense steps to regain our strategic superiority are not out of reach. It is not too late to take them, but if we do not make some drastic changes very soon it *will* be too late. The point of no return is almost upon us. The danger is real. It is pressing.

While fighting a limited war with equally limited success in Southeast Asia, and while witnessing the rapid buildup of Soviet intercontinental nuclear forces, America languors with an illness of euphoria brought on by our leaders who have proclaimed an international détente in the struggle against communism. This détente is unwarranted. It is not shared by our adversaries, who are frantically attempting to pass us in the nuclear weapons race. And they *are* passing us! Yet we sit on our hands, confused and lulled by our leaders.

We have come to that period in our history which John Foster Dulles warned about in his book *War or Peace*. "If at any time in the near future," he wrote, "it seems like the danger of war has passed, that will be the period of greatest peril. Then we may be tempted to relax and get careless and disarm, materially and morally. By so doing, we should expose ourselves to a sudden attack, which is most likely to come at such a time."

The measures we must take to regain and maintain our military superiority are crystal clear. The very first step, of course, is to rid ourselves of those false prophets who have deceived us and who have guided us into the dangerous waters where we now find ourselves. They have been responsible for placing America in danger, and each day that they hold high office America comes closer and closer to oblivion.

The defense of our country has never been easy. But it has been worth any difficulty. And it is worth it today.

No hardship is too severe, no expense too much, and no life too dear to defend this America, the greatest country the world has ever known!

Index